English Result

Pre-intermediate Teacher's Book

Annie McDonald & Mark Hancock

with Rachel Godfrey & Catherine McBeth

OXFORD

UNIVERSITY PRESS

Contents

Introduction

Welcome to **English Result!** We've focussed on making each lesson motivating, attractive, and memorable. We've planned the course to be complete and success-oriented. We treat language as a practical, action-oriented tool for communication. We've made the course transparent and easy to follow, with a clear lesson and unit structure. We hope you enjoy it!

Motivating

English Result is designed to motivate. We believe that quality of learning depends on quality of attention, and students will only pay attention if they are motivated. Student motivation may be extrinsic (they study the subject for external rewards) or intrinsic (they like the subject for its own sake), or a mix of these.

Adult and young adult students often have very good extrinsic reasons for learning English – for work, exams, study, or travel, for example. However, this alone does not guarantee that they will be successful, especially considering that many will have tried to learn English before with disappointing results. We've often heard frustrated students say things like, 'I've studied English for six years and I still can't speak it!'. These students need a fresh new approach, including course material which is intrinsically appealing.

We've written **English Result** with this in mind, by creating material which will act like a magnet to attract students' attention. In our experience, texts and tasks are likely to work as 'attention magnets' if they have one or more of the following properties:

- curiosity
- entertainment
- challenge
- enjoyment
- space for personalization
- space for choice and control

For this reason, we have consciously tried to make sure that at least one of these properties is central to each lesson.

Once the students' attention has been attracted, their motivation needs to be sustained during the lesson and through the course. They need to feel that they are making progress and achieving something worthwhile. This achievement is motivating in itself. We aim to cultivate achievement motivation in a number of ways:

- By providing engaging lessons which begin by stating a practical communicative objective (**How to …**) and provide all the necessary input for the students to achieve that objective.

- By providing tasks which are clear, focussed, challenging, do-able, personalizable, and which offer choices.

- By providing assessment tools for both learner and teacher which are transparent and allow the students to check their own progress against the independent, internationally recognised student attainment levels in the CEFR (the **Common European Framework of Reference**). For more information, go to www.oup.com/elt/teacher/result.

Attractive and memorable

English Result is designed for maximum visual impact. The entire left-hand page of the main lessons consists of a striking combination of picture and text. These 'impact pages' are designed to attract the students' attention. They are the kinds of pages that would probably spark the curiosity of any person thumbing through the book, even someone *not* studying English. These pages are addressed to the reader-as-person, rather than the reader-as-student-of-English, and their impact is not diluted by instructions, explanations, or exercises. The impact page forms the 'centre of gravity' of the lesson, helping to give each lesson a distinct and memorable character.

We believe that variety from lesson to lesson is crucial to maintaining the students' interest, so the impact pages include a wide mix of genres such as the following:

- magazine articles
- comedy sketches
- mystery stories
- games
- puzzles
- personality tests
- general knowledge quizzes
- poems
- art

There is always a strong visual component on the impact pages. We feel that images are very valuable in language learning for a number of reasons:

- In language teaching, a picture is like a text where the students provide the words. As a result, a picture can provide content for a lesson but at the same time leave the students with an active role in constructing the language.

- A picture can provide a very clear context for new language. Often, this context would be impossible to describe in words at the student's level of English.

- Pictures are level-flexible. The more language you know, the more you can say about the picture.

- Pictures are attention magnets.

Success-oriented

English Result is designed for success.

– **Optimum level of challenge**: The course is based on realistic expectations of what the students should be able to achieve in a lesson. For example, we do not expect students to be able to discuss issues in fluent English when they have only been prepared to produce a few basic exchanges. The course is challenging enough to keep a student of this level alert, but not so difficult that they get lost and lose their sense of control. In this way, students are positioned right at the edge of their competence and pushing it forward.

– **Positive approach**: The course takes a positive approach to learning and progress by helping both the student and teacher to focus on what students CAN do rather than what they can't. Language learning is a complex process and we do not expect that, at the end of a lesson, a student will be able to produce a flawless performance in a communicative task. Instead, we take a positive approach to learning by helping teachers and students focus on elements of communication which are successful, rather than viewing an utterance as something to be corrected. In this way, students can see how far they've come and not only how far they've got to go.

– **Support**: In **English Result Pre-intermediate**, students are given plenty of support in all skills. For example, for spoken English:

– New words and phrases are modelled on the audio component to help with pronunciation.

– Often, functional dialogues are printed on the page so that students can see a printed model for their own oral communication.

– Students are given the opportunity to prepare and plan before freer communicative tasks.

– All of this kind of scaffolding means that students are not simply 'thrown in at the deep end', and success is more than just a matter of luck.

– **Realistic learning load**: The language presented in **English Result Pre-intermediate** is tightly graded and controlled so as not to overwhelm the learner. The grammar and vocabulary input is informed by publications related to the Common European Framework of Reference, based on what is most useful and frequent. In this way, students are not adrift in an endless sea of new language – they are in a pool, and they have a good chance of reaching the other side.

– **Recycling**: New language is continually recycled from lesson to lesson and across the course. In addition to this implicit recycling, there is explicit recycling in the E lessons and Review lessons at the end of every unit. The E lessons are designed to put some of the new language from the unit into action in the context of a carefully staged and supported writing task. The Review lessons give students a chance to revisit all the new grammar and vocabulary in the unit.

– **Feedback on progress**: **English Result** comes with a comprehensive set of assessment material so that students can test their new skills on a regular basis and get reliable feedback on what they're doing well and what they need to do more work on.

Action-oriented and practical

English Result encourages students to see language in terms of what they can do with it, rather than as a body of knowledge. Often, students view language as just a list of words and grammar structures and they end up in the frustrating position where they know a lot about the language but they still can't speak it. In our experience, most students would like to imagine themselves coming out of a course being able to say, 'I can use English', rather than, 'I know the past tense of irregular verbs in English.' To help move towards this, we have tried to show how the new language is used to create meaning and to communicate:

– The **How to** titles of all the lessons indicate a practical purpose for the language in the lesson, showing the students that they are not simply learning new vocabulary and structures 'because they are there'.

– New grammar and vocabulary are presented within the flow of a lesson, as part of an overall practical objective, and not just for their own sake.

– The **Can do** bar at the end of each lesson reminds students that they are learning practical abilities, not passive knowledge.

Complete

The **English Result Pre-intermediate** syllabus is closely informed by Council of Europe publications and includes a comprehensive coverage of the various competences outlined in them. A strong A1-level student who has worked successfully through **English Result Pre-intermediate** should be able to place themselves at or above A2 for listening, reading, spoken interaction, spoken production, and writing. For more information, go to www.oup.com/elt/teacher/result.

– **Communicative tasks**: The English Result Pre-intermediate lesson themes are functional in nature, and are based on activities described as being appropriate for an A2-level learner. In this way, the student can easily see the use of the language they are learning, and it is pitched to their level to provide an optimum degree of challenge.

– **Skills**: In addition to the traditional four skills of listening, reading, speaking, and writing, **English Result** follows the CEFR by regarding the speaking skill as comprising both spoken interaction (conversation) as a skill in its own right, and spoken production (for example, giving a short self-introduction) as a separate skill. This helps to ensure that the students experience a balanced range of speaker roles so that they really can come away from the course being able to 'speak English'.

– **Strategies**: **English Result** pays explicit attention to the various strategies students can use to overcome difficulties in communicative situations, such as asking for clarification or listening and identifying clues to meaning. In this way, students will be empowered and not left helpless whenever they hit a communication problem.

– **Language competence**: **English Result** has clearly identifiable grammar, vocabulary, and pronunciation strands, which are highlighted at the top of each lesson page as well as in the contents pages. In addition, attention is paid to sociolinguistic competence (namely aspects of culture such as appropriate ways of addressing people) and pragmatic competence (for example being able to make and respond to suggestions appropriately or using linkers to join ideas together). This gives students a full picture of what the language is and how it works.

Clear unit structure

All 12 units of **English Result Pre-intermediate** have the same six-lesson structure:

- Lessons A–D each consist of two pages: the impact page on the left and the lesson page on the right.
- Lesson E is one page, reviewing the language in the unit and building up to a written output task.
- Each unit ends with a one-page Review lesson, providing extra practice of the grammar and vocabulary covered in the unit.

This clear structure means that you know where you are at a glance, making the course clear and easy-to-use.

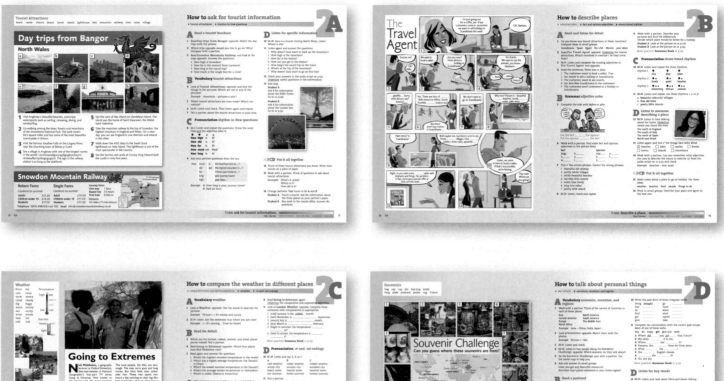

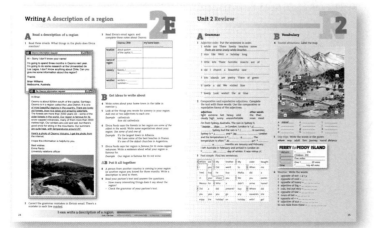

How English Result works

How to ...

The **How to** provides a clear focus and makes the practical learning outcome absolutely transparent to the student.

Left-hand impact page

Every A to D lesson includes a whole page of visual stimulation to keep motivation high.

Many different genres, from news articles to adverts, cartoon strips to mystery stories, quizzes to games, help to provide variety and keep the material fresh.

Visual help

Images are used extensively to make texts and new language more accessible and memorable for the students.

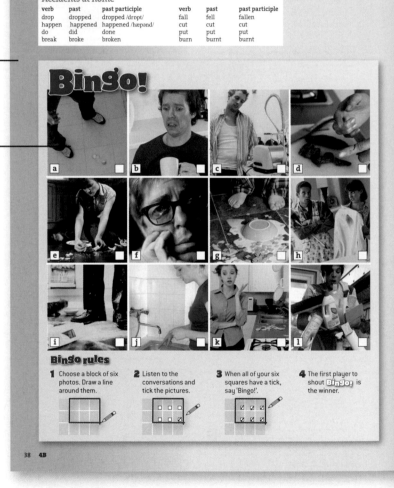

GVP bar

The grammar, vocabulary, and pronunciation content of each lesson is clearly signposted so teachers and students know what to expect.

Vocabulary

The vocabulary input is manageable and relevant – high-frequency, useful language that is of immediate practical value.

Students are given the opportunity to expand their vocabulary in areas which are relevant for them. This helps them to talk about their own life and circumstances.

Vocabulary is constantly recycled across lessons, helping students to fix it in their minds.

Grammar bank

The **Grammar Bank** at the back of the book provides clear reference notes plus extra exercises for students who need more controlled practice.

Reading and listening skills

Receptive skills, sub-skills, and strategies appropriate for a student aspiring to reach level A2 or A2+ are made explicit in the section headings. Teachers and students know what they are practising and why.

Both audio and textual materials are true to their genre. For example, casual conversation contains features of natural speech such as hesitation. Scripted dialogues contain authentic sound effects so students are exposed to the contrasting varieties of spoken English they might expect to hear both in the media and on the street.

Pronunciation

Pronunciation sections flow naturally from the How to, grammar, or vocabulary of each lesson, helping students see how pronunciation fits into the wider picture.

Equal weight is given to segmental features such as sounds and to supra-segmental features such as sentence stress. In this way, students get balanced practice of English pronunciation both receptively and productively.

Pronunciation exercises take a meaning-based approach wherever possible, so that students can see how pronunciation can change meaning.

Productive Skills

The **Put it all together** section at the end of every A–D lesson gives students the chance to put new language into action in a speaking or interaction activity. This provides an opportunity for freer oral practice of the new language.

The students are given plenty of support and preparation for these activities to help give them the best possible chance of success.

The Put it all together section at the end of every E lesson is a piece of written work that has been carefully prepared, step-by-step, throughout the whole lesson. In this way, students have plenty of ideas, strategies, and appropriate language before they start writing. Students are also shown stages involved in the writing process.

Grammar sections

Students always see new grammar in context before it is actively presented to them. This shows the grammar in action and demonstrates how it contributes to meaning, before they focus on the form.

Students are encouraged to work out rules and patterns of language for themselves so that the presentation is more memorable.

Reflection

The **Can do** bar at the end of each lesson reminds students what the lesson has been about and invites them to reflect on how much they have learnt. This helps them to self-assess their achievement realistically and positively.

Sample lesson page (4B)

How to say what's happened

G present perfect for recent events V accidents at home P short form of *have*

A Vocabulary accidents at home

1 Look at the **Bingo!** photos opposite with a partner. What can you see?
Example There's a knife in picture d.

2 Match 1–6 with a–f. There may be more than one correct answer.

1 drop *a, c, d* a your toast
2 break b your finger
3 fall c a cup
4 cut d an egg
5 put e salt in your coffee
6 burn f off the shelf

3 Look at the photos again. Make sentences and say which picture or pictures they are describing.
Example He's broken his glasses – picture f

1 He's broken an egg.
2 He's dropped her finger with a knife.
3 She's cut his glasses.
4 He's put his shirt.
5 He's burnt salt in his coffee.

B Grammar present perfect for recent events

4 Look at the grammar box and complete the examples.

past action	present result
He's dropped an egg.	(I can see an egg on the floor.)

Use the present perfect to talk about a past action when you are interested in the present result.

Examples

past action	present result
1 She's *cut her finger*	(I can see blood on her finger.)
2 He's _____ salt.	(The coffee is horrible.)
3 She's _____.	(I can see a cup on the floor.)
4 She's _____.	(There is milk all over the floor.)
5 The bottles have _____.	(They're on the floor.)
6 He's _____.	(The toast is black.)

5 Look at the grammar box. Underline the correct words in the rule below.

subject	have	past participle	object
I/You/We/They	've (have)	broken dropped	a cup an egg
He/She/It	's (has)		

The past participle is always/not always the same as the past simple form.

6 Look at **Accidents at home** opposite. Decide which group A–D each verb is in.

A regular (+*ed*)		
drop – dropped – dropped		

B irregular	C irregular	D irregular
all three forms are the same	past simple = past participle	past participle is different from past simple
cut – cut – cut	burn – burnt – burnt	break – broke – broken

7 Look at **Bingo!** opposite. Work with a partner.
A Say sentences about the photos.
B Say the photo.
Example A He's dropped the sugar. B i!
More practice? **Grammar Bank** ›› p.139.

C Listen and play a game

8 **4B.1►** Listen and read this conversation. Tick ✓ the picture.
M Oh no!
W What's happened? What have you done?
M I've burnt the toast.
W Yeah, I can smell it!

9 How did you know which picture to tick? Underline the key words in the conversation.

10 Read and follow **Bingo** rules opposite.

11 **4B.2►** Play the **Bingo!** game. You will hear conversations. Listen for key words and tick ✓ the pictures.

D Pronunciation short form of *have*

12 Match the contractions and the phonemic spelling.
you've he's I've she's
1 /aɪv/ I've cut my hand.
2 /jəv/ _____ burnt the toast.
3 /ʃiz/ _____ dropped an egg.
4 /hɪz/ _____ broken a glass.

13 **4B.3►** Listen and repeat the sentences in exercise 12.

14 Look at audio script 4B.2 on ›› p.152. Choose five of the conversations. Act them with a partner.

ABCD Put it all together

15 Work with a partner and describe your picture. Find the differences.
Student A Look at the picture of the kitchen on ›› p.127.
Student B Look at the picture of the kitchen on ›› p.135.

I can say what's happened.
Tick ✓ the line. with a lot of help with some help on my own very easily

39

What else does English Result offer?

Student's Book

Workbook
with MultiROM

Workbook
with Answer Key Booklet
and MultiROM

Teacher's Book
with DVD

Class Audio CDs

For students: extra practice material **www.oup.com/elt/result**
For teachers: extra resources **www.oup.com/elt/teacher/result**

Teacher's Book

The **English Result** Teacher's Book has been designed as a resource:
- for planning before the lesson
- for quick reference during the lesson
- for step-by-step guidance during a lesson

The Teacher's Book is interleaved with the Student's Book so that the teaching notes are on the page facing the corresponding classroom material. This, together with strong section headings, clear answer keys, and colour-coded extra activities, makes for easy navigation and fast cross-referencing.

A Read and understand the writer's aim

In this section, students analyse a note to determine why it has been written.

1 Check students understand the title of the section. Go through the instructions and the questions. Direct students to the note. Set a short time limit for students to skim and scan to answer the questions. Go over answers as a class.

> 1 Phillipa's house (maybe in the kitchen)
> 2 Phillipa   3 She's not home to welcome Ana.

2 Ask students to read items 1–6 and check vocabulary. Do the example to make sure students understand the activity. They compare in pairs before you go over answers as a class.

> 2 perhaps   3 yes   4 no   5 perhaps   6 yes

Extra activity
Ask students for examples from Phillipa's letter which indicate that it's an informal note to a friend, e.g. *Hi!, use of short sentences – one on each line, imperatives, contracted forms.*

What's in it?

The teacher's notes for each lesson are in three main sections:
- **Orientation** This gives you all the background information about the language and content of the lesson so that you can see 'the bigger picture'.
- **Step-by-step lesson notes** These guide you through the lesson.
- **Assessment guide** At the end of the lesson, this helps you assess student performance so that you and your students can see how far they've come.

Orientation

These notes appear in the first column of a set of notes for each lesson, and provide you with a variety of lesson-appropriate information: the context of situation, the language focus of the lesson, and what will happen in the *Put it all together*. The section ends with practical preparation ideas and warmer suggestions.

- **Context notes** This is a an overview of what the students will mainly focus on during the lesson, along with a brief summary of the input material to help you quickly 'tune in' to the material.
- **Culture notes** These are brief notes on aspects of everyday culture such as different politeness conventions or different expectations of how to be a good guest. You can use this information to help your students become more inter-culturally aware. For more information, go to www.oup.com/elt/teacher/result.
- **Language focus** This is an 'at-a-glance' boxed summary of main language areas of the lesson (grammar, vocabulary and phrases, pronunciation and discourse), along with an indicator of language points being previewed, recycled or which should be treated as for recognition purposes only. This helps you distinguish between areas of language which needs greater attention and language which is incidental to a particular lesson.
- **Language notes** These notes give extra information about aspects of the new language that often confuse students, such as structures which may be different in their own language, or false friends. In this way, you'll be prepared for those 'difficult' questions.
- **End-product notes** These notes provide a summary of the final task: what students will be doing, what materials they can look back to for support, and how they will work together to do it. This means you know in advance what the whole lesson is building towards.
- **Preparation notes** These notes tell you what you can do before the lesson to make it run more smoothly, such as asking students to bring dictionaries or preparing a few questions. This helps to ensure you're not caught unprepared.
- **Warmer notes** The Warmer section provides topic-opener activities for you to get your students thinking and talking about the topic and to introduce the How to ..., the communicative task focus and aim of the lesson.

Step-by-step lesson notes

Numbered exercise notes

These notes accompany the exercises in the Student's Book, following the same numbering system for ease of navigation. The notes include:

- Advice on **classroom management**, for example how students should be grouped.
- **Teaching techniques**, for example concept-checking. There are a wide variety of techniques to help you vary your teaching style and discover which procedures best suit you and your class.
- Tips on when and how to give **feedback** on students' performance, and what aspects of their performance to focus on. The notes also advise you where not to expect accuracy or correct error. For more information go to www.oup.com/elt/teacher/result.
- **Text orientation** For the listening and reading sections in each lesson, we provide a mini-orientation to the topic of a text, a summary of the sub-skills being developed, and supplementary information on the genre of a written text or the qualities of a listening text.

Extras

These notes are in colour so that you can distinguish them from the procedural notes. They include:

- **Language notes** on typical problem areas in the focus language.
- **Teaching tips** to give you extra ideas for dealing with different teaching points.
- **Extra help** for dealing with students who are having difficulty.
- **Extra activities** in case you have extra time and would like to give more practice.
- **Extra plus**: ideas to provide more challenge for those students who need it.
- **Early finishers**: extra activities for mixed ability classes or where some students finish earlier than others.
- **Answer keys**: For more open-ended exercises which don't have a single correct answer, suggested answers are given so you know the kind of answer the students are expected to produce.

Student performance

At the end of each lesson, you will find an **assessment checklist** to help you to assess and give feedback on student performance, and to focus student attention on specific criteria when they are deciding where to place themselves on the **Can do** bar.

Student performance

Students should be able to use simple sentences to give information.

Use this checklist for monitoring and feedback or to assess students' performance.

Fluency	Do students say what's happened without a lot of hesitation? exercise 13
Vocabulary	Do students use verbs and nouns appropriately? exercise 3
Pronunciation	Do students mostly pronounce *he's* and *she's* as one word? exercise 14

I can say what's happened.
Students tick *on my own* if they can describe the picture without looking at >> **p.38**. They tick *with some help* if they need to look back to >> **p.38** once or twice to check the verb list.

- **Balanced** The list gives you a menu of criteria by which to judge performance, for example accuracy, fluency, vocabulary, or coherence. The criteria are systematically varied from lesson to lesson so that your assessment and feedback is balanced and not dominated by only one aspect, such as grammatical accuracy for example.
- **Practical** When you assess student performance, it is impossible to focus on all aspects at once. For this reason, there are only a few criteria specified in each assessment checklist, in order to make the task more manageable. In addition, for each criterion, a very concrete and specific feature is specified for you to listen out for, helping to make your assessment more focussed and objective rather than impressionistic.
- **Appropriate** The task checklists in **English Result Pre-intermediate** are based on the scales at A2 in the Common European Framework of Reference. This means you can be confident that the assessment criteria are relevant and appropriate to the students' level.
- **Transparent** The assessment checklists are transparent for both teacher and student alike. They make it easy for you to explain and for students to understand exactly what they're doing well and what could be improved. A final note in the Student Performance section gives more advice on helping students self-assess on the **Can do** bar at the bottom of the page. For more information, go to www.oup.com/elt/teacher/result.

Notes for Review Lessons

The Review lessons in the Student's Book provide a set of familiar, free-standing exercises which students can use to review the main grammar and vocabulary in a unit. The accompanying TB notes provide a wealth of extra activities and exercise types to help tailor the material to your students' needs. For further information, go to www.oup.com/elt/teacher/result.

The **Review** lessons can be used in a variety of different ways. For example:

- You can have a quiet class, to allow students to work at their own pace, and make yourself available to attend individual questions.
- Students could work through all the exercises in pairs or small groups.
- Students could chose which exercises they want to do.
- You could also use the **Review** activities at an appropriate point in your lesson to give students further controlled practice.
- You could set the **Review** exercises as homework, possibly asking students to choose two or three exercises, and give students parts of the answer key for them to self-correct.

In each set of Teacher's Book **Review** lesson notes, you will find:

- A Review Lesson **Warmer**, with an exercise or activity based on ten key phrases from the unit.
- **Warm-up activities** for each exercise: suggestions for optional short (often whole-class) activities which get students thinking about a language point before they do the exercise.
- **Set-up notes** for each exercise: practical advice and answer keys.
- **Follow-up notes** for each exercise: suggestions for optional activities which usually have a more student-centred focus.
- **Early finishers**: suggestions for further activities which students can do individually, often giving them the opportunity for personal reflection on their work on the unit as a whole.

Also in the Teacher's Book

Unit Tests

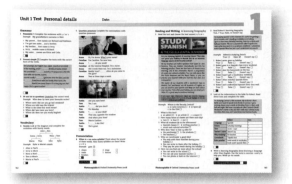

- One photocopiable Test per SB unit (see p.162)
- Each Test includes Grammar, Vocabulary, Pronunciation Awareness, and Reading and Writing sections.
- Easy to administer with clear instructions and examples for students and marking guidelines for teachers.

DVD

Key features:

- 30 minutes of classroom footage and author commentary to show you how the material works in the classroom.
- Accompanying teacher training worksheets www.oup.com/elt/teacher/result.

Other components

Workbook

- One page of grammar, vocabulary, and pronunciation practice exercises for each Student's Book lesson (with **Can do** self-assessment).
- Two pages of **Skills practice** every unit to develop students' reading, writing, and listening skills.
- **Self Check tests** for every unit to help students reflect on their learning and measure their progress.

MultiROM

- **Student's MultiROM** with interactive listening, vocabulary, and pronunciation practice plus downloadable study documents.

Website

The **Result Website** provides extra interactive and downloadable materials, including:

- Listening tests
- Speaking tests
- CEFR support
- English Result Portfolio
- Worksheets to accompany the DVD
- Extra practice for students

Teacher's site: www.oup.com/elt/teacher/result
Student's site: www.oup.com/elt/result

Assessment in English Result

English Result contains a coherent, comprehensive, flexible, and reliable set of assessment materials for both teachers and students. These materials can be found in various components in **English Result**: the Student's Book, Workbook, Workbook MultiROM, Teacher's Book, and Website.

We take a broad view of assessment and provide a set of resources we think will be useful for both teachers and students. We believe that one of the main purposes of assessment is to show what has been achieved, and so, in keeping with the key values of the course, we have provided material to help you to provide reliable feedback and to credit students for what they are able to do. In other words, as well as providing traditional tests, we also offer assessment materials which are success-oriented and informative. We hope the result will be a positive impact on motivation and learning.

For teachers: We provide a set of traditional tests which comprehensively assess language and skills on a unit-by-unit basis, and which are easy to administer and mark. To help teachers feel that they are being fair and consistent in their assessment, we also provide clear answer keys with suggestions on how to allocate marks and what to focus on when assessing the writing and speaking skills. For more information, go to www.oup.com/elt/teacher/result.

For students: We provide a range of materials which will encourage students to reflect on their progress in relation to their personal learning needs and current learning goals. Our aim is to help teachers to help students to take greater responsibility for their own learning. At the end of the course, students who want to will be able to see how their progress in **English Result Pre-intermediate** relates to the Council of Europe 'Can do' descriptions in relation to level A2 for Listening, Reading, Spoken Interaction, Spoken Production, and Writing.

Assessment for teachers

Put it all together tasks

In the Teacher's Book lesson notes, we provide a general description of the type of activities students do in the **Put it all together** section in each lesson. We also offer some task-specific criteria to help you focus on particular aspects of students' language. The checklists offer different criteria on a lesson-by-lesson basis, and using these will help you become more confident in using a range of criteria for speaking and writing tasks. If you want to use the criteria to give your students a mark for their performance, you should also add an overall evaluation of how well you felt students performed the task.

Unit tests

The **Unit tests** give students the chance to show how much they can do. On pp.162–185 of the Teacher's Book, there are photocopiable **Unit tests**. There are three sections, testing Grammar, Vocabulary and Pronunciation Awareness, and a further two sections with Reading Comprehension and Writing tasks. There are 60 marks in total for this part of the test, divided equally between language and skills. Overall, each test takes about 40 minutes, and is easy to administer, with clear instructions and examples which demonstrate to students what they have to do. The listening and speaking tests, with 20 marks allocated to each skill, can be found on www.oup.com/elt/teacher/result.

All the questions and activities are based on the material students have covered in the corresponding Student's Book unit. The grammar and vocabulary content of a unit test is closely linked to the unit's Review lesson, with a range of testing questions designed to help to build students' confidence before they embark on more specific exam training courses, for example if they plan to sit internationally recognised language tests.

We have designed the speaking tests so that you can choose to focus on either spoken interaction or spoken production, testing students in groups of two or three. There are role cards for students, with clear instructions for each part of the test. There are also step-by-step instructions, and a user-friendly mark record sheet to help you assess your students' performance reliably and with confidence.

Samples of the **Unit tests** and answer keys were trialled in different countries, and we looked carefully at how the students answered questions and what the teachers had to say about the material. The insights we gained informed development of the tests and the answer keys.

The answer keys

The **Unit test** answer keys on pp.186–189 of the Teacher's Book, include guidance on how to deal with students' mistakes in relation to the testing focus of particular questions. For example, in order to help you be sure you are responding to students' answers objectively and consistently, we suggest that it is best if no half marks are awarded. In a reading comprehension test, for example, we advise that an answer which shows a student has understood a text should not be penalised for spelling mistakes. This isn't to say that accurate spelling isn't important – students will be required to demonstrate this in another part of the test.

In the answer keys, we also include assessment criteria to help you assess students' writing and speaking skills, plus advice on how to distribute marks for the different areas. The task-specific assessment criteria have been anchored to A1 descriptions of ability in the CEFR, and they follow a similar format to the assessment checklists in the Teacher's Book notes. You could use information you collect to diagnose and build up a picture of strengths and weaknesses on a class basis or for individual feedback. By showing students how you assess, you can help them develop criteria to evaluate their own work and identify areas needing further attention.

Assessment for students

The Can do bar

At the end of each lesson in the Student's Book, students are invited to reflect on their performance in the task and mark their self-assessment on the **Can do** bar at the bottom of the page. The bar is worded to encourage a positive outlook and is a simple learner-training device. With regular use, it should:

– engage students in the learning process
– make the link between their own learning experiences and progress
– help students identify their personal learning goals
– develop the ability to become more realistic in their self-assessment
– increase student motivation

The Teacher's Book lesson notes offer some assessment criteria which you could use to help students reflect on their performance before they mark the **Can do** bar. There is also a brief description of the abilities of a student who might be considered to be at one of the middle positions on the scale – *with some help* or *on my own*. The other positions, *with a lot of help* and *very easily*, can be described relative to the middle positions.

Students can return to their initial self-assessment and review their position on the bar after they have worked with other **English Result** materials, for example the Workbook. Students can transfer their self-assessment to the Biography in the **English Result Portfolio Practice Book** at regular intervals. Later, these

can be transferred to the Passport, which has descriptions of ability in the five skills based on the CEFR. Thus, the bar acts as a personalized record of both achievement during the lesson, and progress over the course.

The Self Check tests

In addition to on-going self-assessment using the **Can do** bars at the end of each lesson, students are given the opportunity to think about their progress by using the **Self Check tests** after each unit of the Workbook. Students are given an answer key, and encouraged to use the tests as a do-it-yourself diagnostic tool.

The questions are based on grammar, vocabulary, and pronunciation awareness. Once students have checked their answers, they are encouraged to reflect on their performance and self-assess their achievements. The notes which follow the Self Check activities help students reflect on language and skills achievement. Using these, students can determine personal study objectives and are given information which guides them to corresponding Student's Book, Workbook, and MultiROM activities for further practice.

The Portfolio Practice Book

The **English Result Portfolio Practice Book** is based on the principles behind Council of Europe accredited models. It is for students who want to keep records of their work, to record and reflect on their learning experiences, to monitor their progress, and to see how their learning progresses during the course.

Students reflect on their ability to perform communicative tasks they practise at the end of each lesson. Later, they will be shown how to use this information for more global self-assessment using skill-specific descriptions for levels A1, A1+, A2 and A2+. These provide students with a stepping stone to CEFR level descriptions in an officially accredited European Language Passport.

Teacher's notes explain the purpose of the different sections in the portfolio, and how to integrate them with the course. For more information, go to www.oup.com/elt/teacher/result.

2   **Contents**

Contents 5

WHAT'S IN A NAME?

a

b

c

d

e

1 In **Iceland**, people don't have a family surname. They use their father's first name. For example Björk Guðmundsdóttir is the daughter of Guðmund.

2 In **Russia**, people have both their father's name and a surname. For example, the second name in Maria Yuryevna Sharapova comes from her father's name, Yuri.

3 **British and American** people usually have a first name, a middle name and the surname of their father. They often write their first name and middle name as initials. For example, the writer Joanne Kathleen Rowling is called J. K. Rowling on her books.

4 In **Spanish-speaking** countries, children use the surnames of both their parents. For example, Gabriel García Márquez's father's surname was García. His mother's surname was Márquez.

5 People from **China** write their surname before their first name. For example Jackie Chan's name is Chan Kong-Sang. 'Jackie' is just a nickname.

FAMOUS SURNAMES QUIZ

You know the **names**, but do you know the **people**?

How to talk about names

Orientation

Context

In this lesson, students will practise talking about their names and how names are 'composed' in their own country.

The names of the five people in the photos in *What's in a name?* are examples of how names are formed in Britain, America, Spain, China, Iceland, and Russia. In *Famous surnames quiz*, students must match the names of well-known people with their photos.

Culture note

Phrases for parts of names don't always translate. In English, 'first name' refers to a name at the beginning, while 'surname' is the last name. In English names, a 'middle name' is a second Christian name.

Language

Focus grammar	possessives 's, s'
Preview grammar	questions: *Have you got ...?, Is ...?, Do you like ...?, Does your name ...?*
Focus words	family and names: *cousin, first name, middle name, nickname, surname, etc.*
Focus phrases	*Just call me ...!*
Recognition vocabulary	words: *common, female, male* phrases: *it's short for, we call her*
Recycled language	nationality: *English, Chinese, Russian, Spanish, etc.* family: *daughter, father, grandmother, husband, etc.* jobs: *actor, singer, tennis player, writer* present simple: *be affirmative and question forms* spelling: *letters of the alphabet, capital, double, small*

End product

In *Put it all together,* students mingle and have short conversations with five others about their names, based on audio script 1A.3 on >> p.150. Students look at exercises 5 and 13 for help.

Preparation

Take a soft ball (or several pieces of paper scrunched up into a ball) to the lesson.

Choose English names of famous people your students will know, to show the meaning of *first name, middle name, surname, nickname,* e.g. use David and Victoria Beckham. Victoria Caroline Adams is known as Victoria Beckham or by her nickname *Posh.* Beckham's full name is David Robert Joseph Beckham, his nickname is *Becks.*

Warmer

If students don't know each other, stand them in a circle and throw the ball to a student as you say your name. Students continue. Next, students throw the ball to each other, saying the name of the person they are throwing to. If students can't remember a name, encourage them to use *Sorry, what's your name?* Finally, students throw the ball to someone but say another person's name, to indicate who the ball should be thrown to next.

If students already know each other, write their initials on the board. In pairs, students see if they can name all their classmates. With a multilingual class, check students can pronounce each other's names intelligibly.

Write *How to talk about names* on the board.

A Read and use what you know

In this section, students activate background knowledge of a topic before skimming and scanning short texts for gist and detail.

1 Direct students to the photos on >> p.6, *What's in a name?* and tell them to cover the text. See if students can name the people in the photos before they read texts 1–5. Check students remember vocabulary for jobs and do the example together to check understanding. Set a short time limit for the activity and elicit answers around the class. Do not overcorrect for precise pronunciation, but check students can understand each other.

> a J.K. Rowling   e Björk   d Jackie Chan   c Maria Sharapova

2 Ask about the people, encouraging students to guess their nationality and job. Do the example as a class. Monitor and help as necessary as students continue in pairs or small groups. Ask for volunteers to give information and see if the class agrees.

3 Direct students to texts 1–5 and photos a–e in *What's in a name?* on >> p.6. Do the first matching item with the class. Students continue individually and compare in pairs before you check answers as a class.

> a 3   b 4   c 2   d 5   e 1

4 Go through items 1–6 and check students understand name vocabulary, e.g. *first name, surname,* etc. by using examples of famous people your students know. Go through the example as a class, reminding students that they don't need to understand every word in the texts. Ask for answers around the class.

> 2 Joanna, Maria   3 Kathleen   4 Guðmundsdóttir, Yuryevna
 5 Márquez   6 Jackie

5 Ask students to read questions 1–7 and put them in pairs to ask and answer. Demonstrate the first item if necessary. Monitor and help as necessary. Ask for volunteers to tell the class some information about their partner.

Extra plus

Nominate students to ask and answer the questions.

B Grammar possessive 's

6 Draw a simple family tree with examples of family members for the words in the box on the board. Elicit or give the words as you go along. Direct students to the column headings, *male, female* and elicit or give examples to show the meaning. Check answers around the class and help with pronunciation as necessary. Ask *Who are my cousin's mother and father? (my aunt and uncle)* and model pronunciation /kʌsn/.

> **male:** son   brother   grandfather   **female:** wife   aunt

Teaching tip

Always be aware that every now and then the topic of family is one that might be sensitive or difficult for some students. Make it clear in the instructions that students should only tick the family members they are happy to talk about.

7 Go through the example. Monitor and check pronunciation as students continue the activity in pairs. Remind them to use the *I've got* structure.

8 Direct students to the grammar box and column headings. Write the first sentence from each column on the board, highlighting *'s* and *s'* to show how punctuation carries singular or plural meaning. Direct students to the rules below the box before they complete the examples. Elicit and write the correct answers on the board.

> grand**mother's**   daugh**ters'**

9 In pairs, students ask and answer about the family members they talked about in exercise 6. Go through the example to demonstrate if necessary. Monitor and check students pronounce the final /s/ sound.

Extra help
Students repeat the activity with a different partner.

Extra plus
Students tell the class about their partner's family.

10 Ask students to read the text quickly and to tell you how many family members the writer talks about. *(Five.)* Check vocabulary, and go through the first item as a class before students do the exercise individually. Monitor and help as necessary and make a note of any problem areas to go over when you check answers as a class.

> I've got two brothers. Their names are Ruy and Edson. Ruy's middle name is José. Edson's middle names are Pedro and Paulo. My sister's name is Nélida but we call her Nelly. My parents' names are João and Maria.

Extra activity
Students write names of these people on a piece of paper: their best friend; a common name in their country; the surname of a teacher they like(d) at school; the surname of a teacher they didn't like at school; a first name to give a daughter; a first name for a son. In pairs or small groups, students ask each other about the names, e.g. *Who's Tiggy? She's my …* etc.

C Listen for key words

In this section, students listen intensively to two texts, a name quiz for key words and an informal dialogue for detail.

11 1A.1 Direct students to *Famous surnames quiz* on **>> p.6** to see if they can name any of the people. Go through the instructions and ask students when they might have to spell their names. *(On the telephone, talking to someone who speaks a different language, when giving information to an official to complete a form.)* Tell students they will hear five more names and play the audio. Pause after each name and elicit the answer. Play the audio a second time for students to write the names. Check answers on the board to elicit the meaning of the words *double*, *small*, and *capital* for describing letters, and *apostrophe* for the punctuation mark.

> 2 Lacoste   3 Hilfiger   4 Schweppes   5 McDonald's

Extra help
In pairs, students take turns to spell full names of others in *Famous surnames quiz*. Remind them to ask for repetition.

12 1A.2 Divide the class into small teams and tell students they will hear clues about five famous people. Play the audio, pause after each item and give teams time to write their answer. After listening, nominate team members to write the names on the board, and invite others to say if the answer is right and the name spelt correctly. Play the audio a second time, pausing after each item to give the answer.

> 1 Chanel   2 Ericsson   3 Suzuki   4 Warner   5 Ferrari

Extra plus
In pairs, students choose a famous name and use audio script 1A.2 on **>> p.150** to write a simple quiz question for another pair, group or the class.

Extra activity
See if students know the first names of the other people in the quiz. They are: Henry Ford, Christian Dior, Torakusu Yamaha, André and Édouard Michelin, Tommy (Thomas Jacob) Hilfiger, Rene Lacoste, Enzo Ferrari, Ferdinand Porsche, Soichiro Honda, Jacob Schweppe.

13 1A.3 Ask *How many names has Chico got?* and ask students to read the conversation quickly to find the answer. *(Three, or four if you count his nickname.)* In pairs, students guess the gapped words before listening to the audio to confirm their guesses. Do not give answers at this stage.

14 Direct students to audio script 1A.3 on **>> p.150** to check answers.

> 2 first   3 short   4 surname   5 father's   6 call

15 Before students have the conversation, write *How do you spell that?* on the board and remind them to ask if they don't understand. In pairs, students practise reading the dialogue. Monitor and encourage them to look less and less at their book to become more confident and independent. Monitor and check pronunciation of the final /s/ and make sure they swap roles.

ABC Put it all together

16 Explain to students that they will stand up and walk around to ask five other people in the class about their names. Tell them to try and ask the questions from memory or to look at exercises 5 and 13 for help if necessary.

Student performance
Students should be able to have short informal conversations.

You can use this checklist to monitor and give feedback or to assess students' performance.

Content	Do students ask about all parts of a name? exercise 15
Communication strategy	Do students ask for spelling, if necessary? exercise 11
Pronunciation	Do students mostly pronounce the final /s/? exercise 9

I can talk about names.

If students haven't used the *I can* self-assessment bar before, make sure they realize that they mark what *they*, not you as their teacher, think about their ability to do the task. To illustrate this, draw a thought bubble on the board and write *You*. Now draw a line and use smilies for different points on the bar (one = *with a lot of help*, two = *with some help*, three = *on my own*, four = *very easily*). Students could repeat exercise 16 before self-assessing. Help them use the *Can do* bar, encouraging them to think positively.

Students tick *on my own* if they have found out about at least three students in the class, if they have looked at exercises 5 and 13 occasionally for key words. They tick *with some help* if they have read two or three questions from the exercises.

Early finishers
In pairs or small groups, students role play being one of the famous people in *Famous surnames quiz*, who meet at a party. Give each student a card with a different name.

Additional material

www.oup.com/elt/result for extra practice material
www.oup.com/elt/teacher/result for extra teacher resources

How to talk about names

G possessive *'s*   V family; parts of names

A Read and use what you know

1 Look at **What's in a name?** opposite. Match the people in photos a–e with these names.

- [b] Gabriel García Márquez, writer
- [ ] J. K. Rowling, writer
- [ ] Björk, singer
- [ ] Jackie Chan, film actor
- [ ] Maria Sharapova, tennis player

2 What do you know about the people in exercise 1? Tell a partner.

Example Gabriel García Márquez is from Colombia.

3 Read **What's in a name?** opposite. Match photos a–e with texts 1–5.

4 Match these names with sentences 1–6. Work with a partner.

Jackie   Rowling   Joanna   Yuryevna
Kathleen   Marquez   Maria   Guðmundsdóttir

1 This is a surname. *Rowling, Yuryevna, Márquez*
2 These are first names.
3 This is a middle name.
4 These names come from a father's first name.
5 This is a mother's surname.
6 This is a nickname.

5 Ask and answer with a partner.

1 Have you got a middle name?
2 How many surnames have you got?
3 Have you got a nickname?
4 Is any part of your name the same as your father or mother's name?
5 Do you like your name?
6 Is your name common in your country?
7 Does your name mean anything?

B Grammar possessive *'s*

6 Complete the box.

male	female
father	mother
	daughter
husband	
	sister
uncle	
	grandmother
cousin	

7 Tell your partner about your family. Use *I've got*.

Example I've got three brothers.

8 Complete the grammar box.

singular nouns	plural nouns
My father's name is Jerry.	My brothers' names are Ben and Tom.
My grand_____ name is Alice.	Our daugh_____ names are Kylie and Nina.

To make a singular noun possessive, add *'s*.
To make a plural noun possessive, add *s'*.

9 What about your family's names? Ask and answer with a partner.

Example **A** What are your sisters' names?
             B Maria and Sonia.

10 Complete the text with *s*, *'s*, or *s'*.

I've got two brother___¹. Their name___² are Ruy and Edson. Ruy___³ middle name is José. Edson___⁴ middle name___⁵ are Pedro and Paulo. My sister___⁶ name is Nélida but we call her Nelly. My parent___⁷ name___⁸ are João and Maria.

More practice? **Grammar Bank** ≫ p.136.

C Listen for key words

11 **1A.1▶** Listen to the spellings. Find the names in the **Famous surnames quiz** opposite.

Audio H-O-N-D-A   **You** Honda!

12 **1A.2▶** Listen to five quiz questions. Say the surname.

13 **1A.3▶** Listen and complete.

A What's your ¹ *name* ?
B Chico.
A Is that your ² _____ name?
B Yes. It's ³ _____ for Francisco.
A Oh. And what's your ⁴ _____?
B My surnames are Oliveira Cardoso.
A Oliveira Cardoso?
B Yes. Oliveira's my mother's surname and Cardoso's my ⁵ _____ surname.
A Oh I see. So it's Francisco Oliveira Cardoso?
B That's right. but just ⁶ _____ me Chico!

14 Check your answers in the audio script on ≫ p.150.

15 Say the conversation with a partner. Then say it again with information about you.

ABC Put it all together

16 Ask other people in the class about their names. Use the questions in exercises 5 and 13 to help you.

I can talk about names.

Tick ✓ the line.   with a lot of help   with some help   on my own   very easily

You're the detective!

ticket

letter

envelope

note

driving licence

passport

business card

credit card

I.D. card

badge

How to give and understand personal details

Orientation

Context

In this lesson, students will practise giving information about their daily routines.

You're the detective! shows a collection of documents and objects belonging to a woman called Caroline Watt. Some of the documents are labelled.

Culture note

In the UK people aren't obliged to carry personal identification with them all the time but in other countries this is a legal requirement.

Language

Focus grammar	present simple affirmative: -s or -es ending
Focus words	documents: *badge, card, credit card, driving licence, envelope, ID card, letter, membership card, passport*
Recognition vocabulary	words: *awful, cookery, dress-making, helmet*, etc.
Recycled language	personal details: *address, first name, marital status, married, surname, Mr, Miss, Mrs, Ms.* times: *at half-past six*, etc. everyday routines: *get up at, have a shower, start work at, go to bed at*, etc. hobbies and interests: *dance, go swimming, play tennis, sing, watch football*, etc.
Pronunciation	when is -s an extra syllable? *reads* vs *dances*, etc. **1B.2**
Discourse	linkers: *and, then*

Language note

Students often have problems remembering the third person *–s* or *–es*, as it doesn't carry meaning. In many languages, the verb ending shows who or what the subject is, but in English a noun or pronoun is used to indicate this. Some linguists predict this feature of English will eventually disappear altogether.

The third person singular spelling rule is closely connected with pronunciation. It is impossible to pronounce /s/ directly after /tʃ/, /ʃ/, /s/. It has to be pronounced /ɪz/. This is looked at in section D.

End product

In *Put it all together*, students give three short descriptions of other students' daily routines. They use the notes they have made in exercise 13 and link information with *and* and *then*.

Preparation

Take a few personal documents you are happy to use as realia (optional for exercise 1) and calculate Caroline's age from the details in her passport for exercise 2. Make sure students have dictionaries.

Warmer

Write *How to give and understand personal details* on the board and play a team game. Draw a very simple silhouette of a person's head and shoulders on the board and put a question mark above it. Put students into small teams and say *You're a detective.* Give an example, *(Sherlock Holmes)* so students understand. Set a three-minute time limit and direct students to **≫ p.8** to find information about the owner of the items. Elicit suggestions around the class and give one point for each piece of information.

A Vocabulary documents and personal details

1 Show the class some of your documents or point to examples on **≫ p.8**, and elicit the word *document*. In pairs, students show or tell each other about any documents or cards they have with them. Monitor and help with pronunciation as necessary and make a note of any problems for exercise 3.

Extra help

Students repeat the exercise with a different partner.

2 Direct students to the form and check vocabulary. Elicit or remind students that *marital status* refers to whether or not a person is married. Go over the use of *Mr, Miss (unmarried), Mrs (married)*, and *Ms (either)*. Do the example together and set a short time limit for students to complete the form individually. Students compare in pairs before you ask for volunteers to give answers.

> 2 Caroline   3 she was born in 1981 so her age depends on the current date   4 British   5 12 Oct 1981, Lincoln   6 29 Weldon Street, Louth, Lincolnshire   7 509 483 8927   8 married   9 nurse   10 Louth County Hospital   11 reading French, playing the guitar, cats, tennis, sewing, cookery, listening to music, painting

3 Go through the instruction and example, pointing out the labels on the picture. Students continue in pairs. Monitor and help them to use the vocabulary from the table in exercise 2. Go over the answers as a class. Help with pronunciation of document vocabulary if necessary, with the stress falling on the first syllable, except for *ID card* /aɪ ˈdiː/.

> 1 credit card/driving licence   2 credit card/driving licence   3 passport   4 passport   5 passport   6 envelope/driving licence   7 business card   8 business card   9 badge   10 badge   11 iPod: music, tennis ball: tennis, etc.

Extra activity

Students tick the information on the form a detective would find out about them from the documents they are carrying. See who has the most and least ticks.

B Listen for key information

In this section, students listen for specific information in a short, natural-sounding monologue.

4 **1B.1** Tell students they will hear Caroline talking about herself and they should tick the information she gives on the form in exercise 2. Explain that the information on the audio is not in the same order as the form. Play the audio. Students compare answers. Play the audio a second time. To check answers, read through the words on the form, pausing for students to say *yes* or *no* according to whether she talked about them.

> ✓ surname   first name   nationality   date and place of birth   marital status   job   interests (cycling, tennis, cooking)

5 Direct students to the table and go through the information in the first column. Ask students about the type of information they will listen for to complete the second column, checking the meaning and use of *then* and *and*. Play the audio and check answers as a class.

> get up at: 6.30am and have breakfast   start work at: 8.00am
> finish work at: 5.00pm   evening: cook   go to bed at: about
> 11.00pm

Extra activity

In small groups, play the audio again for students to find
and point to connected items on >> p.8 (*passport, note from
husband Paul, hospital ID card, book about cats, bike, tennis, Thai
cookbook*).

6 Help students complete the *Me* column, if necessary. As
students compare in pairs, monitor and see how well they use
the present simple, but do not correct at this point. Encourage
students to join sentences using *and* and *then*.

Extra plus

Students tell the class about their normal day.

C Grammar present simple -*s* or -*es* ending

7 Before you do the exercise, use concept questions and draw
a timeline on the board to remind students that the present
simple is used for everyday routines.

> past ————————————— now ——————————— future
> X X X X X X X X X X X X X X X X X X X

Point to one X and say *I get up at six o'clock.* Then point to
other Xs and say *Monday, Tuesday, ...* Ask *Is this is the same
routine every day for me? (Yes.)* Ask a student what time they
get up, and repeat with *He/she gets up at ...* to demonstrate
spelling of the third-person -*s*. Point to the second column
heading and remind students that the verb *go* is spelt with
es in the third person. Elicit or explain that *have* and *be* are
irregular in the present simple. Students complete the box
individually. Check answers and write the verbs in two
columns on the board.

> -*s*:   start – starts   read – reads
> -*es*: finish – finishes   watch – watches

8 Check vocabulary and do one or two examples as a class before
students, in pairs, put the spelling rule into practice. Ask for
volunteers to give the answers and point out that most verbs
just take -*s*, apart from verbs ending in -*ch*, -*sh*, -*x* and -*s*.

> -*s*:   arrive sing dance make paint draw play eat drink think
> -*es*: teach   push   wash   kiss

Extra help

Direct students to >> p.8 and re-elicit sentences about Caroline's
interests. If students forget the third person -*s*, write a big
colourful 'S' on the board. Point to it every time you
hear it omitted. After a while, you will only need to turn in the
direction of the 'S' for students to remember it.

D Pronunciation when is -*s* an extra syllable?

9 1B.2 Go through item 1 as a class. Ask *How many syllables?* Play
the first item on the audio and tap the table. Repeat with the
second item. Continue with items 3–6, pausing after each pair
of sentences to give students time to count and decide whether
the number of syllables is the same or different. Play the audio
a second time, stopping after each pair of sentences. Elicit
answers around the class.

> 3 4/5 (different)   4 5/6 (different)   5 4/4 (same)   6 5/6 (different)

10 Play the audio again for a whole class choral drill. Nominate
small groups, pairs, or individuals to repeat.

11 Students write the verbs from exercise 9, according to whether
-*s* is pronounced as an extra syllable or not. Go through the
example and do another one, e.g. ask *Closes – box 1 or box 2?*
(*Box 2.*) *Opens – box 1 or box 2?* (*Box 1.*) Check answers as a class
and point out that the rule here is closely connected with the
spelling rule from section C.

> -*s* is not an extra syllable: reads   sings   opens   goes   starts
> -*s* is an extra syllable: watches   closes   finishes

Language note

Sometimes spelling and pronunciation issues are hard to
disentangle. *Dance* is spelt with an 'e' at the end but it finishes
with an /s/ sound. The -*s* ending must be spelt and pronounced
as an extra syllable.

Extra help

Students label the columns A/B and say a verb to test a partner.

12 Put students into different pairs from those they were in for
exercise 6. Go through the example and remind students to use
and and *then*. Monitor and be rigorous about accuracy of both
grammar and pronunciation. Remember to praise students
when they produce accurate sentences.

Extra plus

Students change pairs again and repeat exercise 12, using the
pictures on >> p.8 only.

ABCD Put it all together

13 Students copy the table in exercise 5. Ask them to mingle and
talk to three others. Check they are collecting all the information
and are making notes rather than writing full sentences.

14 Go through the instructions and the example. Put students into
groups of three or four and remind them to use *and* and *then*
to link their sentences.

Student performance

Students should be able to give a short description.

You can use this checklist to monitor and give feedback or to assess
students' performance.

Content	Do students include all the information? exercise 5
Coherence	Do students use *and* and *then* to link some ideas? exercise 6
Pronunciation	Do students usually add an extra syllable for -*es*? exercise 12

I can give and understand personal details.

Students tick *on my own* if they can give descriptions of three
people using their notes. They tick *with some help* if they need to
check the pronunciation of one or two verbs in section D.

Early finishers

Students use a dictionary and the picture page to write a list of ten
items in an imaginary 'top drawer'. They swap lists with a partner
and work out what information a detective may learn about them.

Additional material

www.oup.com/elt/result for extra practice material
www.oup.com/elt/teacher/result for extra teacher resources

How to give and understand personal details

G present simple -s or -es ending   V documents and personal details   P when is -s an extra syllable?

A Vocabulary documents and personal details

1 What documents have you got with you now? Show or tell a partner.

2 Look at **You're the detective!** opposite. Complete this form about the person.

1	Surname	Watt
2	First name	
3	Age	
4	Nationality	
5	Date and place of birth	
6	Address	
7	Telephone	
8	Marital status	
9	Job	
10	Place of work	
11	Interests	

3 How do you know the information in 1–11? Say which documents helped you.

Example   We know her birthday from her passport. We know her age from ...

B Listen for key information

4 **1B.1▶** Listen to Caroline. Which pieces of information from exercise 2 do you hear? Tick ✓ them.

5 Listen again. Complete the information for Caroline. Compare with a partner.

	Caroline	me
get up at		
then	have shower	
and		
start work* at		
finish work* at		
evening	play tennis	
go to bed at		

* or school / university

6 Complete the 'Me' column and tell a partner about yourself.

Example   I get up at 7 o'clock and then I brush my teeth.

C Grammar present simple -s or -es ending

7 Add these verbs to the grammar box.
finish start watch read

-s		-es	
I/you/we/they	he/she/it	I/you/we/they	he/she/it
get	gets	go	goes

irregular	
I/you/we/they	he/she/it
have / are	has / is

8 Do you add -s or -es to these verbs? Decide with a partner.

arrive dance draw drink eat kiss make paint play push sing teach think wash

More practice? **Grammar Bank** >> p.136.

D Pronunciation when is -s an extra syllable?

9 **1B.2▶** Do these pairs of sentences have the same or different numbers of syllables? Listen and count.

1 I sit and read. [4]   She sits and reads. [4] *same*
2 You sing and dance. [4]   She sings and dances. [5] *different*
3 We watch football. [ ]   He watches football. [ ]
4 They open and close. [ ]   It opens and closes. [ ]
5 I go swimming. [ ]   She goes swimming. [ ]
6 You start and finish. [ ]   It starts and finishes. [ ]

10 Listen again and repeat.

11 Write the verbs ending in -s from exercise 9 in this table.

The -s ending is <u>not</u> an extra syllable	The -s ending is an extra syllable
sits	dances

12 Look at your notes in exercise 5. Tell your partner how Caroline is different from you.

Example   Caroline gets up at half past six. I get up at eight o'clock.

ABCD Put it all together

13 Ask three other students in the class about their normal day. Make notes like the table in exercise 5.

14 Work in small groups. Tell the others about the people you talked to in exercise 13. Listen and guess who the people are.

Example   She gets up at eight o'clock. Then she ...

I can give and understand personal details.

Tick ✓ the line.   with a lot of help   with some help   on my own   very easily

Office Life

Episode one

1
Justin Hi. Are you new?
Anna Yes.
Justin When did you start?
Anna On Monday.

2
Justin Where do you work?
Anna Just along the corridor. What do you do?

3
Justin I'm a computer technician. I check the system for viruses.
Anna How often do you check it?
Justin Not very often. They don't pay me enough!

4
Anna So what are you doing now?
Justin I'm playing a computer game. Why not? The boss isn't looking!

5
Anna What's the boss like?
Justin I don't know her. She's new. But people say she's horrible.
Anna Really? What's her name?

6
Justin Anna Conde. But we call her Anaconda.
Anna Why do you call her that?
Justin Why do you think?!

7
Anna Where does she come from?
Justin I don't know. The zoo, probably!

8
Anna Hmm. And what's your name?
Justin Justin. And you?

9
Anna I'm Anna Conde – the new boss. And by the way, I think you've got a virus.
Holly Ouch!

Question words

Who? Where? When? What? Why? Which? How?

How to ask questions about people

Orientation

Context

In this lesson, students will focus on asking questions to get to know people.

Office Life is a photo strip story from a make-believe TV situation comedy. The main characters are Justin and Holly. (*Office Life* appeared in *English Result Elementary*, lessons 4D and 12C).

In this episode, Justin and Holly meet Anna, a new person to the office. Justin tells her about his work, and talks critically about their new boss, whom he hasn't actually met yet.

Culture note

In Britain, as in many countries, certain topics of conversation are not considered acceptable when you meet someone for the first time or you don't know them very well. These include age, salary, religion, and details of personal relationships.

Language

Focus grammar	question formation: *be, do* pronouns: personal *I, you, he,* etc. possessives: *your, our, their,* etc.
Preview grammar	past simple
Focus words	question words: *how, what, when, where, which, who, why* others: *because, boss, check*
Focus phrases	*What's ... like?*
Recognition vocabulary	*corridor, erase, system, technician, virus, warning*
Recycled language	*family, hobbies, home, study, work,* etc.
Pronunciation	/w/ and /h/ **1C.2** rhythm in questions: *Who was he with? What do they do?* etc. **1C.3**

Language note

In questions where a question word is followed by the full form of the auxiliary and a pronoun, they share the rhythm OooO, e.g. *What do they do?* In cases when the auxiliary is a short form, the rhythm changes to OoO, e.g. *What's your name?*

End product

In *Put it all together,* students ask a partner questions about work, studies, family, home and hobbies.

Preparation

Look back at *English Result Elementary* and make a note of key characters and information for exercise 1.

Check you know where the audience laughs in the cartoon sketch so you can help students with exercise 4.

Warmer

Draw three columns on the board: *at school, at work, at a party.* Tell students to imagine they meet somebody new at one of the places, and they want to get to know them better. Ask them to make a list of topics they would talk about. Set a short time limit and write suggestions on the board. Ask what they wouldn't talk about (see *Culture note* above).

Write *How to ask questions about people* on the board.

A Read a comedy sketch

In this section, students read a cartoon story for gist and detail, identifying humour in what the characters say.

1 Ask students what they remember about *Office Life* from *English Result Elementary.* Write some key characters and information on the board, e.g. Justin and Holly work together, the boss is Mr Minnit, Justin is lazy, always at the coffee machine, etc. Direct students to **» p.10.** Tell them not to read the dialogue but to answer the questions by looking at the photos.

> 1 Justin and Holly are in their twenties. Anna is a bit older.
> 2 Justin and Holly are friends.

2 Go through the instructions, emphasizing that students must choose the *best* title. Check any vocabulary problems in a–c. Set a two-minute time limit to encourage students to skim the text. Students compare with a partner and say why their chosen title is the best.

> The New Boss (This is the main point of the whole story. There is no information about a computer, and we aren't told about other bad days.)

3 Tell students to read questions 1 and 2 and explain that there is more than one answer to question 2. Students reread the text carefully and compare answers in pairs. Go through the answers as a class.

> 1 At the end. 2 Justin tells Anna he doesn't check the system for viruses very often, he doesn't get paid enough, the new boss is 'horrible', people call her Ana Conda (which sounds like a type of snake) and he's playing a computer game and not working.

4 Direct students to the title of the section *Read a comedy sketch* and remind them that the dialogue comes from a TV show. In pairs, students decide where they think the audience will laugh. Nominate or ask for volunteers to read Justin and Anna's parts in frames 1–3. Ask why an audience would laugh after Justin says *They don't pay me enough. (Justin doesn't work hard because he doesn't get much money.)* Help students express the idea if necessary, but do not overcorrect for accuracy at this stage. Monitor and help as students continue in pairs.

5 **1C.1** Play the audio for students to confirm their guesses. Play it a second time, pausing at the laughter places and ask students why people might laugh. Help students get their ideas across.

6 Check students have covered **» p.10** and read through the instructions. Remind them to think about the subject pronoun *(Is it singular or plural?)* and the tense *(present or past?)* to help them. Students compare answers in pairs.

7 Students read the text again to check their answers. Nominate students to read the sentences out. As a quick review, ask students what tense each question is *(1 past simple, 5 present continuous, all the others are present simple).*

> 2 do 3 do 4 do 5 are 6 is/'s 7 is/'s 8 do 9 does 10 is/'s

B Pronunciation rhythm in *Wh-* questions

8 Direct students to *Question words* and the pictures at the bottom of **» p.10**. Do the example as a class, saying *Because!* to elicit the question *Why?* Students continue individually.

When? Now!	How? Carefully!
Who? You!	Which? That one!
Where? Here!	What? Nothing!

9 **1C.2** Draw two columns on the board labelled 1 /w/ and 2 /h/. Play the audio for students to listen and call out 1 or 2. Play the audio a second time and monitor carefully as students repeat.

Teaching tip

/w/ is actually a semi-vowel sound, so some students have problems pronouncing it and try to make it a strong consonant like /g/ or /v/. If this is the case, tell them to form their mouths as though they were going to say /u:/. They can then open out their lips to say /w/.

10 In pairs, students test a partner. Monitor and give positive feedback for clear pronunciation. Give extra help as necessary.

Extra activity

As *question* and *answer* are key pieces of metalanguage, work briefly on pronunciation. Focus on /kw/ in *question* and the silent 'w' in *answer*.

11 **1C.3** Draw the stress pattern OooO on the board and write the first question so the stressed words are under the larger circles. Show or elicit that all the words in columns 1 and 4 are stressed. Play the audio, pausing after each item for students to repeat. Begin by tapping the desk on the two stressed words, to help students make the unstressed words (2 and 3) 'fit into' the rhythm. Encourage students to tap along. Play the audio a second time if necessary.

12 In pairs, students practise the conversation. Monitor and help with rhythm and pronunciation if necessary. Make sure that students swap roles.

Extra plus

After students have practised reading the conversation a few times, they can try to do it from memory. Encourage them to add movement and gesture, exaggerating the characters and their interaction, to bring the drama to life. Ask for volunteers to have the conversation for the class.

C Grammar *be* and *do* in questions

13 Direct students to the headings for the columns and rows in the grammar box. Point to the second column and ask *Be or do?* Go through the items as a class before students complete the questions in the grammar box.

present: are	does	do
past: was	were	did

Teaching tip

English uses auxiliary verbs *be* and *do* to make questions (and form negatives) in the past and present. Ask students how, in their language, they know a person is asking a question or making a negative. This will raise students' awareness and help them understand the importance of the auxiliary verbs *be* and *do* in English.

Extra help

Transformation drill. Say the cue, for students (SS) to transform affirmative into a question.

Present simple. *T He works in a bank. SS Where does he work? T We work in an office. SS Where do you work? T She works in a hospital. SS Where does she work? T They work in a hotel. SS Where do they work?*

Past simple. *T He worked in a bank. SS Where did he work? T She worked in a hospital. SS Where did she work? T We worked in an office. SS Where did you work? T They worked in a hotel. SS Where did they work?*

14 Check students understand the matching activity by doing the example as a class. Students write the letter of the second part of the sentence, rather than drawing lines to connect the two halves. Check answers as a class by nominating a student to say the first half and another student or group of students to complete the sentence.

2 e	3 g	4 f	5 d	6 b	7 a	8 c

15 Put students in pairs and go through the instructions, checking that they understand that they should invent a character for the new worker. Monitor and help as necessary and make sure students swap roles. Give positive feedback.

Extra plus

Volunteers do the role play for the class.

ABC Put it all together

16 Direct students back to the question words in exercise 8 and tell them to write one question for each of the topics.

17 Put students into pairs. Students ask each other their questions and make a note of their partner's answers. Remind students to ask for repetition, if necessary. Ask each student to tell the class one fact about their partner.

Student performance

Students should be able to ask personal information questions.

Use this checklist for monitoring and feedback or to assess students' performance.

Accuracy	Do students use auxiliary verbs *be* and *do* appropriately? exercise 15
Vocabulary	Do students use four or five different question words? exercise 10
Pronunciation	Do students try to use rhythm in questions? exercise 11

I can ask questions about people.

Students tick *on my own* if they can ask questions from memory. They tick *with some help* if they have read two or three of the questions from exercise 11.

Early finishers

In small groups, students choose one or two of the areas in exercise 16. They ask other students to find a person who is similar.

Additional material

www.oup.com/elt/result for extra practice material
www.oup.com/elt/teacher/result for extra teacher resources

How to ask questions about people

G *be* and *do* in questions   V question pronouns   P rhythm in *Wh-* questions

 A **Read a comedy sketch**

1 Work with a partner. Look at the photos opposite. Guess the answers to these questions.
   1 How old are the people?
   2 Are they friends?

2 Read **Office Life** opposite. Choose the best title for this episode. Compare with a partner.
   a The New Boss
   b Justin's Computer
   c Another Bad Day

3 Answer the questions with a partner.
   1 When does Justin understand that he's speaking to the new boss?
   2 Anna is angry. Why?

4 **Office Life** is a comedy sketch. Where do you think the audience will laugh? Write L.

5 **1C.1▶** Listen and check.

6 Cover the page opposite. Complete these questions from the story. Use *did*, *does*, *do*, *is*, and *are*. Then answer the questions with a partner.
   1 When ___did___ you start?
   2 Where _____ you work?
   3 What _____ you do?
   4 How often _____ you check it?
   5 What _____ you doing now?
   6 What _____ the boss like?
   7 What _____ her name?
   8 Why _____ you call her that?
   9 Where _____ she come from?
   10 What _____ your name?

7 Read and check.

B **Pronunciation** rhythm in *Wh-* questions

8 Look at **Question words** opposite. Match them with these answers.
   _Why?_____ Because!
   _____ Now!
   _____ You!
   _____ Here!
   _____ Carefully!
   _____ That one!
   _____ Nothing!

9 **1C.2▶** Listen and check. Which questions begin with /w/ and which begin with /h/?

10 Cover exercise 8 and test a partner.
   Example A Where? B Here!

11 **1C.3▶** Listen and repeat these questions. Keep the ●●●●rhythm.

●	●	●	●
Who	was	he	with?
Where	were	your	keys?
When	does	she	start?
What	do	they	do?
Why	are	you	here?
Which	is	her	desk?
How	did	it	end?

12 Act the **Office Life** conversation with a partner.

C **Grammar** *be* and *do* in questions

13 Write the red words from exercise 11 in the grammar box.

	questions with verb *be*		questions with other verbs	
	he / she / it	you / we / they	he / she / it	you / we / they
present	Where _is_ her car?	What _____ their names?	What _____ he do?	Where _____ you work?
past	Where _____ he born?	Who _____ you with?	When _____ they arrive?	

14 Match 1–8 with a–h.
   1 What's _h_   a she sit?
   2 Where do   b the boss?
   3 Which is   c the toilets?
   4 When did   d you before?
   5 Where were   e you sit?
   6 Who's   f you start this job?
   7 Where does   g your computer?
   8 Where are   h your name?

15 Work with a partner. Do a role play. One of you is a new worker in the office and the other is Holly. Use questions from exercise 14 or think of others.
   More practice? **Grammar Bank >>** p.136.

ABC **Put it all together**

16 Write questions to ask your partner about their work, studies, family, home, and hobbies. Use the question words from exercise 8.
   Examples Where do you work? What do you study?

17 Change partners and ask your new partner about their partner from exercise 16.

I can ask questions about people.

Tick ✓ the line.   with a lot of help   with some help   on my own   very easily

In the dictionary

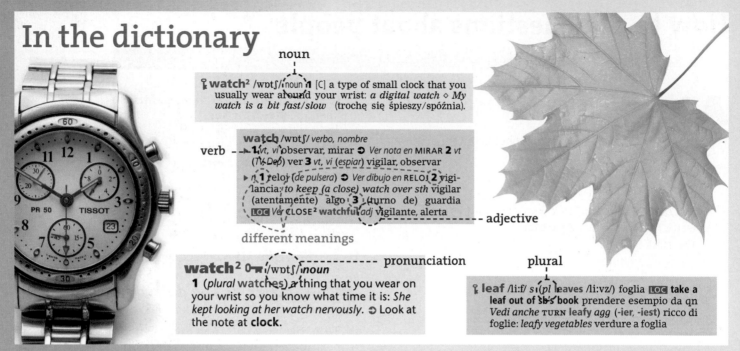

noun

 watch² /wɒtʃ/ *noun* **1** [C] a type of small clock that you usually wear around your wrist: *a digital watch* ◇ *My watch is a bit fast/slow* (trochę się śpieszy/spóźnia).

verb

watch /wɒtʃ/ *verbo, nombre*
▸ **1** *vt, vi* observar, mirar ➲ *Ver nota en* MIRAR **2** *vt* (*TV, DVD*) ver **3** *vt, vi* (*espiar*) vigilar, observar
▸ *n* **1** reloj (*de pulsera*) ➲ *Ver dibujo en* RELOJ **2** vigilancia **to keep (a close) watch over sth** vigilar (atentamente) algo **3** (turno de) guardia **LOC** *Ver* CLOSE² **watchful** *adj* vigilante, alerta

adjective

different meanings

pronunciation

watch² 0━━/wɒtʃ/ *noun*
1 (*plural* watches) a thing that you wear on your wrist so you know what time it is: *She kept looking at her watch nervously.* ➲ Look at the note at **clock**.

plural

 leaf /liːf/ *s* (*pl* leaves /liːvz/) foglia **LOC** **take a leaf out of sb's book** prendere esempio da qn *Vedi anche* TURN **leafy** *agg* (-ier, -iest) ricco di foglie: *leafy vegetables* verdure a foglia

Extracts from *Oxford Pocket Słownik Kieszonkowy*, *Diccionario Oxford Pocket para estudiantes de inglés*, *Oxford Wordpower Dictionary* and *Dizionario Oxford Study per studenti d'inglese*.

Definitions!
Which one is *wrong*?

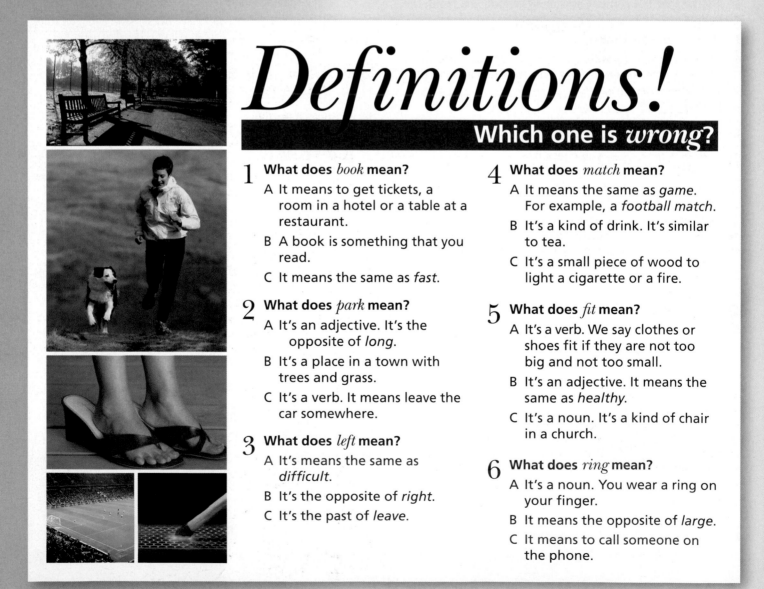

1 **What does *book* mean?**
A It means to get tickets, a room in a hotel or a table at a restaurant.
B A book is something that you read.
C It means the same as *fast*.

2 **What does *park* mean?**
A It's an adjective. It's the opposite of *long*.
B It's a place in a town with trees and grass.
C It's a verb. It means leave the car somewhere.

3 **What does *left* mean?**
A It's means the same as *difficult*.
B It's the opposite of *right*.
C It's the past of *leave*.

4 **What does *match* mean?**
A It means the same as *game*. For example, a *football match*.
B It's a kind of drink. It's similar to tea.
C It's a small piece of wood to light a cigarette or a fire.

5 **What does *fit* mean?**
A It's a verb. We say clothes or shoes fit if they are not too big and not too small.
B It's an adjective. It means the same as *healthy*.
C It's a noun. It's a kind of chair in a church.

6 **What does *ring* mean?**
A It's a noun. You wear a ring on your finger.
B It means the opposite of *large*.
C It means to call someone on the phone.

How to talk about vocabulary

Orientation

Context

In this lesson, students will practise explaining the meanings of words.

The fragments from bilingual and monolingual dictionaries in *In the dictionary* illustrate that one word can have different meanings and grammar. They also show how a dictionary provides information on pronunciation. The labels help students talk about the features in a dictionary.

In the magazine quiz, *Definitions!*, there are three definitions given for six words and the task is to identify the wrong definition for each word. The quiz is based on a famous BBC radio programme called *Call my bluff!* in which a team member gives three plausible definitions for obscure words and phrases. A member of the opposing team guesses the correct definition.

Language

Focus grammar	parts of speech in the dictionary
Preview grammar	past simple
Focus words	word classes: *adjective (adj), adverb (adv), noun (n), verb (v)* grammar: *singular (s), plural (pl)*
Focus phrases	definitions: *a kind of, is the opposite of, is the past/present of, means the same as, sounds the same as, What does .... mean?*
Recognition vocabulary	*definition, meaning, pronunciation, similar, uncountable*
Recycled language	present simple: *third person* words with two meanings: *change, fit, left, match, park, watch,* etc.
Pronunciation	pronunciation in the dictionary, using phonemic symbols 1D.1

End product

In *Put it all together*, students read short explanations for the meanings of three words, based on *Definitions!* on ≫ **p.12**, and audio script **1D.2** on ≫ **p.150**. Their partner identifies the incorrect definition.

Preparation

Take some different types of dictionary to class.

Prepare sets of vocabulary cards if you want to do the *Early finishers* activity at the end of the lesson.

Warmer

Show students some different kinds of dictionaries, e.g. big, small, bilingual, monolingual and picture dictionaries. Ask them which kind of dictionaries they have, which they prefer and why. Ask *What information can you find in a dictionary? (Meaning or definition, pronunciation, grammar, example sentences.)* Do not correct for accuracy, but help students get their ideas across.

Write *How to talk about vocabulary* on the board.

A Think about words and meanings

In this section, students are shown that some words have more than one meaning, or the same word can be used as a different word class.

1 Direct students to *In the dictionary* on ≫ **p.12** and show that if students follow the line from the words they will find an example. Put students in pairs and tell them to look carefully at the fragments. Go over the answers as a class.

> 2 watch   3 watchful   4 watches, leaves

2 Tell students that sometimes words in English have more than one meaning or use. To demonstrate this, do item 1 together as a class, showing that the words for the small pictures are both nouns and verbs. Students continue in pairs. Go over the answers as a class and clarify the relationship between the pictures and the words in the answers.

> 1 I'm going to watch a football match on TV.
> 2 I'm going to ring the restaurant and book a table.
> 3 Oscar always leaves his car in a car park.

Teaching tip

Set a short time limit for exercise 2, to encourage a light, game-like introduction to the topic.

3 Go though the instructions and each of the words in turn and see if students know two meanings for each word. Write the word *book* on the board. Explain or elicit that it is either something you read, or something you do, e.g. *book a table/ holiday*. Students check to see if this information is in their dictionaries. Do the example as a class and put students in pairs to continue. Monitor and help as necessary.

> 2 park   3 leaves   4 book   5 watch   6 book   7 leaves   8 park
> 9 watch   10 cook

B Pronunciation in the dictionary

In this section, students are introduced to ways in which a dictionary can help with pronunciation.

4 Ask *Is it easy to pronounce words in English from spelling? (Not always.)* Ask students to look at item 1 and show how the symbols represent *write* and *right*, they are spelt differently but sound the same. Students, in pairs or individually, continue the activity. Monitor and help students use dictionaries, if necessary. Write the answers on the board, drawing students' attention to the page in their dictionaries which gives a list of all pronunciation symbols (found either in the front or at the back).

> 2 son, sun   3 wait, weight   4 buy, bye   5 knew, new
> 6 meet, meat

5 Introduce the activity with a word students know, e.g. *climb*. Write it on the board and ask students to say it. Now write /klaɪm/, and point out that the phonetic symbols show that the final letter *b* isn't pronounced. Explain that the words in the exercise are new and they will find out how to pronounce them. Tell students they will listen and check but give positive reinforcement as students work out the pronunciation.

6 **1D.1** Play the audio and pause to give students time to think and check. Play the audio a second time if necessary. Write the words on the board and underline the silent letters.

C Read definitions and respond

In this section, students practise reading dictionary-style definitions in the form of a multiple-choice quiz.

7 Direct students to *Definitions!* on » **p.12**. Explain that it's a magazine-type quiz and a radio game. Ask students to read questions 1–6 only to find the words. Elicit *book, park, left, match, fit, ring* and write them on the board. Direct students to the first question and ask *Which definition is wrong?* Read options a, b, and c with the class, and check vocabulary. Students continue in pairs. Monitor and help as necessary.

8 1D.2 Play the audio, pausing before each answer. Gesture for students to call out their answer. Continue for students to hear the answer and explain if necessary, as you go along.

Extra help

The question *What does .... mean?* is a useful piece of classroom language for students. Drill it a few times, then follow it up by eliciting more examples: say *left* to elicit *What does left mean?*

9 Direct students to the phrases in the middle column of the table. Tell them that these phrases are used in dictionaries to explain what words mean and that they can also be very useful if students need to describe a word they can't remember. Ask students to underline one example sentence for each phrase in *Definitions!*

Students read the words in the first and last columns. Check vocabulary. Go through the example and do the exercise together as a class, asking for volunteers to make a definition from the table. Check pronunciation of the third person /s/ where appropriate. Ask the class to listen carefully and say *right* or *wrong* after each definition before you respond.

Write sounds the same as *right*.	*Son* sounds the same as *sun*.
Salmon is a kind of *fish*.	*Little* means the same as *small*.
Left is the past of *leave*.	*Easy* is the opposite of *difficult*.
Left is the opposite of *right*.	*Apple* is a kind of *fruit*.

Extra help

In pairs, one student says a word from the first column. A partner completes the definition. Students swap roles.

Extra activity

Write *What does 'orange' mean?* on the board and put students into pairs to write a new quiz question for the word *orange*. Monitor and help, using these examples if necessary: *a It's a colour between red and yellow. b It's a kind of animal. It lives in Indonesia. c It's a kind of fruit, similar to a mandarin and a lemon.*

D Grammar in the dictionary

In this section, students are shown more abbreviations used in dictionaries to indicate the grammar of a word.

10 Explain that most dictionaries use *abbreviations* to show the grammar of a word. Write *adj* on the board and elicit *adjective*. Direct students to *In the Dictionary* on » **p.12** and elicit an example of an adjective. Ask for one or two more examples from the first column of the table. Check students understand the column headings before they complete the table and compare in pairs. Go over the answers as a class.

short for: n – noun, v – verb
examples: adverb – slowly, plural – children, past tense – bought

Extra activity

In pairs, students test a partner. They take turns to write an abbreviation. Their partner says what it's short for and gives an example.

11 Direct students to the text and say *The story is about Justin, Anna, and Holly. True or False?* Tell students to read and ignore the blanks. *(False. The text only mentions Justin and Anna.)* Go through the instructions, the word pool and the example to check students understand the activity and the vocabulary. Students continue individually and can compare in pairs before you go over the answers as a class. Read the text aloud, pausing at each space, for the class to say the missing word.

2 office   3 checks   4 viruses   5 lazy   6 job   7 well
8 stopped   9 asked   10 questions   11 rude   12 new   13 boss

Extra plus

In pairs, students prepare a short text based on personal information from 1C. They choose three words to blank, and write the text again using the abbreviations. Pairs swap texts.

ABCD Put it all together

12 Put students into groups of four and give each pair within the group a letter, A or B. Explain that they will write quiz questions similar to those in *Definitions!* on » **p.12**. Check pairs are looking at the correct page. When students have finished, give them time to rehearse saying the definitions.

13 Students play *Definitions!* If necessary, encourage students to explain, very simply, why an answer is wrong.

Student performance

Students should be able to make short, simple statements.

Use this checklist for monitoring and feedback or to assess students' performance.

Fluency	Do students say definition phrases without a lot of hesitation? exercise 9
Vocabulary	Do students use different word classes? exercise 11
Pronunciation	Do students pronounce the /s/ on the third person? exercise 9

I can talk about vocabulary.

Students tick *on my own* if they have prepared and read one of their quiz questions without a lot of hesitation. They tick *with some help* if they hesitated occasionally in all their quiz questions.

Early finishers

Write the following words on cards: *lemon, saw, wrong, thin, slept, push, give, fantastic, old, boss, slowly, thought*. Give a set of word cards to each pair of students. They take it in turns to pick up a card and ask *What does ... mean?* The partner answers using phrases from exercise 9.

Additional material

www.oup.com/elt/result for extra practice material
www.oup.com/elt/teacher/result for extra teacher resources

How to talk about vocabulary

G grammar in the dictionary   V definition words   P pronunciation in the dictionary

A Think about words and meanings

1 Look at **In the dictionary** opposite. Find an example of each.

   1 a noun = *leaf*   3 an adjective =
   2 a verb =   4 a plural =

2 Complete the sentences with a partner. Use the pictures to help you.

   1 I'm going to ⌚ a football 🎾 on TV.

   2 I'm going to ⭕ the restaurant and 📖 a table.

   3 Oscar always 🍂 his car in a car 🌳 .

3 Complete the sentences. Use each word twice.

   book   cook   leaves   park   watch

   1 My mum works in a restaurant. She's a _cook_ .
   2 You can't _____ your car there.
   3 The train _____ at twelve.
   4 I often read a _____ before going to sleep.
   5 Shall we _____ a DVD?
   6 Did you _____ a room in the hotel?
   7 The garden is covered in _____ .
   8 We went for a walk in the _____ .
   9 My _____ says the time is 3.15.
   10 You can _____ this in the microwave.

B Pronunciation in the dictionary

4 Match these words and their pronunciation. Then check in a dictionary.

   buy son meet ~~write~~ knew sun
   wait meat ~~right~~ new weight bye

   1 /raɪt/ *write, right*   3 /weɪt/   5 /njuː/
   2 /sʌn/   4 /baɪ/   6 /miːt/

5 Find the pronunciation of these words in the dictionary. Try to say the words.

   debt receipt quay rough

6 **1D.1▶** Listen and check.

C Read definitions and respond

7 Look at **Definitions!** opposite. Work with a partner. Read the quiz and decide which definition (a, b or c) is wrong.

8 **1D.2▶** Listen and check your answers.

9 Make definitions from the table.

Write	means the same as	leave
Salmon	sounds the same as	sun
Left	is the opposite of	fruit
Son	is a kind of	difficult
Little	is the past of	small
Easy		right
Apple		fish

Example   *Write* sounds the same as *right*.

D Grammar in the dictionary

10 Write these words in the table.

   bought verb ~~adjective~~ slowly noun children

	short for ...	example
adj	*adjective*	slow
adv	adverb	
n		child
pl	plural	
v		buy
pt	past tense	

11 Complete the story with these words. Use a dictionary to help you.

   asked boss checks job lazy new office questions
   rude stopped viruses well ~~works~~

   Justin is a computer technician. He ¹ _works_ (v) in an
   ² _____ (n) and he ³ _____ (v) the system for
   ⁴ _____ (pl). He's ⁵ _____ (adj) and doesn't do his
   ⁶ _____ (n) very ⁷ _____ (adj). Yesterday, Anna
   ⁸ _____ (pt) at his desk and ⁹ _____ (pt) him some
   ¹⁰ _____ (pl). Justin said some very ¹¹ _____ (adj)
   things about the ¹² _____ (adj) boss. He didn't know
   it, but Anna *is* the new ¹³ _____ (n)! The moral of the
   story is 'Always find out who you are talking to!'

   More practice? **Grammar Bank** ≫ p.136.

ABCD Put it all together

12 Work in a four, organized as Pair A and Pair B. Pair A look at **Definitions!** on ≫ p.126. Pair B look at **Definitions!** on ≫ p.132. Add a wrong definition in questions 2 and 3 and complete the missing example in question 3.

13 Take turns to be A and B.
   A Read out a question and the three possible answers, a, b and c.
   B Guess which definition is wrong.

I can talk about vocabulary.

Tick ✓ the lines.   with a lot of help   with some help   on my own   very easily

Writing A learning biography

A Read for general meaning

1 Read the text. Don't worry about the spelling mistakes! What language is Cleo studying?

I'm studying _____ at the moment. It's the most important langage in West Africa, and I want to travel to Senegal and Mali next year.

I go to evening classes three times a week. We have a coursebook, and I aways study it if I've got a free moment, on the bus for exampl. I also have a vocablary notebook, and I writ new words in there, with an example sentence. I've got some CDs for listening practice, and I lisen to them when I'm in the house cooking or cleaning. I somtimes listen to Radio Paris too, and I can undestand a little.

Cleo Roberts

2 Read the sentences. Are they *true* or *false*?
In the text, Cleo tells us ...
1 she wants to travel to Senegal next year. *True*
2 she goes to classes three mornings a week.
3 she reads her coursebook on the bus.
4 she reads her vocabulary notebook when she's cooking.
5 she listens to French radio.

3 Ask your partner these questions.
1 Why are you learning English?
2 When do you study your coursebook?
3 What do you write in your notebook?
4 How do you practise listening?

B Think about learning English

4 Work with a partner. What verbs can you use to talk about learning a language?
1 _write, read, send_   email
2 _____ songs
3 _____ DVDs
4 _____ books
5 _____ computer games
6 _____ my notes
7 _____ other students
8 _____ the radio

5 Why and How? Answer the questions.
1 Why is Cleo studying this language?
2 How does she study it?

6 Here are some points about learning English. Do they answer the question *Why do you study?* or *How do you study?*
1 I write new words in a notebook. *How*
2 I want to visit Canada.
3 I listen to CDs in English on the bus.
4 I watch DVDs in English.
5 I need English in my work.
6 I need to read books in English at university.
7 I meet English speakers in a pub in my town.
8 I learn the words of songs in English.

7 **1E.1▶** Luisa is studying English. Listen and write *why* and *how* notes in the table.

Studying English		Luisa	me
Why?			
How?	lessons		
	study		
	practice		

8 Write notes for you in the table.

C Check spelling

9 Correct the mistakes in Cleo's writing. Add one letter to each underlined word.

ABC Put it all together

10 Write a learning biography for you. Use your notes from exercise 8 to help you.

11 Check your spelling.

12 Give your paragraph to your partner. Do you do the same things?

I can write a learning biography.

Tick ✓ the line.   with a lot of help   with some help   on my own   very easily

Orientation

Context and language

In this lesson, students will read about why and how people learn languages to enable them to write a personal learning biography.

Recycled language	words: *classroom language* phrases: *verbs and nouns: play games, read a book, send an email*, etc. grammar: *present simple tenses; question pronouns*
Recognition language	places: *Mali, Senegal, West Africa*

End product

In *Put it all together*, students write a short paragraph using their notes (about 65–75 words). They review spelling and capitals and swap texts with a partner to compare ways of studying.

Warmer

Write *biography* and *diary* on the board. Ask *What's the difference?* Set a short time limit for students to brainstorm ideas *(a diary is more private, a biography more public)*. Ask why people write a language learning biography *(to reflect on what they know and, how they learn)*. Write *How to write a learning biography* on the board.

A Read for general meaning

In this section, students scan a text for specific information.

1 Read the question. Direct students to the gap in the first sentence. Ask them to read quickly to find the answer *(French)*.

2 Go through the instructions. Ask students to read items 1–5 and check vocabulary. Students continue individually and compare in pairs. Go over the answers with the class, asking for volunteers to correct any false facts.

> 2 False. (evening classes)   3 True   4 False. (She listens to CDs.)
> 5 True

3 Read through questions 1–4 and give students time to make notes. Monitor and help with ideas. In pairs or small groups students exchange information. One person from each group reports to the class.

B Think about learning English

4 Go through the instructions and the example as a class. Put students in pairs to continue. Monitor and help as necessary. Ask for answers around the class.

> 2 sing, listen to, write, understand   3 watch, understand
> 4 read, understand   5 play   6 read, review, study   7 listen to, talk to, practise with   8 listen to

Extra activity

Read down the list of nouns, asking for a show of hands for each item if students use these for their learning. Nominate students to use one of the verbs to say what they do.

5 Write *Why?* and *How?* on the board. Ask *Which word do you answer with because?* *(Why)*. Students answer the questions individually. Check answers as a class. Elicit more reasons for learning a language and write key words on the board, e.g. *work, pleasure, it's a school subject, for qualifications.*

> 1 To travel to Senegal and Mali. It's the most important language in West Africa.
> 2 She goes to evening classes, studies in her free time, writes vocabulary in her notebook, listens to CDs and the radio.

6 Read through the instructions and the example. Do one or two more items together before students continue individually. Monitor and help as necessary. Check answers as a class.

> 2 Why   3 How   4 How   5 Why   6 Why   7 How   8 How

Extra activity

In small groups, students brainstorm other ways of studying, e.g. *practising speaking in the mirror, sending emails in English, writing new vocabulary on sticky notes and labelling things around the house.* Ask students if they've tried these ideas.

7 1E.1 Check students understand the activity and the table. Play the audio for them to make notes. Students compare in pairs. Play the audio a second time if necessary. Check answers.

> **Why:** wants to visit Canada
> **How:** two lessons a week, does homework, practises speaking in an Irish pub, watches English TV there too

8 Tell students to complete the final column for themselves. They can use dictionaries to help. Monitor and help as necessary.

C Check spelling

9 Direct students to Cleo's learning biography and elicit that the red underlining indicates typing mistakes. Go through the example as a class before students correct the other mistakes. Ask for volunteers to spell the words correctly. Remind them of the importance of checking their own work for spelling.

> always   example   vocabulary   write   listen   sometimes   understand

ABC Put it all together

10 Tell students to say *why* they are studying before they explain *how*. Remind them to refer back to exercise 8 if necessary.

11 Encourage students to use dictionaries to check spelling and capital letters.

12 Students, in pairs, swap biographies. Ask them to report similarities back to the class

Student performance

Students should be able to write a paragraph following a simple plan.

Use this checklist for monitoring and feedback or to assess students' performance.

Organization	Have students written an introduction saying why they are studying?
Content	Have students given three different ways of learning?
Punctuation	Have students spelt words correctly?

I can write a learning biography.

Students tick *on my own* if they have included all the information in the correct order. They tick *with some help* if they have made a few spelling mistakes.

Early finishers

Students compare ideas in small groups. They choose another *how* to try for the next unit.

Additional material

www.oup.com/elt/result for extra practice material
www.oup.com/elt/teacher/result for extra teacher resources

Warmer

Remember who

Read sentences 1–10 below. Students write who said or wrote them and then check in unit 1.

1 Yes, it's short for Francisco.   2 I'm from Louth.   3 I'm a computer technician.   4 What's the boss like?   5 Ouch!   6 I've got some CDs for listening practice.   7 I'm learning English because I want to go to Canada.   8 My husband's name is Paul.   9 I'm playing a computer game.   10 There's an Irish pub in my town.

1 Chico	4 Anna Conde	7 Luisa	10 Luisa
2 Caroline Watt	5 Holly	8 Caroline Watt	
3 Justin	6 Cleo	9 Justin	

A Grammar

1 Possessive 's 1A exercises 6–10

Warm-up: Write one or two sentences about yourself and your family on the board, omitting the *'s*. Ask students to suggest corrections.

Set-up: Go through the instructions. Do the first item together and tell students to write a dash (–) in spaces where they don't need to add a letter.

1 –	4 names	7 parents'	10 –
2 sisters	5 brother's	8 surnames	11 father's
3 sisters'	6 –	9 mother's	12 surnames

Follow-up: Students write a couple of sentences about themselves and their family, including one false fact. They can use the text in 1A exercise 10 for help if necessary. Students swap sentences with a partner, who asks questions to find the false fact.

2 Present simple -s or -es endings 1B exercises 7, 8

Warm-up: Say verbs from the word pool for students to say the third person singular form. Monitor for pronunciation. If you can't hear the final 's' sound, draw a big letter 's' on the board.

Set-up: Say a couple of the verbs and nominate students to spell the third person singular form.

2 goes	4 takes	6 finishes	8 reads	10 play
3 has	5 starts	7 watches	9 sings	

Follow-up: In pairs, students create three gap-fill sentences. Students swap with another pair and complete the sentences. They check each other's answers.

3 be and do in questions 1C exercises 13–15

Warm-up: Write these letters on the board: *e, i, a, e, w, d, o, i, s, r.* Set a short time limit for students to make auxiliary verbs, using letters more than once.

is, are, was, were, do, does, did

Set-up: Ask students to read questions 1–7 and check any vocabulary problems.

2 did   3 are   4 were   5 do   6 does   7 is

Follow-up: Go through the question words *What?, Where?, Who?* and ask for an example answer. Put students in pairs. They choose four questions to ask a partner.

4 Pronouns and possessive adjectives 1C exercises 11, 13

Warm-up: Tell students to imagine they are talking about Flavio. Tell them to use the information in exercise 1 to make sentences, e.g. *His name's Flavio.* Ask for volunteers to say their sentences. Monitor for accuracy of pronouns and possessive adjectives.

Set-up: Go through the first item as an example with the class.

1 Their   2 My   3 your   4 His   5 Our, We

Follow-up: Students choose two people from the unit and write three sentences about each one. They read their sentence in pairs or small groups for the others to guess who it is.

5 Grammar in the dictionary 1D exercises 10, 11

Warm-up: Write the following abbreviations on the board: *n, v, adj, pl, adv*. Ask what they mean and for an example of each.

Set-up: Go through the instructions and the example to check students understand the activity.

2 plural noun   3 adverb   4 noun   5 adjective   6 past tense

Follow-up: In pairs, students write a list of ten words from unit 1. They join with another pair and ask what type of word it is.

B Vocabulary

6 Personal details 1B exercise 2

Warm-up: Pair work. Set a short time limit of about two minutes for students to write types of personal information. Give one or two examples from the first column in the table.

Set-up: Direct students to the table and check vocabulary in the first column.

Students' own answers

Follow-up: In pairs, students ask each other two or three questions.

7 Documents 1B exercise 3

Warm-up: Write the following words on the board: *credit card, driving licence, passport* and ask students what personal information each one contains.

Set-up: Choose one of the items to do together as a class.

1 note   2 ticket   3 envelope   4 licence   5 initials   6 card
7 badge   8 passport

Follow-up: Students empty their pockets and bags and see how much information somebody could find out about them from the documents they are carrying. They tell a partner.

8 Question pronouns 1C exercise 8

Warm-up: Write these letters on the board: *w, o, e, r, n, a, t, y, i, c, h.* Set a short time limit for students to write question pronouns. They can use the letters more than once.

who, what, where, why, when, how, which

Set-up: Go through the example. Tell students to look at the answer to help find the word.

2 Who   3 What   4 When   5 How   6 Which   7 Why

Follow-up: Pair work. Students ask each other one question using each pronoun. They use questions from exercise 8, or their own ideas.

Early finishers

Students write *My language and English* and draw two columns with the headings *same* and *similar*. They go through unit 1 to find words to put in both columns. In the second column students write a translation. They can add any other words connected to the topic that they know.

A Grammar

1 **Possessive 's** Add *s*, *'s*, *s'* or nothing in the spaces in this text. There are nine missing letters.

My name___¹ is Flavio. I've got two sister___² and a brother. My sister___³ name___⁴ are Maria and Celia. My brother___⁵ name___⁶ is Lucio. In my country, we take both our parent___⁷ surname___⁸. Our mother___⁹ surname___¹⁰ comes first and our father___¹¹ surname___¹² comes second. My surname___¹³ are Arantes and Ferreiro.

2 **Present simple *-s* or *-es* endings** Complete the text with the correct form of these verbs.

take   watch   ~~get up~~   go   finish
sing   have   start   read   play

Keira ¹*gets up*_____ early and ²_____ running. She ³_____ breakfast and ⁴_____ the train to work. She ⁵_____ work at 9.00 and ⁶_____ at 5.30. In the evening, she ⁷_____ TV or ⁸_____ a book. At the weekend, she ⁹_____ and ¹⁰_____ the piano in a band.

3 **be and do in questions** Complete the questions with these forms of *be* and *do*.

is   are   ~~was~~   were   do   does   did

1   What *was* on TV last night?
2   What _____ you do last weekend?
3   Where _____ my glasses?
4   Where _____ you born?
5   Where _____ you live now?
6   Where _____ your family come from?
7   Who _____ your favourite actor?

4 **Pronouns and possessive adjectives** Underline the correct word.

1   I've got a sister and a brother. They / Their names are Carol and Colin.
2   I / My parents' names are Pedro and Paula.
3   What's you / your name?
4   Chan Kong-Sang is from China. He / His nickname's Jackie.
5   We / Our names are Marta and Pablo. We / Our're from Spain.

5 **Grammar in the dictionary** Look at the underlined words in the text. Write the number next to the type of word.

adjective ☐   adverb ☐   noun ☐
plural noun ☐   verb ☐1☐   past tense ☐

Run is a verb. When people move¹ their feet² faster than walking they are running. People move quickly³ when they run. A cat⁴ can run faster⁵ than a mouse. Yesterday, a mouse ran⁶ into my garden.

B Vocabulary

6 **Personal details** Complete the form with your personal details.

1	Surname	
2	First name	
3	Age	
4	Nationality	
5	Date and place of birth	
6	Address	
7	Telephone	
8	Marital status	
9	Job	
10	Place of work	
11	Interests	

7 **Documents** Find the words.

1   enot _____
2   kittec _____
3   volpenee _____
4   cencile _____
5   ilastini _____
6   drac _____
7   gebda _____
8   sportsap _____

8 **Question pronouns** Complete each question with a different question word.

A ¹*Where*_____ do you live?
B In Prague.
A ²_____ do you live with?
B Nobody. I live alone.
A ³_____ time do you get up?
B Eight o'clock.
A ⁴_____ do you start work?
B Half past nine.
A ⁵_____ do you get to work?
B By bus.
A ⁶_____ day of the week is your favourite?
B Sunday.
A ⁷_____?
B Because I can relax.

Day trips from Bangor

North Wales

1 Visit Anglesey's beautiful beaches, and enjoy watersports such as surfing, canoeing, diving, and windsurfing.

2 Go walking among the lakes, forests and mountains of the Snowdonia National Park. The park covers 823 square miles and has some of the most beautiful countryside in Britain.

3 Visit the famous Swallow Falls on the Llugwy River, near the charming town of Betws-y-Coed.

4 See a village in Anglesey with one of the longest names in the world: Llanfairpwyllgwyngyllgogerychwyrndrobwyllllantysiliogogogoch. The sign in the railway station is as long as the platform!

5 See the ruins of the church on Llanddwyn Island. The island was the home of Saint Dwynwen, the Welsh Saint Valentine.

6 Take the mountain railway to the top of Snowdon, the highest mountain in England and Wales. On a clear day, you can see England in one direction and Ireland in the other.

7 Walk down the 400 steps to the South Stack lighthouse on Holy Island. This lighthouse is one of the most spectacular in the country.

8 See the famous old castle at Conwy. King Edward built the castle in only four years.

Snowdon Mountain Railway

Return Fares

Llanberis to summit

Adults	£21.00
Children under 15	£14.00
Students	£17.00

Single Fares

Llanberis to summit

Adult	£14.00
Children under 15	£11.00
Students	£11.00

Journey times

One way	1 hour
Round trip	2½ hours
First train	9.00a.m.

Distance
4½ miles (7½ kilometres)

Telephone 0870 4580033 ext 100 **Email** info@snowdonmountainrailway.co.uk

10 miles
10 kilometres

Holy Island
Anglesey
Conwy
Bangor
Llanddwyn Island
Llanberis
SNOWDON
3,560 ft
1085m
Betws-y-Coed

How to **ask for tourist information**

Orientation

Context

In this lesson, students will focus on asking for information about tourist attractions.

Day trips from Bangor is a tourist brochure advertising attractions and day trips around Bangor, in North Wales. The photos of places of interest illustrate the vocabulary panel, *Tourist attractions*. Specific details of a trip on the Snowdon Mountain Railway are given below the brochure page, e.g. prices and length of trip.

Culture note

Britain (or Great Britain) includes England, Scotland and Wales, and with Northern Ireland it forms the United Kingdom (UK). Welsh is the official language of Wales, spoken by about 700,000 people at home and for official purposes. All schools in Wales are obliged to teach Welsh and all road signs and markings are written in Welsh, usually with the English below. Many Welsh sounds are difficult for English people to pronounce, e.g. 'dd' is pronounced /ð/, and 'f' is /v/. Wales, like the rest of Britain, still uses imperial measures, e.g. *feet, miles* rather than the metric system of *metres, kilometres*.

Language

Preview grammar	superlative: *the highest, the longest,* etc.
Focus words	tourist sights: *castle, countryside, desert, forest, lighthouse, ruins, village* day trips: *fare, journey, one-way, return, round trip, single* adjectives: *far, high, long, much, old* prepositions of direction: *from, to*
Focus phrases	*How high is it?, How much is the fare?, It's a bit expensive.*
Recognition vocabulary	*charming, countryside, famous, kilometres, man-made, metres, natural, ruins, spectacular, summit*
Recycled language	numbers: *4 miles, 2 hours, 1000 metres* places and buildings: *beaches, church, island, lake, mountain, park, railway station, river* grammar: *prepositions of place in, on, at*
Pronunciation	rhythm in *How* questions 2A.2

End product

In *Put it all together,* students take turns role playing a tourist and a tourist information officer. They have a short conversation similar to *Pairwork* on >> **p.126** and >> **p.132**, asking and answering three questions. They can ask for repetition and can use cues on the board to help.

Preparation

Collect some authentic holiday brochures (optional for exercises 1 and 15), but essential if you want to do the *Extra activity* in exercise 7.

Think about a tourist attraction to describe to the class for exercise 7.

Warmer

Direct students to the map of North Wales and ask *How many lakes are there in the area? How many islands are there? What is Snowdon? How far is Anglesey from Bangor?* Do not overcorrect for accuracy at this stage, but help students get their ideas across.

Write *How to ask for tourist information* on the board.

A **Read a tourist brochure**

In this section, students practise scanning and more detailed reading in a semi-authentic tourist brochure.

1 Begin by raising interest and showing some authentic holiday brochures, if you have some. Elicit the word *tourist brochure* or use the section heading and ask students what kind of information they expect to find in one. Direct them to *Day trips from Bangor* and picture a. Do the first item as an example if necessary. Set a short time limit to encourage students to scan rather than read each text carefully to match the descriptions with the photos. Check answers quickly as a class.

> a 2 b 7 c 8 d 3 e 1 f 6 g 4 h 5

2 Ask students to look at the photos again, and to number three trips they would like to go on (1 first choice, 2 second choice, 3 third choice). Students compare with a partner and tell the class about their first choice. Tell them not to worry about correct pronunciation of place names and monitor for correct use of prepositions of place *in, on,* and *at*. If necessary, give examples of places in the text, for students to say the preposition and find and underline the phrase.

3 Tell students they will find out about the Snowdon Mountain Railway trip, using the map and the brochure information. Go through questions 1–4 and check vocabulary. Ask *What do we call the top of a mountain? (Summit.) What do we call a single and return journey together? (Round trip.) What do we call the price of train, plane or bus journey? (Fare.)* Go over the answers as a class.

> 1 3560 feet/1085 metres   2 4.5 miles/7.5 km   3 2.5 hours
4 £11.00

Extra help

If necessary, review numbers at this point. Write the following on the board: *a 3.5 b 35,000 c 35 d 335 e 3,500 f 3,000 g £3.50.* Read the numbers out in random order for students to call out a letter corresponding to the figure you say. Gradually increase the speed you say the numbers until students recognize them quickly. Change the numbers to generate more practice (e.g. 7.5, 75,000, etc.) if necessary. Elicit and drill pronunciation and put students in pairs to continue.

Extra activity

Ask the class which they would prefer to do: *walk up Snowdon, take the mountain railway up and down, or take the railway up and walk down.* See which activity is the most popular.

B **Vocabulary** tourist attractions

4 Direct students to *Tourist Attractions* and do the example together. Tell students that one of the words isn't in the pictures *(desert)*. Students complete the activity. Go over answers as a class. Ask *Are there any deserts in Great Britain? What's the weather like in a desert?* Monitor pronunciation for stress on the first syllable, making sure students don't pronounce it as *dessert* /dɪˈzɜːt/!

beach e	island h	railway f
castle c	lighthouse b	river d
church h	lake a	ruins h
desert (not in picture)	mountain f	village g
forest a		

How to describe places

Orientation

Context

In this lesson, students will practise giving a description of a typical holiday destination.

The Travel Agent photo story is about a couple who want to go on a safari holiday and a travel agent who is trying to promote holidays to Scandinavia (Norway, Sweden, and Denmark). The travel agent tries to convince the customers to change their plans, and finally suggests Oslo zoo. The couple leave without booking a holiday.

Language

Focus grammar	adjective order in noun phrases (fact and opinion): *lovely blue water*, etc.
Focus words	opinion adjectives: *fine, horrible, interesting, lovely, nice, pretty*, etc.
Focus phrases	*Are you sure?, How about a ...?, to book a holiday*
Recognition vocabulary	*animals, insects, palm trees, pyramids, safari, zoo*
Recycled language	adjectives: *blue, little, long, quiet, white*, etc. compass directions: *north, south, east, west* tourist attractions: *beaches, forests, islands, lakes, ruins*, etc.
Pronunciation	stress-timed rhythm 2B.3–4

Language note

The stress-timed rhythm of English means that unstressed syllables become very reduced and are usually either pronounced as /ɪ/ or /ə/, both very weak sounds, e.g. *-es* in *beaches* and *villages* is pronounced /ɪz/, and *ful* in *beautiful* and *colourful* is pronounced /fəl/.

End product

In *Put it all together*, students describe a place for a holiday in small groups. Students' descriptions are based on a listening text, and notes they have made about the weather, beaches, food, people and things to do in the place.

Preparation

See if you can find any colourful and detailed tourist brochures for holidays in Africa and Scandinavia, for the *Warmer*.
Think about tourist attractions in the places in exercise 1.

Warmer

Write *Scandinavia* and *Africa* at the top of two columns on the board and set a short time limit for students to brainstorm why people go to these places on holiday. Ask for suggestions around the class and write them on the board.
Show the brochures if you have any. Ask *Which place would you prefer? Why? Have you ever been on a safari? Have you ever been to Scandinavia?* Do not correct for accuracy at this stage, but help students get their ideas across, providing vocabulary as necessary.
Write *How to describe places* on the board.

A Read and listen for detail

In this section, students read a cartoon story and read for detail and follow the order of a conversation.

1   Go through the instructions and elicit a few examples of tourist attractions in North Wales (lesson 2A). Read the list of countries and put students in small groups to do the activity. Encourage students to add one or two places of their own. Set a short time limit then ask for suggestions for each place. Ask each group to tell the class about one more place.

2   Students read the photo story. Tell them to identify the tourist attractions and underline them. Then they identify which countries they come from. Students compare answers in pairs before you go over answers as a class.

> palm trees, beaches: the USA   pretty villages, fine castles: Spain   Aztec ruins: Mexico   pyramids: Egypt

3   2B.1 Play the audio for students to listen for the missing adjectives.

> Frame 3 nice   Frame 6 horrible, big   Frame 8 white, blue   Frame 9 white, old   Frame 11 long

4   Go through the example as a class and ask students to find the information in the dialogue. Ask them to read items 2–5 and check vocabulary. Students continue individually correcting any sentences they think are false. Students compare answers in pairs before you go over them as a class. Check any vocabulary in the dialogue and ask students if they would go to this travel agent's.

> 2 True   3 False. The customers want to see animals.   4 True
> 5 True

B Grammar adjective order

5   Direct students to the cartoon and ask *Who likes the insect? (The woman.)*, and *How does she describe it?* Write *a lovely little insect* on the board. Repeat for the man, and write *a horrible little insect*. Ask students whether *lovely* and *horrible* are opinions *(Yes)*, and whether *little* is an opinion *(no, fact)*. Go through the rule with the class, eliciting the answer before students complete the gaps.

> Put the fact **after** the opinion.
> Put the opinion **before** the fact.

6   Books closed. Ask students what two false facts Jen told the customers about Scandinavia. Elicit or give *It has pretty white villages.* and *It has fine old castles.* Ask which words are facts *(white, old)* and which are opinions *(pretty, fine)*. In pairs, students complete the activity. Ask around the class for answers.

> **fact:** big white blue old long
> **opinion:** horrible beautiful pretty fine

7   Go through the instructions and the first item as a class. Students work individually and compare their answers in pairs.

8 2B.2 Play the audio for students to confirm their answers. Play it a second time and pause after each item for students to repeat the phrases. Encourage students to say the phrases at a natural speed, as they are said on the audio (rather than as three clearly separate words).

> 1 ✓ 2 ✓ 3 beautiful white beaches 4 ✓
> 5 lovely blue water 6 nice long safari 7 ✓

Extra help

Class back-chain drill. Choose a couple of the phrases from items 1–7. Say the last word, for students to repeat, e.g. *railway*. Next, say the fact adjective and the noun for students to repeat, e.g. *old railway*. Finally, say the whole phrase for students to repeat, e.g. *beautiful old railway*.

Extra plus

Books closed. Say the nouns only in items 1–7 randomly and nominate students to say the complete phrase from memory. Students continue in pairs.

9 Go through the instructions and check understanding. Give A and B students time to look at the pictures on **>> p.126** and **>> p.132** and make notes to describe the places using adjectives. Tell them they can use their dictionaries and monitor and help them think of phrases to describe the places, e.g. *Picture A: a lovely quiet/small beach, a pretty little village, horrible dirty factories; Picture B: horrible crowded beach, lovely quite lakes, beautiful green forests*. At the end of the activity, see which place is the most popular.

C Pronunciation stress-timed rhythm

10 2B.3 Draw circles representing the three rhythms on the board. Point to a rhythm and tap the table, keeping the strong taps at roughly regular intervals whether you are tapping rhythm 1, 2, or 3. This helps show how the weaker taps have to 'fit in' with the strong ones. Play the audio, and pause after each phrase for students to repeat. Each phrase is said three times. Give extra practice if necessary.

11 2B.4 Play the audio, pausing after each set. Ask *Rhythm 1, 2, or 3?* Play the audio a second time for students to listen and repeat.

> a rhythm 3   b rhythm 1   c rhythm 2

Extra plus

In pairs, students say a phrase from exercises 10 and 11, for a partner to say which rhythm.

D Listen to someone describing a place

In this section, students listen to an authentic-sounding description of a place for gist.

12 2B.5 Draw a simple compass on the board and review the directions *north, south, east, west*. Read the instruction and options, pointing out that the definite article is used when the direction words are nouns but not adjectives. Play the audio.

> The north of Spain

13 Direct students to the words and ask if the north of Spain has all these attractions *(Yes)*. Play the audio. Students compare with a partner before you give the answers.

> ✓ forests, towns, mountains

14 Put students into pairs and set a short time limit for them to recall the adjectives Sara used to describe the nouns in exercise 13. Students can listen to the audio again before they look at audio script 2B.5 on **>> p.151** and check.

> **forests:** lovely, big   **towns:** beautiful, old
> **mountains:** high, nice

Extra activity

Ask if students know or like the north of Spain. If they visited as a tourist, ask if they liked it. If they haven't been, ask if they'd like to go there on holiday. Why? Why not? Help them express their ideas but do not overcorrect for accuracy.

ABCD Put it all together

15 Write the five topics on the board. Elicit one or two examples of words and phrases associated with each one and write them on the board. Give students time to make notes and rehearse saying their descriptions.

16 Put students into small groups to describe their places. Ask for a volunteer from each group to tell the class which place they thought was the best and give one reason.

Student performance

Students should be able to give a short description.

Use this checklist for monitoring and feedback or to assess students' performance.

Accuracy	Do students mostly use fact and opinion adjectives in the correct order? exercise 8
Vocabulary	Do students use different adjectives in their descriptions? exercise 9
Pronunciation	Do students try to use rhythm in noun phrases? exercise 11

I can describe places.

Students tick *on my own* if they have given a description of all aspects of a holiday using their notes. They tick *with some help* if they have looked at the notes on the board and read a few phrases from exercise 7.

Early finishers

Put students in pairs and give them time to prepare a conversation like *The Travel Agent,* using the places they talked about in exercise 16. Pairs act the conversation for the group.

Additional material

www.oup.com/elt/result for extra practice material
www.oup.com/elt/teacher/result for extra teacher resources

How to describe places

G adjective order   V fact and opinion adjectives   P stress-timed rhythm

A Read and listen for detail

1 Do you know any tourist attractions in these countries? Compare ideas in small groups.

Scandinavia Spain Egypt the USA Mexico *your ideas*

2 Read **The Travel Agent** opposite. Underline the tourist attractions. Which countries in exercise 1 do they come from?

3 **2B.1▶** Listen and complete the missing adjectives in **The Travel Agent** text opposite.

4 Read the sentences. Write *true* or *false*.
1 The customers want to book a safari. *True*
2 Jen wants to sell a holiday in Scandinavia.
3 The customers want to see insects.
4 Jen describes Scandinavia to the customers.
5 The customers aren't interested in a holiday in Scandinavia.

B Grammar adjective order

5 Complete the rule with *before* or *after*.

Put the fact _____ the opinion.
Put the opinion _____ the fact.

6 Work with a partner. Find more fact and opinion adjectives in the picture story.

fact		opinion	
long	b_____	*nice*	p_____
b_____	o_____	h_____	f_____
w_____	l_____	b_____	

7 Tick ✓ the correct phrases. Correct the wrong phrases.
1 beautiful old railway
2 pretty white villages
3 white beautiful beaches
4 horrible little insects
5 water blue lovely
6 long nice safari
7 pretty little island

8 **2B.2▶** Listen, check and repeat.

9 Work with a partner. Describe your pictures and find the differences. Decide which place would be better for a holiday.
Student A Look at the picture on ≫ p.126.
Student B Look at the picture on ≫ p.132.

More practice? **Grammar Bank** ≫ p.137.

C Pronunciation stress-timed rhythm

10 **2B.3▶** Listen and repeat the three rhythms.

rhythm 1	●	●	●
	nice	blue	lakes
rhythm 2	●•	●•	●•
	lovely	quiet	beaches
rhythm 3	●••	●••	●••
	interesting	African	animals

11 **2B.4▶** Listen and repeat. Are these rhythms 1, 2, or 3?
a **beau**tiful **co**lourful **vil**lages
b **fine old** trees
c **pret**ty **litt**le **is**lands

D Listen to someone describing a place

12 **2B.5▶** Listen to Sara talking about her home. Underline where you think she lives.
The north of England
The south of Italy
The north of Spain
North-east Brazil

13 Listen again and tick ✓ the things Sara talks about.
✓ beaches ☐ lakes ☐ castles ☐ forests
☐ towns ☐ islands ☐ mountains

14 Work with a partner. Can you remember what adjectives she uses to describe the nouns in exercise 13? Read the audio script on ≫ p.151 and check.

Example beaches – nice, quiet

ABCD Put it all together

15 Make notes about a place to go on holiday. Use these ideas:

weather beaches food people things to do

16 Work in small groups. Describe your place and agree on the best one.

I can describe a place.
Tick ✓ the line.   with a lot of help   with some help   on my own   very easily

Weather

Noun	Adj
rain	rainy
snow	snowy
cloud	cloudy
fog	foggy
storm	stormy
sun	sunny
wind	windy
heat	hot
cold	cold

Temperature

high — hot
— warm
— cool
low — cold

Rainfall

heavy — wet
light —
— dry

a
b
c
d

London Weather

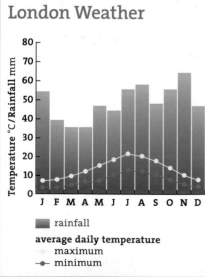

rainfall
average daily temperature
maximum
minimum

Afro hair

Going to Extremes

Nick Middleton, a geography lecturer at Oxford University, likes bad weather. In National Geographic's four-part TV series *Going to Extremes*, Nick travels to the places with the most extreme weather in the world — the hottest, coldest, wettest, and driest places.

In one episode of the series, Nick visits the Danakil in North East Ethiopia. The Danakil is a desert of salt. It's 100 metres lower than sea level and it's hot! The temperature is often higher than 50 degrees. The highest recorded temperature in the world is 57° in Libya. But the Danakil has the highest average temperature. In summer, it's never lower than 40°.

The local people, the Afar, are very tough. The men carry guns and long knives. But Nick finds their softer side: hair. These men spend two hours a day working on their big *Afro* hair. In this heat, they say, their hair is better than a hat.

In another episode of the series, Nick travels to the world's coldest inhabited place. In Oymyakon, Siberia, the average winter temperature is lower than minus 25°. Only Antarctica is colder, but nobody lives there. Nick also visits the wettest place in the world, Mawsynram in India, and the driest place, Arica in Chile.

How to compare the weather in different places

Orientation

Context

In this lesson, students will practise using comparatives and superlatives to compare weather in different places.

Going to Extremes is a magazine article which introduces a new geography-based TV series about the most extreme weather conditions in the world. The main picture shows a member of the Afar tribe, nomadic people from the north east region of Africa, and the small picture is Oymyakon in Siberia.

The four small photos in *Weather* show different places in London (the River Thames, Hyde Park. a main shopping street and Tower Bridge) and illustrate the weather vocabulary. The graph, *London Weather*, shows London rainfall and temperatures.

Culture note

The weather is considered Britain's favourite topic of conversation, but it's probably true to say that it's a universal topic. It's a neutral, non-controversial subject, especially for polite conversation with a stranger and a typical conversation opener might be *It's a lovely day, isn't it?* Many people associate the weather in England with being cold, rainy and foggy much of the time, but, in recent years the summers have become hotter, drier and longer.

Language

Focus grammar	comparative and superlative adjectives, *more, most*
Focus words	weather: *foggy, rain, rainy, storm, temperature, 5 degrees, -25 degrees*, etc. seasons: *summer, winter*
Recognition vocabulary	*Afro, average, episode, hair, rainfall, recorded, TV series*
Recycled language	months: *in January, in March*, etc. numbers: *5, 20*, etc. grammar: *comparative and superlative adjectives; be present; present simple and continuous: It's raining., It's windy., There is/aren't*
Pronunciation	*-er* and *-est* endings 2C.2

Language note

When there is a consonant cluster in phrases, e.g. *windiest city/ hottest summer*, the 't' at the end of *-est* often disappears.

End product

In *Put it all together*, students use their notes to tell their partner about the weather in places they know, giving four or five pieces of information about different times of the year. They refer to audio script 2C.3 on >> p.151 to make their notes, and are given rehearsal time before doing the activity.

Preparation

Find a picture or map of Australia for exercise 12 and collect pictures of extreme weather.

Warmer

Draw some weather symbols and temperatures on the board. Elicit simple weather vocabulary, e.g. *rain, sunny, hot, cold* and ask about the day's weather. Write *England, Ethiopia, Siberia* and *Australia* on the board, and ask what kind of weather students associate with each place. Point out that the weather isn't always bad in England.

Write *How to compare the weather in different places* on the board.

A Vocabulary weather

1 Direct students to pictures a–d on >> p.20 and check their understanding of weather vocabulary. Ask *Are there any clouds in picture b? Is the weather warm in picture c? In which pictures is the weather wet? Can you see the sun in any of the pictures? Do you think the temperature is high or low in picture b? Is the rain in picture d heavy or light? Is the weather stormy in any of the pictures?* Students continue the matching exercise. Ask for volunteers to give the answers.

> b It's hot and dry.   c It's cold and snowy.
> d It's foggy and rainy.

2 2C.1 Explain the activity and play and pause the audio for students to respond as a class. Play the audio a few times until students are responding quickly.

Extra help

Write the sentences from audio script 2C.1 on >> p.151 on the board and remind students of the use of the verb *be* in the present continuous tense in *It's raining.* and *It's* + adjective *(It's hot)* and *There is/are* + noun *(There isn't any wind)*. Students make their own true/false statements about the weather like the ones in exercise 2. They read them to their partner, who says true or false.

B Read for detail

In this section, students practise skimming a magazine article for gist and scanning for specific information.

3 Elicit the names of places which have very dry, very wet, extremely hot, and extremely cold weather. Students talk to a partner about the weather in places they have visited. Ask for volunteers to tell the class.

4 Tell students they will read an article about a new TV series *Going to Extremes*. Ask the class to look at the pictures and predict what it might be about. Elicit a few ideas, and ask students to read the article very quickly to see if they were correct. Student read it again quickly and find the names of four places Nick visits. Direct them to the small picture at the end of the article and ask *Where? (Siberia.)*

> The Danakil in NE Ethiopia; Oymyakon, Siberia; Mawsynram, India; Arica, Chile

5 Read questions 1–5 to check vocabulary. Ask students *Are you going to read the text in detail? (No.)* Direct them to question 1 and ask *What type of information do you need to look for to answer the question? (A number.)* Show them that they read and find a number, and then look at words on either side to check they have found the correct information. Set a short time limit and check answers as a class. Ask students if they would watch the programme.

> 1 57°   2 the Danakil   3 40°   4 lower than -25°   5 Antarctica

Extra help

Write the answers on the board in random order. Students match the answers to the questions and check in the text.

Extra activity

In pairs, students choose three or four new items of vocabulary in the text. They guess the meaning of each word and check and confirm in their dictionaries.

Souvenirs

bag   cap   cup   fan   key ring   knife
mug   plate   postcard   poster   rug   T-shirt

Souvenir Challenge
Can you guess where these souvenirs are from?

NORTH AMERICA

— The USA

— Mexico

CENTRAL AMERICA

Panama —

SOUTH AMERICA

Peru —

UK —   — Germany
        — Austria
EUROPE
            THE
            MIDDLE
            EAST
Tunisia —   — Jordan
NORTH AFRICA   — Egypt

Russia —

ASIA

China —

Postcard

Hi James

Having a great time here in Cairo.

Today we visited the Khan el-Khalili Bazaar. It's one of the biggest bazaars in the world and we got lost! There are thousands of shops. I bought a leather jacket and a rug. We spent an hour in a carpet shop and the man gave us tea. Then he wasn't very happy because we left without buying anything!

Tomorrow, we're going to visit the Cairo opera on the island of Gezira.

See you next week

Love from Petra (and Bernie!)

How to talk about personal things

2D

Orientation

Context

In this lesson, students will focus on talking about holiday souvenirs and personal belongings.

Souvenir Challenge is a travel magazine article which invites readers to see how much they know about the world by guessing which countries different souvenirs come from. The places are shown on the world map accompanying the article.

Postcard shows the back of a postcard that a woman called Petra has written to her friend James. She mentions the Khan el-Khalili Bazaar in Cairo which is one of Cairo's most important shopping areas.

Language

Focus grammar	past simple: affirmative, negative, yes/no questions, *Wh*-questions regular and irregular verbs: *bought, go, spend, visit, want, write,* etc.
Focus words	souvenirs: *cap, cup, fan, key ring, mug, postcard, poster,* etc. countries and regions: *India, North Africa, South America,* etc.
Focus phrases	*Better than nothing!, Oh well!*
Recognition vocabulary	*challenge, duty free shop, Pisces*
Discourse	using topically-related vocabulary in conversation

End product

In *Put it all together*, students have conversations in pairs about personal possessions, e.g. about the place of origin and who bought the item. They have rehearsed a similar conversation before, and can use notes of key words from the listening in exercise 12.

Preparation

Take some souvenirs to the class. They can be like the ones on >> p.22 or, for example, stones from a beach or postcards.

Warmer

Put students into small groups and ask them to write a list of the type of holiday presents people buy. Ask around the class for examples. Show your souvenirs if you have any and ask *What's more important, things or memories?* Do not overcorrect for accuracy but help students express their ideas. Direct students to the pictures around the map to see which items they mentioned.

Write *How to talk about personal things* on the board.

A Vocabulary souvenirs, countries, and regions

1 Tell the students to look at the map on >> p.22. Put students in pairs, and go through the instructions and the example. Give them three minutes to brainstorm names of countries for each of the areas. Ask around the class for suggestions and see if students have visited any of the places.

> **Suggested answers**
> **Asia:** China, India, Japan, etc.
> **Central America:** Mexico, Guatemala, etc.
> **Europe:** Greece, Spain, Poland, etc.
> **North Africa:** Morocco, Sudan, Egypt, etc.
> **North America:** Canada, Cuba, the USA, etc.
> **South America:** Brazil, Argentina, Chile, etc.
> **The Middle East:** Iran, Iraq, Israel, etc.

2 Students work individually, matching pictures 1–12 with the words in *Souvenirs*, before comparing in pairs. Do not give answers at this stage.

3 2D.1 Play the audio, pausing after each item for students to check their answers. Explain that the words are in sentences.

1 fan	4 key ring	7 plate	10 T-shirt
2 rug	5 cup	8 poster	11 bag
3 mug	6 knife	9 cap	12 postcard

Extra help
Say the picture numbers for students to call out the words. Monitor and give extra pronunciation practice, if necessary.

4 2D.2 Go through the instruction and tell students to listen carefully as the conversation is very short. Play the audio and give students the option of listening a second time. Direct them to audio script 2D.2 on >> p.151 and divide the class in A/B halves to practise the conversation aloud and swap roles.

> caps from the USA (New York City)

5 Direct students to *Souvenir Challenge*. In pairs, students guess where the souvenirs were bought. Ask for answers and see if the class agrees before confirming or giving the correct answer.

1 China	4 London/UK	7 Mexico	10 Panama
2 Egypt	5 Austria	8 Moscow	11 Peru
3 Germany	6 Jordan	9 New York	12 Tunisia

6 Put students into pairs to answer the questions and monitor conversations. Help quieter groups by asking some questions to keep the conversation going. Ask for volunteers to tell the class about themselves and others in the group.

B Read a postcard

In this section, students read a postcard for specific information and detail.

7 Ask students what type of information people write on a postcard and write suggestions on the board. Give them one minute to read the postcard and ask *Who's it to? (James), Who sent it? (Petra)* and *Where is she? (Cairo), Is she having a good holiday? (Yes).* Students read the postcard again to find the souvenir Petra bought.

> a rug

Abilities

do crosswords, puzzles, jigsaws
make dinner, clothes, a fire
play the guitar, golf, table tennis, chess

read a map, Arabic, music
ride a bike, a horse, a motorbike
use a sewing /ˈsəʊwɪŋ/ machine, a computer

Rabbit Kekai
the 85-year-old beach boy

WAIKIKI BEACH, HAWAII

Albert 'Rabbit' Kekai could surf when he was five. Now, 80 years later, he can still surf and he can still win competitions. Rabbit is a great-grandfather, but he's still physically fit. 'The water is so good,' he says. 'It keeps me young.'

Albert got the nickname 'Rabbit' because he was fast. He says that he could run the 100 metres in 9.6 seconds. When he was six, he could already ride the big waves with the older boys. In those days, the surfboards were very long and heavy, compared with today, but Rabbit was able to control the board with his quick footwork. Today's best surfers can't use those heavy old surfboards. 'They look like beginners,' says Rabbit.

In 80 years of surfing, you see a lot of different things. Rabbit was out on his board in World War Two when the first bombs fell on Pearl Harbour in 1941. 'We could see all the smoke,' he says. During the war, Rabbit worked as a scuba diver in the US army. In 1945, he returned home and started surfing again.

He taught many of Hollywood's most famous actors to surf – stars such as Gary Cooper and Kirk Douglas. More recently, he taught Kirk's son, Michael Douglas. Rabbit says Michael learned quickly. He could surf after just four lessons.

Now, Rabbit Kekai still surfs every day and he still gives lessons. He travels a lot to competitions around the world, and his wife Lynn often goes with him. With his fashionable sunglasses and Bermuda shorts, he looks like a real beach boy. He's 85 years old but he doesn't plan to stop surfing. 'I'm still looking for 100.' he says.

How to **talk about your abilities**

Orientation

Context

In this lesson, students will focus on talking about past and present abilities.

Rabbit Kekai ... is a magazine article about a man who is still surfing at the age of 85 and is decorated with pictures showing him in action.

Abilities gives verb and noun collocations for various activities.

Language

Focus grammar	*can, can't, can you ...?, could, couldn't, could you ...?*
Focus words	*chess, fire, jigsaws, sewing machine*
Focus phrases	*I didn't know you ..., Really?, What about you?, What do you like ...ing?*
Recognition vocabulary	*Bermuda shorts, bomb, great-grandfather, physically, sunglasses*
Recycled language	words: *bike, computer, crosswords, golf, guitar, map, nickname, puzzles, table tennis,* etc. collocation: *do crosswords,* etc. *make dinner,* etc. *play the guitar,* etc. *read a map,* etc. *ride a bike,* etc. *use a sewing machine,* etc. grammar: *past tenses; time phrases: in 1941, when he was six,* etc.
Pronunciation	stressing the negative: *can't, couldn't* 3B.1
Discourse	*but* to introduce a contrast

Language note

Accurate pronunciation of *can/can't* and *could/couldn't* is important in terms of recognition and production. When a person says, e.g. *I can't drive,* the 't' at the end of *can't* often disappears. However, comprehension doesn't break down because the vowel sound in negatives is also given its full, stressed form.

End product

In *Put it all together,* students have a conversation with a partner about things they can and can't, could and couldn't do. The activity is based on a listening, and students have the conversation from their notes.

Preparation

Take some realia to class, such as chess pieces, a tennis ball, and a dice, to set the context of games.

Warmer

Write some activities from previous lessons on the board. Ask students to put them in order and then label them according to the phrases on the *Can do* bar at the end of each lesson. Example activities: *play football, tennis, guitar, ride a bike, make dinner, do crosswords, read Chinese,* etc. Put students into groups to compare abilities. Do not correct for accuracy but make a note of how well students use *can* and *could* for ability and if they use verb/noun collocations appropriately.

Write *How to talk about your abilities* on the board.

A Vocabulary abilities

1. Start students thinking about collocation. Tell them to tick the things they can do, and to use a dictionary to check any new vocabulary. Ask them which words they would look for *(the nouns, not the verbs)*. Put students into pairs to ask and answer. Monitor and help with pronunciation as necessary.

2. Do the first item as an example. Direct students to *Abilities* to find an example of another language. Elicit the verb and tell students to continue individually, using the examples on **>> p.28** to help them if necessary. Students compare answers in pairs before you go over answers as a class.

read: Chinese	**do:** a Sudoku puzzle
ride: a camel	**play:** tennis
use: a digital camera	**make:** a cheese sandwich

   Extra activity

   Students check their dictionary to see if it gives this information. They might find it in an example sentence after the definition of the word or on a separate page which gives common verb/noun collocations.

3. Ask students to look at the verbs and nouns in *Abilities* and ask *What type of words do we use with* do? Elicit or tell students that *do* is generally used with games and quizzes on paper. Repeat for the other verbs. Set a time limit for students, in pairs or small groups, to add more nouns to the lists. Elicit answers briskly around the class and give positive feedback.

   Extra help

   Give students time to study their lists. Call out a noun for students to say the verb. Students continue testing a partner.

B Read a magazine article

In this section, students anticipate the content of a text from visual clues, before reading for gist and detail.

4. Direct students to the title of the text on **>> p.28** but tell them not to read it. Put students into pairs and set a short time limit to discuss ideas. Ask for suggestions around the class and write key words on the board.

5. Give students time to read the text and put a tick by any of their guesses.

6. Go through the instructions, emphasizing the word *main*. Ask students to read items a–d to check vocabulary and tell them that all the facts are in the text. Go over the answer as a class and ask students to explain why.

   b is the main point of the text. Rabbit still surfs, wins competitions, gives lessons, and he plans to continue surfing until he's 100 years old.

7. Focus students' attention on key factual information. Go through the instructions and the example as a class. Check students understand the difference between *false* and *doesn't say* (Students write *false* if there is different information, and *doesn't say* if there is no information in the text.) Students read items 2–6. Check any vocabulary problems. Students complete the activity. Monitor and help as necessary. Go over the answers as a class, asking students to give you information from the text to explain their answer.

   2 True   3 True   4 False   5 True   6 Doesn't say

C Grammar ability

8 Read the instructions and direct students back to the text to find *can*, *could* and *couldn't* in context. Set a time limit of about three minutes for students to work individually. They compare in pairs, and count how many of each example they have found in the text (*can = two, could = five, able to = one*). Elicit examples of sentences from the text. Point out that *be able to* is also used to talk about ability. Do not focus on this now, as students will be taught how to use it in the next level.

9 Read through the grammar rules together as a class. Students complete the grammar rules. Check answers as a class.

> Use **can/can't** to talk about ability in the present.
> Use **could/couldn't** to talk about ability in the past.

Extra help
Choral controlled practice. Use *Abilities* on >> p.28 and make sentences in the present for students to transform into the past or vice versa, or give affirmative sentences to be transformed into questions, e.g. *T He can play the guitar. Past tense? SS He could play the guitar. T She could play chess. Question? SS Could she play chess?* etc. Students continue in pairs or small groups.

10 Direct students to the cartoons. Point to the first picture and ask *Can the boy swim?* Elicit *Yes, he can.* Ask *And when he's older?* Ask for suggestions of other activities people can usually do when they are young but not when they are older, e.g. touch their toes, do daredevil activities or extreme sports. Do the first item as a class and show how the words around the blank will help them find the answer. Students complete the text individually and compare answers in pairs. Do not give answers at this stage.

11 3B.1 Play the audio, pausing after each line for students to check their answers.

> 1 could   2 couldn't   3 can   4 can   5 can't

12 Go through the instructions and check students understand the activity. Play the audio and go through the rule together. Play the audio a second time for students to say the verse, pausing at the end of each pair of lines for students to repeat.

> **couldn't** and **can't** are stressed.
> **could** and **can** are not stressed.

Extra help
Model and drill the modal verbs in isolation and check students are producing weak forms /kən/ and /kəd/ and strong forms /kɑːnt/ and /kʊdnt/. Draw oO on the board to show the pattern for *can swim* and *could swim*. Contrast this with *can't swim* and *couldn't swim*, and draw OO and OoO on the board. Ask students to 'shadow read' the poem, reading it quietly alongside you or the audio.

Extra plus
Ask students to read the poem slowly, loudly, quietly, quickly, in a whisper and so on, maintaining natural stress and rhythm.

13 Go through the instructions and the activities. Elicit the verbs used with each topic (*cooking = make; sports = play; computers = use; games = do, play; languages = read, speak, understand*) before reading the example. Students continue in pairs. Monitor and ask for clarification if you can't distinguish between the positive and negative forms. At the end of the activity, ask for volunteers to say a sentence about their partner.

D Listen for specific information

In this section, students listen to a conversation for specific information.

14 3B.2 Introduce the listening and read the question to the class. Play the audio while students listen for the answer (*Ben*).

15 Go through the instructions. Ask students to put a tick or a cross by the activities if they can remember any information from the first listening. Play the audio and ask students to compare their answers in pairs. Play the audio a second time if necessary before you go over answers as a class.

> Sarah can windsurf.   Sarah can't surf, read maps.
> Ben can ski, climb, do mountain walking.   Ben can't surf.

16 Go through the instructions. Tell students that items 1–4 are the words Ben and Sarah used, and items a–d are the conversation reasons why they ask them. Check students understand this idea by referring to some of the lesson titles, e.g. *How to apologize, ... start a conversation, ... ask for information.* Do the first item before students continue in pairs. Monitor and help, directing students to audio script 3B.2 on >> p.151, if necessary. Play the audio a second time, pausing after each item a–d. Check answers. In pairs, students role play the conversation.

> 1 b   2 d   3 c   4 a

Teaching tip
Don't let students spend a lot of time on this. They should understand that Ben and Sarah play an active part in the conversation and respond as interested listeners to the information the other gives.

17 Direct students to audio script 3B.2 on >> p.151. Give them time to read it through individually. Divide the class into pairs. Students practise the conversation with their partner. Ask pairs to act the converation for the class.

ABCD Put it all together

18 Go through the instructions as a class. Give students time to complete the table with two or more examples for each box. Ask a volunteer to read the example conversation to demonstrate.

Student performance
Students should be able to have a short conversation and respond as interested listeners.

Use this checklist for monitoring and feedback or to assess students' performance.

Interaction	Do students ask a few questions to show interest? exercise 16
Accuracy	Do students use *can/could* appropriately? exercise 13
Pronunciation	Can you hear the final /t/ sound in negatives? exercise 13

I can talk about my abilities.

Students tick *on my own* if they can have a conversation about their present and past abilities and interact appropriately looking at phrases in exercise 16 once or twice. They tick *with some help* if they have to refer to exercise 16 more than twice.

Early finishers
Students change partners one or twice and see if they can find somebody who has the same abilities in the present and past.

Additional material
www.oup.com/elt/result for extra practice material
www.oup.com/elt/teacher/result for extra teacher resources

How to talk about your abilities

G ability V abilities P stressing the negative

A Vocabulary abilities

1 Look at the **Abilities** phrases opposite and tick ✓ the ones you can do. Ask about your partner's skills.
   – Can you do crosswords?   – No, I can't.

2 Which verbs can you use with these things?
   Chinese a camel a digital camera
   a Sudoku puzzle tennis a cheese sandwich

3 Add more words to the lists for the six verbs.

B Read a magazine article

4 Work with a partner. Look at the photos opposite. What do you think the text is about?

5 Read **Rabbit Kekai** opposite and check.

6 The author's main point is that ...
   a Rabbit is 85 years old.
   b an 85-year-old can still surf.
   c some famous film stars have had surf lessons.
   d modern surfers can't use the heavy old boards.

7 What do we learn about Rabbit Kekai? Write *true, false,* or *doesn't say*.
   1 He's over 80 and he can still surf. *True*
   2 He's got great-grandchildren.
   3 He was able to surf when he was five.
   4 Surfers today use very long and heavy surfboards.
   5 He could see the smoke from the bombs in Pearl Harbour.
   6 Kirk Douglas learned surfing quickly.

C Grammar ability

8 Underline examples of *can, could,* and *able to* in the text.

9 Complete the grammar rule below.
   Use _____ to talk about ability in the present.
   Use _____ to talk about ability in the past.
   You can also use *be able to* to talk about ability, but it is less common than *can*.

10 Complete the text with *can, can't, could,* or *couldn't*.
   When I was five
   I was able to dive
   I ¹_____ swim really well
   But I ²_____ drive

   Now, I ³_____ cook
   And I'm able to drive
   I ⁴_____ swim quite well
   But now I ⁵_____ dive

11 **3B.1▶** Listen and check.

12 **Pronunciation** Listen again. Are the words *can, can't, could,* and *couldn't* stressed? Complete the rule and practise saying the text.
   _____ and _____ are stressed.
   _____ and _____ are not stressed.

13 Tell your partner about your abilities now and in the past. Use these ideas to help you.
   cooking sports computers games languages
   Example When I was five, I could make a milkshake but I couldn't make a cake.

   More practice? **Grammar Bank** ≫ p.138.

D Listen for specific information

14 **3B.2▶** Listen to Ben and Sarah. Who likes mountain sports?

15 Listen again. Complete the table with these activities.
   ski windsurf climbing
   read maps surf mountain walking

	can do it	can't do it
Sarah		
Ben	swim	

16 Work with a partner. Why do Ben and Sarah say these things? Match the sentences and reasons.
   1 Windsurfing? I didn't know you were a windsurfer.
   2 Really?
   3 What about you? Do you do any water sports?
   4 What, like climbing?

   a to ask for clarification
   b to ask for more information
   c to change the focus to the other person
   d to show surprise

17 Read the audio script on ≫ p.151. Act the conversation with a partner.

ABCD Put it all together

18 Write notes to complete the table with your abilities in the past and now. Then tell a partner why these things are/were important to you. Is your partner similar to you?

at age	things you could do	things you couldn't do
	things you can do	things you can't do
NOW		

   Example A When I was 10, I could play football quite well.
             B Really? Can you play now?

I can talk about my abilities.
Tick ✓ the line. with a lot of help with some help on my own very easily

Nothing to do

The **carpet's green**
The **sof**a's **blue**
The **TV**'s **bor**ing
And **you** are **too**

I could **go** to **town**
And **meet** some **friends**
But **no** one goes **out**
Ex**cept** at week**ends**

We could **switch** it **off**
And **go** to the **park**
But there's **nothing** to **do**
In the **park** in the **dark**

This **pro**gramme's so **bor**ing
Oh, **what** shall we **do**?
Let's change the **chan**nel
And **find** something **new**

Nowhere to **go**
Nothing to **do**
Watching **TV**
On the **sof**a with **you**

Jessica

Jack

TV Guide

TVC1	TVC2	Channel 3
18.00 News and weather	**18.00** Cartoon The Simpsons	**18.00** Series Belfort Road There's a surprise for Greg when Martha comes to visit.
18.30 The South Tonight Local news, weather and sports update	**18.20 Golf** Highlights of the US Open Championship.	**18.30** Comedy Three's a Crowd
19.00 National Geographic 'Going to Extremes' Nick Middleton travels to Siberia.	**19.20 Perspective** 'Climate change documentary'	**19.00 News** **19.20 Sports Week**
19.55 Poem for the Day A Walt Whitman reading		
20.00 Comedy Mad House More fun and games from the Mad House team.		**20.00 National Lottery**
20.30 Film Anaconda! Big snakes attack!	**20.30 Regional news** **20.50 National news**	**20.30 Big Brother** Who's going to leave the house today?
	21.20 Home improvements More practical ideas to make your house look better.	**21.15** Quiz Show Win a Million! Celebrity guests raise money for charity.
	22.00 The Money Programme What's it Worth? Buying foreign currency: Where to go for the best exchange rates.	**22.00** Film Psycho Hitchcock season – a classic thriller
22.45 Police Action Series **Crime Scene** Lost documents help police solve this week's crime.	**22.30 Change your Husband!**	

How to suggest what to do

Orientation

Context

In this lesson, students will focus on using *could* for possibility to suggest things to do.

The TV guide gives a typical night's viewing for three channels, with pictures to generate interest in three of the programmes.

The poem, *Nothing to do,* reflects the mood of the two teenagers sitting on the sofa.

Language

Focus grammar	*could* (possibility)
Focus words	*boring, channel, interesting, new, old, programme*
Focus phrases	*Good idea!, go out, How about …?, Let's …, nothing to do, nowhere to go, Shall we …?, stay at home, switch off, switch on, We could …, What shall we …?*
Preview language	*action, comedy, nothing, nowhere, something, somewhere, thriller*
Recognition language	*dark, except, news, reality show, series, too (as well)*
Recycled language	times: *18.00, at 6 o'clock* activities: *go to a restaurant, go to the cinema, listen to music, play a game, watch the news, watch TV*

Language note

There are subtle differences in use between the phrases for making suggestions. *What shall we do?* is used to invite suggestions and *Shall we …?* is used to offer a suggestion tentatively and to keep the discussion going. Both *How about …?* and *Let's …* are used in informal contexts to make suggestions. *Let's … (Let us …)* is used to make a suggestion which includes the speaker, whereas *How about …?* can also be used to suggest actions for others. It is always followed by *…ing*. *We could …* is used to make a tentative suggestion and can be used in formal and informal situations.

End product

In *Put it all together,* students make and respond to suggestions. In pairs, they generate ideas before having conversations in small groups. They should reach consensus on what to do for the evening.

Preparation

Take a TV guide, an empty DVD or video box or other small realia related to free-time activities to class.

Warmer

Put students into small groups to brainstorm typical teenage activities, e.g. going out with friends, playing computer games and use the realia to get students thinking. Write suggestions on the board. Ask students about the activities and use mime to teach the words *interesting* and *boring*.

Write *How to suggest what to do* on the board.

A Read and find

In this section, students read a poem for specific information. They also scan a TV guide and then read for detail.

1 Direct students to the picture of Jessica and Jack on **» p.30** and elicit some ideas about what they are doing and how they are feeling. Write the title of the poem on the board to introduce the context and put students into pairs or small groups. Write short sentences for the thought bubbles and ask students for ideas and see how well they can use language for suggestions. Take a class vote on the best suggestions.

2 3C.1 Say each of the phrases with the class and elicit the opposites to activate vocabulary before students read and listen to the poem. Direct students to the poem, and play the audio for students to find the opposites.

> old/new   light/dark   switch on/switch off
> interesting/boring   something to do/nothing to do
> stay at home/go out   somewhere to go/nowhere to go

Extra activity

In pairs, students test each other on vocabulary opposites.

3 Remind students about sentence stress and rhythm. Play the audio for students to read the verse aloud as they tap along.

Extra plus

Students read and add a 'lazy' feeling to the poem. Their pronunciation will help carry the meaning of the poem.

4 Direct students to the *TV Guide* on **» p.30** and give them time to familiarize themselves with the programmes. Point out the three columns and check they understand the difference between *channel* and *programme*. Ask students how people read these texts (quickly at first to look for things of interest, then more carefully for detail).

Set a two-minute time limit for students to read the TV guide and find four or five programmes which interest them. In pairs, students then choose three programmes to watch together. Ask for volunteers to tell the class which programmes they chose.

B Listen for specific information

In this section, students listen to two authentic-sounding conversations for specific information and detail.

5 3C.2 Go through the instructions and tell students to listen out for the names of programmes and to underline them in the TV guide. Play the audio, pausing after each conversation to give students time to compare their answers in pairs. Play the audio a second time if necessary.

> 1 The Money Programme   Anaconda   Change your Husband
> 2 The National Lottery   Mad House   Anaconda   Big Brother

6 Go through the instructions as a class, and check students understand they will need to make notes on *why* or *why not* for each question. Students complete the activity. Ask each question and elicit reasons around the class. Alternatively, play the audio again for students to listen and check.

> 1 No, she doesn't. She wants to watch the *Money Programme* (the film finishes after the *Money Programme* starts).
> 2 Yes, he does. The woman suggests videoing it.   3 No, he doesn't. It's boring.   4 No, he doesn't. He's seen it before.

C Vocabulary making suggestions

7 Students match sentence halves to make functional expressions they have heard in conversations. Do the first matching item as a class and set a short time limit for students to complete the activity. Do not give answers at this stage.

8 3C.3 Play the audio and pause after each expression for students to check. Play the audio a second time for students to repeat until they are saying them fairly fluently. At the end of the pronunciation phase, remind students that *How about* is used to suggest a general idea (with or without the speaker's involvement) and is followed by an *-ing* verb form. Do not focus on the grammar of the other phrases, it is sufficient for students to be able to use them as chunks at this level.

1c 2e 3b 4a 5d

Extra plus
Focus on the different ways the phrases are used. Refer students to the poem and audio script **3C.2** on **>> p.151** and ask *Which one do we use to ask for a suggestion? (What shall we …?); Which ones are used to suggest ideas which include the speaker? (Let's … We could … Shall we …). Which one is used to make a suggestion which doesn't automatically include the speaker (How about …?).*

9 Read the instructions and direct students to the first two turns. Read the first part of the conversation and ask *What will the next speaker do – say yes or no, or give a suggestion? (Give a suggestion.)* Read the second part of the conversation. Students continue the activity individually. Monitor and help them think about what type of response would come next. Do not give answers at this stage.

10 3C.4 Play the audio and pause after each turn to see if students can say what comes next. Ask for volunteers to read the conversation out in open pairs. Put students in pairs to have different conversations. Monitor and check that students give appropriate responses and help as necessary.

Extra help
Class drill. Ask *What shall we do?* and use realia such as the DVD, video or TV guide to elicit suggestions with *Shall we …, Let's … How about …? We could …* Students pass the realia around to practise asking the question *What shall we do?* and answering in different ways.

11 Put students into pairs to try to have the conversations from memory. Encourage students to write some key words on a piece of paper, before they close their books. Remind them to listen to their partner carefully so they can respond appropriately. Remind them to ask for repetition or clarification if necessary. Monitor and help, giving positive feedback for fluent use of suggestion phrases.

Extra activity
Put students into groups of three. Two students have the conversation and the third listens and helps by saying the first word of the next line if necessary.

D Grammar *could* (possibility)

12 Contrast the use of *could* for ability and possibility. Draw two columns on the board labelled *past* and *now*. Remind students of Rabbit Kekai from 3B and elicit or write the sentence *Rabbit could surf when he was five.* Direct students to the grammar box and read the past ability examples in the first column as a class. Point out the use of time phrases like *as a child* and *when he was three.*

Remind students of expressions for making suggestions in the previous section and elicit *We could watch Sports Week.* Go through the other examples in the second column in the grammar box.

Ask students to read sentences 1–8 and check any vocabulary. Do the example and one or two items as a class. Monitor and help as necessary as students continue individually. Students compare in pairs before you go over answers as a class.

2 possibility   3 possibility   4 ability   5 possibility
6 ability   7 ability   8 possibility

Teaching tip
Stress that *can* is not used for possibility when we are talking about the actual chance of something happening. It is wrong to say *That film can be good.* Ask students to compare this in their own language.

13 Go through the instructions and model the activity by setting up a chain drill. Nominate a student to read A's part, another to read B's, and gesture for A to continue. Elicit a few more A/B turns and stop the activity. Ask students for phrases to use to show they agree and elicit examples like *OK. Good idea! Sounds good! I'd like to do that, too.* and write them on the board. Monitor and give positive feedback for appropriate responses as students continue the controlled practice activity.

ABCD Put it all together

14 Put students into pairs. Students make notes of things to do for a night out.

15 Set up the activity up by allocating A/B/C roles to three students and ask them to read the conversation for the class. Put students into groups of three or four to plan a night out using their notes from exercise 14.

16 Ask for one volunteer from each group to tell the class what they have decided to do. The class decides which plan is best.

Student performance
Students should be able to make suggestions.

Use this checklist for monitoring and feedback or to assess students' performance.

Coherence	Do students respond appropriately? exercise 11
Fluency	Do students use some suggestion phrases without a lot of hesitation? exercise 8
Vocabulary	Do students use different suggestion phrases? exercise 11

I can suggest what to do.
Students tick *on my own* if they can contribute to the conversation without looking at exercise 7. They tick *with some help* if they need to look at the phrases in exercise 7 once or twice.

Early finishers
Students change groups and talk about a class visit or a day out.

Additional material

www.oup.com/elt/result for extra practice material
www.oup.com/elt/teacher/result for extra teacher resources

How to suggest what to do

G *could* (possibility)   V making suggestions   P intonation in suggestions

A Read and find

1 Look at the picture of **Jessica** and **Jack** opposite. What are they thinking? Tell a partner.

2 **3C.1▶** Listen and read **Nothing to do** opposite. Find the opposites of these words in the poem.

old   light   switch on   interesting   something to do
stay at home   somewhere to go

Example old – new

3 Practise saying the poem. Stress the bold syllables.

4 Read the **TV Guide** opposite. With a partner, choose three programmes to watch together.

B Listen for specific information

5 **3C.2▶** Listen to two conversations. Which programmes from the TV guide do they talk about?
a Conversation 1   b Conversation 2

6 Answer the questions. Give reasons.
Conversation 1
1 Does the woman want to watch the film?
2 Does the man want to watch the film? What does the woman suggest?

Conversation 2
3 Does the boy want to watch the lottery?
4 Does the boy want to watch the film?

C Vocabulary making suggestions

7 Match the beginnings and ends of the sentences.
1 ☐ What shall we ...   a off the TV.
2 ☐ Shall we watch ...   b playing a game?
3 ☐ How about ...   c watch?
4 ☐ Let's switch ...   d go out.
5 ☐ We could ...   e the news?

8 **3C.3▶ Pronunciation** Listen and check. Listen again and repeat.

9 Put the conversation in order with a partner.
☐ Let's see. We could watch *Sports Week*.
☐ OK. What's on?
☐1 What shall we do?
☐ No, let's watch the *National Geographic* programme.
☐ OK. Good idea!
☐2 Shall we just stay at home and watch TV?

10 **3C.4▶** Listen and check. Say the conversation with a partner, but change the names of the programmes.

11 Have similar conversations with your books closed.

D Grammar *could* (possibility)

12 Read the grammar box and decide if the sentences below it are about ability or possibility.

could = ability in the past	*could* = possibility in the present
She could sing well as a child.	We could watch *The Simpsons*.
He could play the guitar when he was three.	We could go out tonight.

1 I could swim when I was four.   *Ability*
2 We could stay at home and watch TV if you want.
3 We could watch *Sports Week*.
4 Tom could play chess very well when he was younger.
5 We could have a game of tennis.
6 They could speak French when they were children.
7 She could run very fast when she was young.
8 We could go to the cinema after dinner.

13 Work with a partner. Talk about three or more things you could do tonight.
Example **A** We could watch the news.
          B Oh no. Let's ...

More practice? **Grammar Bank** >> p.138.

ABCD Put it all together

14 Imagine that you're planning a night out with other students in your class. With a partner, write some ideas about:
– where to meet
– places to go
– things to do
– how much to spend
– what to eat and drink
– how to get there

15 Work in small groups and suggest things you could do.
Example **A** What shall we do?
          B We could go to a restaurant.
          C Yes, good idea. Or we could ...

16 Tell the class about your suggestions. Which suggestion is the best?

Types of story

a comedy   a horror story   a novel   a play   a romance
a thriller   an action film   an epic   science fiction

QUIZ OF THE MONTH Classic film moments from the 20th century

1 True or false: Stan Laurel's going to fall.

2 Do you know the name of the other character in this comedy?

3 Someone's going to bite that girl's neck. What's his name?

4 This 1931 horror movie was based on a novel. Who wrote it?
a   Mary Shelley
b   Bram Stoker
c   Arthur Conan Doyle

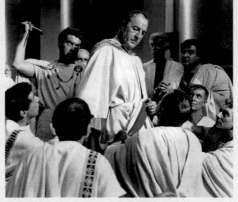

7 The character in the middle's going to die. What's his name?

8 This 1953 epic was based on a play. Who wrote it?
a   Oscar Wilde
b   Agatha Christie
c   William Shakespeare

11 Sean Connery played James Bond in the 1962 spy movie *Dr No*. Name two more Bond actors.

12 What's going to happen in this scene? Say *true* or *false*.
a   The spider's going to walk up Bond's arm.
b   The spider's going to bite Bond.
c   Bond's going to kill the spider.

13 *Blade Runner* is a 1982 science fiction movie set in the future. Here we see Harrison Ford in a difficult moment. What's going to happen? Say *true* or *false*.
a   He's going to fall.
b   He's going to climb up.
c   Somebody's going to help him.

9 Who was the director of the 1960 thriller *Psycho*?
a   Steven Spielberg
b   Alfred Hitchcock
c   Martin Scorcese

10 In this scene, a character's going to kill somebody in the shower. What's the character's name?
a   Norman Bates
b   Frankenstein
c   Jack the Ripper

5 What's the name of this 1939 epic film?
a   *Gone With The River*
b   *Gone With The Money*
c   *Gone With The Wind*

6 What are they going to do?
a   Kiss   b   Cry   c   Fight

14 We all know what's going to happen to the ship, *The Titanic*. But what's going to happen to these two young lovers in this 1997 romance?
a   The boy's going to die.
b   The girl's going to die.
c   They're both going to die.

32   **3D**

How to talk about what's going to happen

Orientation

Context

In this lesson, students will focus on using *going to* to talk about things which are about to happen.

Movie magazine, has a magazine-style film quiz which has questions and scenes from well-known films.

Types of story gives film types from the quiz.

Language

Focus grammar	*going to* (predictions on current evidence)
Focus words	films: *actor, character, director, scene, star, story* types of story: *action, comedy, crime, epic, horror, novel, play, romance, science fiction, thriller* other: *bite, couple, fall, history, lover, movie, ship*
Focus phrases	*based on, set in*
Recognition vocabulary	*classic, movies*
Recycled language	dates: *in 1928, 1931*
Pronunciation	the letter *r* 3D.1

Language notes

The word *actress* is used only for females. However, nowadays the word *actor* tends to be used for both male and female actors.

The words *movie* and *film* are sometimes used as synonyms. *Movies* is used more frequently in American English, and also refers to the cinema. The word *film* is used more frequently in British English and refers to a series of moving pictures, and is also used to describe documentaries.

Going to can be reduced to /gənə/, often written as *gonna* in song lyrics, or /gəʊntə/. The main stress falls at the end of the phrase.

End product

In *Put it all together*, students compare pictures and find differences by explaining what's about to happen based on current evidence.

Preparation

Take some pictures of films, adverts for films or, if you have them, some empty DVD or video boxes. Check the *Warmer* suggestions (see below) and prepare a list of different paired film stars your students will know, if necessary. Prepare some true/false sentences for a different film for exercise 9 if you don't think your students will know about *The Da Vinci Code*.

Warmer

If your students are quite big film-goers, play a film game. Divide the class into teams and give a point to the first team to name the film with these famous film star combinations: Scarlett Johansson and Bill Murray *Lost in Translation*; Antony Hopkins and Jodie Foster *Silence of the Lambs*; John Travolta and Uma Thurman *Pulp Fiction*; Julia Roberts and Richard Gere *Pretty Woman*; Daniel Craig and Eva Green *Casino Royale*; Daniel Radcliffe and Emma Watson *Harry Potter* films. Alternatively, use the visuals/realia to elicit some names of famous films and actors.

Write *How to talk about what's going to happen* on the board.

A Read and do a quiz

In this section, students are introduced to strategies for guessing the meaning of words in context before confirming in a dictionary.

1   Students personalize the topic by discussing the question in pairs or small groups. Ask around the class for favourite types of films and help students express their ideas. Give vocabulary as necessary but do not teach it at this stage as it is the focus of section B.

2   Direct students to *Movie Magazine* on >> p.32 and read the full title. In pairs or small groups, students look at the pictures. Set a short time limit for them to discuss what they know about the films. Go through each picture in turn and elicit what students know. Check they understand *classic* in the title by asking *Are the films famous?* See if students like or think they would like the films.

3   Put students into pairs to do the quiz. Tell them to guess any new vocabulary for the moment. Go over the answers as a class and award one point for each correct answer.

1 False	6 a	11 Roger Moore,
2 Oliver Hardy	7 Julius Caesar	Pierce Brosnan
3 Dracula	8 c	12 c
4 b	9 b	13 c
5 Gone with the Wind	10 a	14 a

4   Tell students to go through the *Movie Magazine* questions again and underline any new vocabulary.

5   Ask students what they do when they see a new word in their own language and elicit ideas around the class. Choose a new vocabulary item for your students from the quiz (e.g. *character* in question 2) and write it on the board. Demonstrate strategies 1–3 using the word on the board. Repeat with another word if necessary to check students understand the strategies. Tell students to choose three of their underlined words, guess the meaning and answer questions 1–3. Monitor and help as necessary, and give encouraging feedback as appropriate.

6   Monitor as students use their dictionaries to confirm guesses. Remind them to use these strategies when reading outside the classroom.

B Vocabulary types of story; films

7   Direct students to *Types of story* on >> p.32 and tell them that these words can be used for books and films. Read the instructions and ask students to read the second column *meaning*. Check any vocabulary. Go through the two examples with the class, demonstrating that students can also use the strategies from exercise 5 to help them. Monitor and help as students continue, individually or in pairs. Ask for answers around the class and help with pronunciation as necessary.

3 a thriller	6 a romance
4 an action film	7 a play
5 a comedy	8 a novel

Teaching tip

Some learners might confuse the words *story* and *history*, often because they pronounce *story* with an intrusive initial vowel sound. Help students by showing the number of syllables in each word (*story* = 2, *history* = 3). Students check the meaning in dictionaries if necessary.

8 Do the first part of the activity as a class and check answers before students continue in pairs or small groups. Monitor and help students find a close (but not perfect) translation of the film name in English, if necessary. Elicit names or information about films or stories around the class.

> 1 Julius Caesar   2 Dracula   3 Psycho   4 Blade Runner
> 5 Laurel and Hardy   6 Titanic   7 Julius Caesar   8 Dracula plus students' own answers

9 Go through the instructions and do the example as a class to demonstrate the activity. Keep the mood light-hearted as you say the name of the film and read statements 1–5 for students to say true or false. Put students into pairs to write their own true/false statements and tell them they can use the information in *Movie Quiz* or their own ideas. Monitor and help as necessary and give students time to practise reading their sentences to each other to prepare for the next activity.

> 1 False. Thriller.   2 True   3 True   4 True   5 False. Ron Howard. (Students don't have to give the name of the director.)

10 Put students into different pairs to read their information. Their partner identifies any false facts. Ask for volunteers to read their information for the class to guess.

11 To introduce the activity, write *Actor, director, or character?* on the board and use the following examples with the class: *T Harry Potter **SS** character T Alfred Hitchcock **SS** director T Johnny Depp **SS** actor T Keira Knightley **SS** actor* (you could accept *actress* but this is less commonly used nowadays). Put students in pairs or small groups to test each other.

C Grammar *going to* (predictions)

12 Direct students to look at the picture under the grammar box and ask *He's going to fall, true or false?* Write the sentence on the board and ask students what *'s* represents *(is)*. Write *subject + is going to + verb* and elicit the negative and question forms. Elicit the sentences to complete the grammar box and monitor for accuracy as students write the answers.

> + I'm **going to be** late. They're **going to kiss**.
> – He **isn't going to fall**. They're not **going to kiss**.
> ? Is he **going to fall**?

13 Go through the instructions and one or two examples as a class. Students continue individually and ask for answers around the class. Monitor for pronunciation of the weak form of *going to* and give further practice if necessary.

Extra help
Backchaining drill. Say a *going to* sentence for students to repeat each word from the last to the first, e.g. *T You're going to watch a film. film. SS film. T a film. SS a film. T watch a film. SS watch a film. T going to watch a film. SS going to watch a film. T You're going to watch a film. SS You're going to watch a film.*

14 Go through the instructions. Say the example sentences and ask students to tell you the films *(Gone with the Wind, Blade Runner)*. Put students in pairs to make sentences and guess the film. Remind them to ask for repetition if necessary.

Extra activity
Students mime simple actions for others to guess what they are going to do. Demonstrate the activity. Ask *What am I going to do?* Mime preparing for an action, e.g. read a book, but stop just before the action itself so that *going to* for prediction is used in a realistic way. Call out for students to continue and whisper an action. Prompts: *You are going to clean your teeth; eat an apple; play the piano*, etc.

D Pronunciation the letter *r*

Teaching tip
Students often overpronounce the letter *r* in spoken English and in this section they focus on instances when English speakers tend not to pronounce the letter *r*. Students can choose which version of *r* they prefer

15 3D.1 Ask students some questions about British and American films, e.g. *Which films do you watch most? English, British or American? Which do you prefer? Why? Which accent do you find easier to understand? Why? Can you recognize whether an accent is British or American?* Tell students that one difference in pronunciation is the way both speakers pronounce the letter *r*. Go through the vocabulary with the class and play the audio, pausing after each word for students to underline the letter *r* if it is not pronounced.

> actor   star   director   thriller   character   horror
> Ford   Hardy   Potter   Star Wars

16 Do the exercise as a class, reading each rule in turn for students to say which rule is correct *(b)*. Drill the words and names if you feel this is an area your students need to work on productively. For most students, recognition will be enough.

ABCD Put it all together

17 Go through the instructions and divide the class into half, A/B. Tell the As to turn to >> p.126 and Bs to >> p.133. Give students time to find the characters and decide what they are going to do. Tell them to look back at *Movie Magazine* for help. Choose two students to read the example conversation before putting students into A/B pairs. Tell them to keep their pictures hidden and ask for clarification if necessary. When students have finished, they look at each other's pictures and check.

Student performance
Students should be able to give short descriptions.

Use this checklist for monitoring and feedback or to assess students' performance.

Content	Do students talk about all the people? exercise 14
Communication strategy	Do students ask for clarification if necessary? exercise 14
Fluency	Do students use *going to* without a lot of hesitation? exercise 14

I can talk about what's going to happen.

Students tick *on my own* if they can make predictions without looking at the grammar box. They tick *with some help* if they look at the grammar box once or twice for help.

Early finishers
Students show or make some simple drawings of clues about what they plan to do after the class, e.g. a bus ticket, car keys, food. In pairs or small groups they predict what they are going to do.

Additional material

www.oup.com/elt/result for extra practice material
www.oup.com/elt/teacher/result for extra teacher resources

How to talk about what's going to happen

G *going to* (predictions) **V** types of story; films **P** the letter *r*

A Read and do a quiz

1 What types of films do you like? Tell a partner.

2 Look at the photos opposite with a partner. Do you know these films?

3 Read **Movie Magazine** opposite and do the quiz.

4 Are there any words you don't understand? Underline them.

5 Choose three of your underlined words. Guess the meanings. Think about these questions:
   1 Can I find the meaning in the pictures?
   2 Can I guess the meaning of the word from the sentence it's in?
   3 Is the word similar to a word in my language?

6 Check the meaning of your three words in a dictionary.

B Vocabulary types of story; films

7 Look at **Types of story** opposite. Find the words in **Movie Magazine** and match them with these meanings.

word	meaning
1 *an epic*	a long story about a time in history
2 *a horror movie*	a very frightening story, about vampires, for example
3 _____	an exciting story about crime, for example
4 _____	a film with a lot of fast action
5 _____	a funny story
6 _____	a love story
7 _____	a story for the theatre
8 _____	a book with a fictional story

8 Find one example of each type of story in the quiz. Try to think of more examples of your own.

9 Work with a partner. Think of three films. Write the titles and some true or false statements.
   Example *The Da Vinci Code*
   1 This is a comedy.
   2 It's set in Paris.
   3 It's based on a novel by Dan Brown.
   4 The main actors are Tom Hanks and Audrey Tatou.
   5 Alfred Hitchcock directed it.

10 Read your statements to a new partner. Can they guess if they are true or false?

11 Test a partner. Actor, director, or character?
   Example **A** Tom Hanks.
   B Actor!

C Grammar *going to* (predictions)

12 Complete the grammar box.

	I	he / she / it	you / we / they
+	I _____ late.	He's going to fall.	They're _____.
−	I'm not going to be late.	He's _____ _____.	They _____ not _____.
?	Am I going to be late?	_____ he _____?	Are they going to kiss?

Use *going to* to predict the future based on what you can see.
Example He's going to fall.

13 Look at **Movie Magazine** again. Underline examples of *going to* in the quiz.

14 Work with a partner. Make sentences with *going to* about the other pictures in the movie quiz.
   Example Vivian Leigh and Clark Gable are going to kiss. Harrison Ford isn't going to fall.

More practice? **Grammar Bank** » p.138.

D Pronunciation the letter *r*

15 **3D.1▶** Listen to a British speaker say these words. Which letters *r* are not pronounced? Underline them.
   acto**r** sta**r** sto**r**y c**r**ime di**r**ector th**r**iller cha**r**acter ho**rr**or Ha**rr**ison Ford Lau**r**el and Ha**r**dy Ha**rr**y Potter Sta**r** Wa**r**s

16 Tick ✓ the correct ending to the rule.
   In British English, you only pronounce the letter *r* ...
   a at the end of a word.
   b before a vowel sound.
   c after a vowel sound.

ABCD Put it all together

17 Work with a partner and find the differences between the film studios.
   Student A Look at the picture of a film studio on » p.126 and say what's going to happen.
   Student B Look at the picture of a film studio on » p.133 and say what's going to happen.

I can talk about what's going to happen.

Tick ✓ the line.   · with a lot of help   with some help   on my own   very easily

Writing An invitation

A Read for information

1 Read these three invitations. Which one would you like to get?

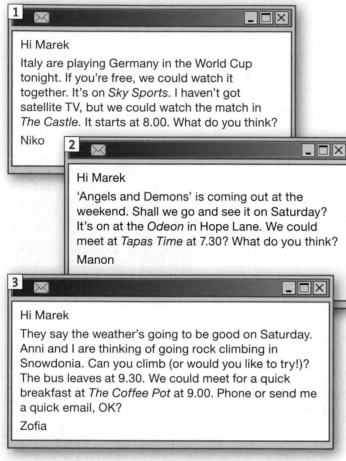

> **1**
>
> Hi Marek
>
> Italy are playing Germany in the World Cup tonight. If you're free, we could watch it together. It's on *Sky Sports*. I haven't got satellite TV, but we could watch the match in *The Castle*. It starts at 8.00. What do you think?
>
> Niko

> **2**
>
> Hi Marek
>
> 'Angels and Demons' is coming out at the weekend. Shall we go and see it on Saturday? It's on at the *Odeon* in Hope Lane. We could meet at *Tapas Time* at 7.30? What do you think?
>
> Manon

> **3**
>
> Hi Marek
>
> They say the weather's going to be good on Saturday. Anni and I are thinking of going rock climbing in Snowdonia. Can you climb (or would you like to try!)? The bus leaves at 9.30. We could meet for a quick breakfast at *The Coffee Pot* at 9.00. Phone or send me a quick email, OK?
>
> Zofia

2 Find names of these places and things in the emails.

1 a cinema *The Odeon*	4 a wine bar	7 a TV channel
2 a café	5 a street	8 a football team
3 a pub	6 a movie	9 a national park

3 Do you think Marek knows the places and things in the emails? Why?

4 Find the parts of the message for emails 2 and 3.

parts of the message	email 1	email 2	email 3
to	Marek		
activity	football match		
invitation	watch it together		
time and place	tonight, *The Castle*, 8.00		
request for answer	What do you think?		
from	Niko		

B Check for missing information

5 What parts of the message are missing in these emails? Use the table in exercise 4 to help you.

> **1**
>
> Hi Marek
>
> I'm having a birthday dinner at *Luigi's* on Friday night. Would you like to come?

> **2**
>
> Hi Marek
>
> There's a Norah Jones concert next weekend. It's at the *Lido* on Saturday at 8.30. What do you think?
>
> Maja

C Put the information into a message

6 Work with a partner. Read the information and complete Marek's email.

Information: Marek has got two tickets to see *The Phantom of the Opera* at the *Palladium*. It's at 7.00 on Thursday evening. He wants to invite Zofia. There's a wine bar near the theatre called *Esperanto's*. It's a good place to meet.

> H__ Z_____
>
> I'___ g___ t___ t_____ t__
> s___ T___ P_____ o__ t___
> O_____ o_ T_____
> e_____. W_____ y___ l_____
> t_ c_____? I_'_ a_ t___
> P_____ a__ 7.00. W__
> c_____ m_____ a__ 6.30 a__
> E_____'_.
> W_____ d__ y___ t_____?
>
> Marek

7 **3E.1** Listen and check.

ABC Put it all together

8 Think of an activity you would like to do next weekend. Write an email to invite another person in the class.

9 Check for missing information and give it to the person.

I can write an invitation.

Tick ✓ the line.   with a lot of help   with some help   on my own   very easily

Orientation

Context and Language

In this lesson, students will think about the information a reader needs in an invitation.

Recycled language	words: *concert, invitation, wine bar* phrases: *suggestions: Would you like to ...?* grammar: *modals: could, can, shall, prepositions: in, on, at*

End product

In *Put it all together*, students write an email invitation following a given structure.

Warmer

Ask *What can people invite you to do?* Make notes of answers on the board, e.g. *go to a party, have dinner, go for a walk, watch a sports event, see a film*. Go through the activities to see which are the most popular. Write *How to write an invitation* on the board.

A Read for information

In this section, students read informal email invitations for gist, inference and detail.

1 Direct students to the emails and ask *Who wrote them? Who are they to?* Read the question and set a short time limit for students to read the emails. Ask *Which email invitation is to watch a film? (2) To go for a day out in the country? (3) To watch a sports event? (1).* Take a class vote and ask students to say why.

2 Go through the activity and check vocabulary. Elicit or give examples of local or well-known places. Do the example, pointing out that they should use the information in the email to help. Set a short time limit and put students in pairs to continue. Monitor and help. Go over answers as a class. Can students give reasons for their answers?

> 2 *The Coffee Pot* (the name, a place for breakfast)
> 3 *The Castle* (pub names often have historical connections)
> 4 *Tapas Time* (people in Spain have 'tapas' or snacks in wine bars)
> 5 Hope Lane (Lane is another name for a type of street)
> 6 *Angels and Demons* (is coming out, something people see)
> 7 *Sky Sports* (watch, the match is 'on')
> 8 Italy / Germany (are playing, World Cup)
> 9 Snowdonia (weather good, climbing)

3 Ask the question to the whole class. Elicit or explain that Marek is the person receiving the invitations. Point out informal phrases, e.g. *Hi, What do you think?* in emails between friends.

> Yes. The writer doesn't explain what or where the places are.

4 Direct students to the table, and ask them to find and underline the information in the first column in Niko's email. Students continue individually for the other two emails. They check in pairs before you go over answers as a class.

> **email 2:** Marek film see it together Saturday at the *Odeon* in Hope Lane (meet at *Tapas Time* 7.30 first) What do you think? Manon
> **email 3:** Marek rock climbing with Zofia and Anni Saturday at *The Coffee Pot* at 9.00 phone, send quick email Zofia

B Check for missing information

5 Go though the instruction and check students understand. Ask *Do you need any more information?* Students continue in pairs. Go over answers as a class.

> 1 The place and time.   2 The invitation itself.

C Put the information into a message

In this section, students practise writing an informal email invitation by transferring given information.

6 Ask students to read the information quickly to say if they would accept or not. Check any new vocabulary. Tell students that they will use the information to complete Marek's email. Explain that there is one blank for each letter of a word, and the first letter has been given. Point out how capital letters and apostrophes can help them guess missing words.

Tell students to use the information and to look back at the three emails in exercise 1 to find typical phrases and expressions used in invitations. Put students in pairs to complete the activity. Monitor and help, encouraging students to think about the grammar of the sentences to help them, e.g. if there is a time and the word before it has two letters and the first one is *o*, they can guess the word is the time preposition *on*. If students are stuck, give them a word to help. Make a note of any common problem areas to go over after exercise 7.

Extra help

Before you begin, direct students to the emails in exercise 1 and ask questions about organization. Ask *How do all the emails start? (Hi.) And how do they finish? (Just with the name.) Are they long or short? (Quite short.) Are they friendly? (Yes.)*

7 3E.1 Play the audio for students to check their answers. Play it a second time, pausing at the end of each sentence if necessary.

Extra activity

Complete cloze team game. Copy the blanks of the email on the board and number them. Put students into small teams. Books closed. Give each team a turn to give a word and number of the blank. Award two points if both pieces of information are correct. Award one point for a correct word but wrong place. Write the words in the blanks until the email is complete.

ABC Put it all together

8 Read the instructions. Direct students back to exercises 1 and 4 if necessary. Pair students to make sure everyone will receive an email for exercise 9.

9 Remind students to review their writing for content and capital letters before giving it to their partner. Ask students to report back on the invitation and if they will accept or not.

Student performance

Students should be able to write a short informal invitation.

Use this checklist for monitoring and feedback or to assess students' performance.

Content	Have students included all the information?
Coherence	Have students used informal expressions?
Punctuation	Have students used capital letters correctly?

I can **write an invitation.**

Students tick *on my own* if they have included all the information in exercise 4. They tick *with some help* if a partner has to ask a question about the arrangement.

Early finishers

Students role play a phone call to accept or turn down an invitation.

Additional material

www.oup.com/elt/result for extra practice material
www.oup.com/elt/teacher/result for extra teacher resources

Hotel rooms

blanket   glass   lamp   remote control   pillow   ashtray   shampoo
sheet   soap   mini-bar   tap   towel   toilet roll   floor

Who steals hotel towels?

Have you ever stolen a hotel towel? One in five Americans has stolen one. Hotels across the U.S. lose $51 million a year in stolen towels.

But hotel guests don't just take towels. The most popular 'souvenirs' are soap, toilet rolls, and mini bottles of shampoo. In fact, most people don't think this is really stealing. But what about glasses and ashtrays? Or bigger things like blankets, sheets, and pillows? And hotel guests sometimes walk away with stranger things – toilet seats, TV remote controls, lamps, and in one case, even the hotel owner's dog.

Hotels sometimes charge for stolen items, such as drinks from the mini-bar, on the guest's credit card. But some guests have found solutions to this problem. For example, they drink the mineral water and then fill the bottle with tap water.

Perhaps the strangest hotel theft is from a hotel near Exeter, England. A couple left the hotel with the shower from their hotel room. Hotel owner Liz Hodges said the stolen shower was worth £300.

The Receptionist

The Guest

How to ask for things in a hotel

Orientation

Context

In this lesson, students will practise having conversations in which they request and offer hotel services.

The magazine article takes a light-hearted look at normal and strange things people steal from hotel rooms and is decorated with an illustration of a hotel room with an en suite bathroom. The photos of a receptionist and a guest have speech bubbles with examples of things each might say.

Culture note

In many other languages and cultures *please* and *thank you* are used differently for requests, regardless of people's status or the size of the favour in question.

Language

Focus grammar	*can / could* (requests)
Preview grammar	present perfect: *Have you ever ...?*
Focus words	hotel: *double, floor, key, room service, shampoo, single, towel,* etc.
Focus phrases	hotel phrases: *Can I help you?, I'd like ..., What time's ...?*
Recognition vocabulary	words: *lamp, lose, owner, receptionist, steal, tap, worth,* etc. phrases: *don't/doesn't work, in one case, walk away with*
Recycled language	adjectives: *hard, old, small, wet* times/numbers: *from 7.30–10 o'clock, at 7.30, €80, room 224* grammar: *comparatives and superlatives* articles: *a hotel room, an alarm call, the second floor*
Pronunciation	guessing words from phonemic transcriptions; final *'s/s* 4A.1

Language note

'*Have you ever stolen a hotel towel?*' occurs in the first line of the text. This is a preview of the present perfect, which will be dealt with in the rest of this unit.

End product

In *Put it all together*, students take turns being a hotel receptionist and a guest, asking for and offering various services. Students use the role card cues for support, and have listened to similar conversations in exercise 11.

Preparation

If possible, write the words for the *Warmer* on the board before the class arrives.

Warmer

Write the following words on the board: *guest, alarm call, key, double room, passport, receptionist, single room* and ask students to sort them into two groups, *things* and *people*. Ask them what the guest might ask for (*alarm call, key, double room*), and what the receptionist might ask for (*your passport*). Direct students to the picture of the hotel room on >> **p.36** and ask if they would like to stay there.

Write *How to ask for things in a hotel* on the board.

A Vocabulary hotel words and phrases

1 In pairs, students talk about their last hotel experience or where they stayed last holiday. After a short time, ask for volunteers to tell the class and help students get their ideas across if necessary.

2 Give students the opportunity to show what vocabulary they already know. Ask students to cover >> **p.36** and set a time limit of about two minutes for them to brainstorm in pairs. Students look at *Hotel rooms* on >> **p.36** and compare lists.

Teaching tip

Tell students to swap partners two or three times. They compare lists and add more words.

3 Students demonstrate they understand meaning by matching *Hotel rooms* vocabulary to the numbered items in the picture. Do the example together, pointing out the number before students continue individually. To check answers, call out numbers for the class to say the words. Do not correct pronunciation at this stage.

1 shampoo	6 toilet roll	11 mini-bar
2 soap	7 ashtray	12 pillow
3 lamp	8 glass	13 sheet
4 tap	9 remote control	14 blanket
5 towel	10 floor	

Extra activity

Students name other things in the picture, e.g. mirror, table.

4 Use the first item to demonstrate the activity. Check students understand that *'s* is the short form of *is* and ask about /bed/, and where they would find this type of text (*in a dictionary*). Look at the second item together and write /ˈblæŋkɪt/ on the board and see if students can pronounce and spell it. Tell students all the words in the poem are in *Hotel rooms* on >> **p.36**. Students continue individually and compare in pairs.

5 4A.1 Play the audio, pausing at the end of each line for students to confirm their answers. Play it a second time for students to repeat. Put them in pairs to practise reading the song aloud. For variety, students could read alternate lines.

2 blanket	3 pillow	4 sheets	5 towel	6 floor	7 taps
8 shampoo	9 lamps	10 ashtray	11 soap	12 control	

Extra plus

Students discuss which problems in the song would be important for them personally.

B Read for specific information

In this section, students guess what an article is about. They scan to confirm ideas before reading for specific information.

6 Books closed. Read the question and check students understand *steal (take without paying)*. Set a short time limit for students to brainstorm ideas in pairs. Ask for ideas around the class.

7 Direct students to *Who steals hotel towels?* on >> **p.36** and tell them to read the text quickly check their ideas. Refer back to the title, and ask students for the answer according to the text. (*One in five Americans.*)

Accidents at home

verb	past	past participle	verb	past	past participle
drop	dropped	dropped /drɒpt/	fall	fell	fallen
happen	happened	happened /hæpənd/	cut	cut	cut
do	did	done	put	put	put
break	broke	broken	burn	burnt	burnt

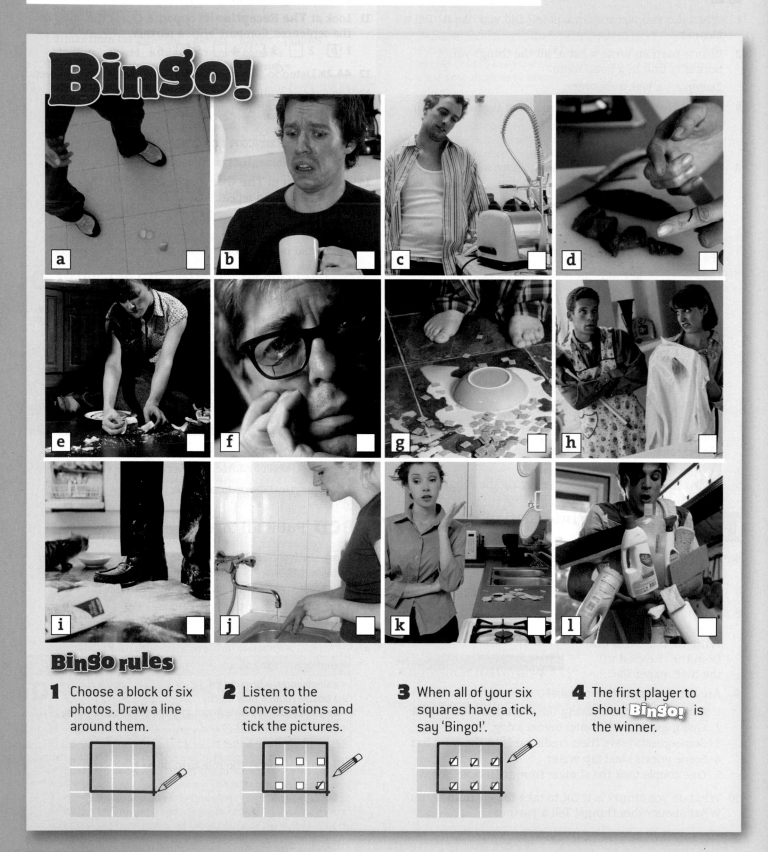

Bingo!

Bingo rules

1 Choose a block of six photos. Draw a line around them.

2 Listen to the conversations and tick the pictures.

3 When all of your six squares have a tick, say 'Bingo!'.

4 The first player to shout **Bingo!** is the winner.

How to say what's happened

Orientation

Context

In this lesson, students will practise using the present perfect to talk about the results of recent events.

Bingo! is a picture-based game board with photos of people suffering minor mishaps at home. These illustrate the vocabulary in *Accidents at home*. The rules of the game are explained at the bottom of the page.

Language

Focus grammar	present perfect (+); past participles of regular and irregular verbs
Focus words	verbs for accidents: *break, burn, cut, do, drop, fall, happen, put*
Recognition vocabulary	words: *blood, floor, horrible* phrases: *Are you alright?, I can smell it., It's not too bad., What a mess!*
Recycled language	*bottles, cup, egg, finger, glasses, iron, milk, plates, salt, shelf, shirt, sugar, toast*
Pronunciation	short form of *have* **4B.3**

Language note

The verbs in *Accidents at home* illustrate the common patterns of spelling of irregular past participles. *Burn* has both regular and irregular alternatives in most dictionaries. *Accidents at home* on **» p.38** gives only the irregular version.

End product

In *Put it all together*, students find picture differences between *Pairwork* **» p.127** and **» p.133** by describing events which have just taken place in a kitchen. Students can ask for repetition and clarification if necessary.

Preparation

Put a plaster on your finger just before class and, if you have a small first aid kit at home or in the school, take it to class as realia.

Remind students to bring bilingual dictionaries for the next lesson (4C).

Warmer

Show your finger and say *I've cut my finger. Now it hurts.* Use mime to show what you mean and gesture to encourage students to ask you questions about how you did it. Now draw a first aid kit (a box with a cross on it) or show a real one, and ask *When do we use this?* Elicit or give *accident.* Ask students *Where do most accidents happen? (In the home.)*

Write *How to say what's happened* on the board.

A Vocabulary accidents at home

1 Give students the opportunity to show what they know and familiarize them with *Bingo!* on **» p.38**. Direct students to photo b and ask *Why does the man look unhappy? What can you see?* and accept different suggestions. Go through the example together. Monitor and help as students continue in pairs by giving the first letter or syllable of words. Elicit answers around the class and help with meaning and pronunciation as necessary. Check students pronounce *finger* as /ˈfɪŋgə/ not /ˈfɪŋə/, and the plural of *shelf* as *shelves* not *shelfs*.

Suggested answers		
a egg, floor	e cup	i sugar
b cup	f glasses	j finger
c toast	g milk	k plates
d finger, knife	h shirt, iron	l bottles

2 Students start thinking about meaning by matching verbs with possible phrases. Go through the example before students continue individually. Check answers around the class by saying the verb and eliciting the noun phrases. Drill the complete phrases and help with pronunciation, if necessary.

2 b, c, d   3 f   4 a, b, d   5 e   6 a, b, d

Teaching tip

Check students understand the concepts by asking *Which are more serious accidents? (break your finger, burn your finger); Which are expensive to fix? (broken glasses); When do you need to clean up? (drop a cup, egg or milk); Which tastes bad? (salt in coffee); Why is the man in photo b unhappy? (He's put some salt in his coffee.)*

3 Students demonstrate they understand the meaning of vocabulary by matching the sentence beginnings and endings to describe the photos. Use the example to check students understand the activity and put them in pairs to continue. To check answers, nominate one student to say the first part of a sentence, and another to continue and a third to say which picture it is. If students ask, explain that in item 6 the subject of the verb is *bottles*, but don't focus on the form of the present perfect yet as it will be covered in the next section.

2 He's dropped an egg . picture a
3 She's cut her finger with a knife. picture d
4 He's put salt in his coffee. picture b
5 He's burnt his shirt. picture h
6 The bottles have fallen on the floor. picture l

B Grammar present perfect for recent events

4 Point to the small picture next to the grammar box. Elicit *He's dropped an egg.* and write the sentence on the board. Check the concept, that we are interested in the direct connection of the past event with its present relevance by asking *Do we know when he dropped the egg? Was it a long time ago? (No.) Can you see the result now? (Yes.)* Say the section heading and ask *What does recent mean? (Not long ago.)* Draw this timeline on the board:

dropped egg EGG ON THE FLOOR!

past ——————— X ——————— now ——————— future

past action   present result

HOW **INDEPENDENT** ARE YOU?

There was a time when young people didn't leave their family home until they got married. In fact, in some languages, the word *married* comes from the word *house*. For example, in Turkish, the word for *house* is *ev* and the word for *married* is *evli*, meaning *with house*. In Spanish, the word for *house* is *casa* and the word for *married* is *casado*.

But times have changed. These days, young people often want to marry later. In Europe, getting married at 29 or 30 is normal. So what do they do before that? Do they stay in the family home or do they become independent? Well, the answer is some people are more independent than others. How independent are young people in your country?

Do this test – choose the best answers for yourself.*

*or for a typical young person in your country

1 **Have you ever lived …**
a alone?
b in another town?
c abroad?

2 **Have you ever paid …**
a for the shopping?
b an electricity, phone, or gas bill?
c rent?

3 **Have you ever bought …**
a a towel?
b knives, forks, and spoons?
c a fridge?

4 **Have you ever had …**
a your own room?
b your own house keys?
c your own home?

5 **Have you ever turned on …**
a the cooker?
b the heating?
c the electricity?

6 **Have you ever cooked a meal …**
a for yourself?
b for your family?
c for guests?

7 **Have you ever put …**
a a battery in a remote control?
b soap in a washing machine?
c a shelf on the wall?

KEY

Count your *yes* answers.
Each *yes* = 1 point.

Age
Under 18? = Add 10 points.
Between 18 and 22? = Add 5 points.
Over 22?= Don't add any points.

Mark your score on the line.

0	VERY DEPENDENT
8	DEPENDENT
16	INDEPENDENT
24	
31	VERY INDEPENDENT

GLOSSARY
1 a*broad* = in another country
2 r_____ = money you pay to the owner of your home
3 h_____ = this is what makes your house warm
4 g_____ = vistors
5 r_____ c_____ = you use this to change the TV channel

How to talk about experiences

Orientation

Context

In this lesson, students will focus on talking about and giving details of experiences.

The introduction to the magazine questionnaire, *How independent are you?*, provides background information about the connection between the words *married* and *house* in two languages.

The questionnaire asks about the type of experiences a person has had. The answers are used to calculate an unmarried person's degree of independence, with scores weighted to take account of their age.

Culture note

On the whole, young British people are fairly independent, generally leaving home sometime between the ages of 18 and 25, often to go to college or university. However, a significant number return to live with their parents after graduating until they are able to get a job and support themselves! They don't generally get married until their late twenties or early thirties.

Language

Focus grammar	present perfect with *ever*; past simple
Focus words	*abroad, ever, lose, never, once, slept, twice*
Focus phrases	*a few times, lots of times, pay a bill/rent,* etc.
Recognition vocabulary	*battery, independent, show, soap*
Recycled language	words: *alone, electricity, fridge, gas, guest, heating, remote control, towel, turn on,* etc. phrases: *last night, last week, last year, yesterday,* etc. grammar: *past tense, wh- questions*

Language note

As well as using the present perfect to link present results to an event which has already taken place, we can use the present perfect with *ever*. The addition of this word broadens the concept to an experience at any time in your life.

End product

In *Put it all together*, students play a game in small groups asking about experiences and for further details. Students' conversation is based on listening texts and a model conversation in *Pairwork on* >> **p.127**.

Preparation

If possible, write the words for the *Warmer* on the board before the lesson.

Warmer

As preparation for section A, write these words on the board: *have, married, home, school, get, leave, buy, rent, get, children*. In pairs, students classify the words into nouns and verbs and match them (*have children, get married, leave school, leave home, buy a home, rent a home*). Go through each one and ask for a show of hands to see if students have done any of these.

Write *How to talk about experiences* on the board.

A Read a questionnaire and respond

In this section, students discuss the topic to activate ideas before reading a questionnaire for detail.

1 Do the first item together to demonstrate the activity. Put students into small groups and give them time to discuss the answers before asking around the class. Help students express their ideas but do not overcorrect for accuracy at this stage.

Teaching tip

In multilingual classes, organize students so that each group has a mix of nationalities to generate cross-cultural comparison. In monolingual classes, there is scope for discussion on the typical ages that people do these things.

2 Direct students to *How Independent Are You?* on >> **p.42** and set a short time limit for them to read and identify the topic (*b leaving home*). Ask for suggestions around the class and words in the text which helped them decide. Ask *Is the word for marriage and house connected in your language?*

3 Direct students to the glossary at the bottom of >> **p.42** and read the first word and definition. Elicit or explain that a glossary is a mini-dictionary for words in a particular text. Ask students to guess the answers first and then scan the text to check. Check answers as a class.

> 2 rent   3 heating   4 guests   5 remote control

4 Explain to students that they can do the questionnaire for themselves or somebody they know. Go through the key with the class and check they understand how to calculate their scores. Monitor and help as necessary as students work through the questionnaire alone. For class feedback, nominate students and ask if they were surprised by their independence rating and to give one example to explain why.

5 4D.1 Tell students that they are going to listen to a young British man answering the questions. Play the audio and pause after each main section for students to mark his answers. Play the audio a second time if necessary and allow students time to calculate his score. In pairs, students discuss whether they are more or less independent than Callum and if any of his answers surprised them.

> Callum scores 11 points, a score which indicates he is not very independent.

B Grammar present perfect with *ever*; past simple

6 Direct students to the two cartoons and ask them to point to the picture in which they can see a recent result (*picture b*). Ask *What's happened? (He's hurt/broken his arm.)* Ask *What's the person pointing to him asking?* and elicit *Have you broken your arm?* Tell students to look at the sentences under the pictures and ask *Which question asks about life experience? (Question 2.) Which question asks about a recent event? (Question 1.)* Match the questions and pictures as a class before students copy the questions in the speech bubbles.

Copy these timelines on the board and ask students which one matches which sentence (1b, 2a). Point out the position of *ever* after the subject but before the past participle.

timeline 1 = recent event

                              broken arm?
past ————————————— X – now ————————————— future

timeline 2 = life experience

                    broken arm?
                    ? – ? – ? – ?
past ————X———X———X———X———now———— future

Extra help

Remind students that in 4B they were focussing on the results of *recent events*. In this lesson they are talking about *life experiences*. To practise the form and show the change in concept with *ever*, elicit and drill *Have you ever ...?* questions about life experience based on familiar vocabulary, e.g. *Have you ever put salt in your coffee? Have you ever cut your finger?*

7 Students practise manipulating the grammar. Go through the example with the class and remind students that they can find past participle lists on >> p.148. Monitor and help if necessary as students continue individually. To check answers, ask for volunteers to ask you the question and give your reply using some of the expressions in exercise 8. Check students understand the meaning of *once* and *twice* and encourage them to ask follow-up questions and respond with more detail.

Have you ever
2 ... stolen a hotel towel?
3 ... lost your house keys?
4 ... paid a bill with a credit card?
5 ... bought something on the Internet?

8 Go through the instructions and the example. Answer questions about the experiences in the box. Put students into pairs to interview each other, and monitor and help with word order in questions as necessary. Do open-class pairwork at the end and ask follow-up questions to students' replies.

9 Use the information from the open pairwork and write an affirmative sentence about one of the students on the board, e.g. *Hana has lost her house keys a few times.* Ask *Did this happen in the past? (Yes.) Do we know when? (No.) Is the time or the experience important? (the experience)* to check the concept of this use of the present perfect again. Ask students *When?* and amend the sentence on the board, *Hana lost her house keys last year.* Direct students to the grammar box, example sentences and the time phrases. Go through questions 1–4 together as a class and see if you can elicit the rule for item 5.

1 No 2 Yes 3 No 4 Yes 5 Present perfect

10 Ask students to read items 1–5 and do the first item as a class. Point out the time clause at the end of the sentence and in the grammar box in exercise 9. Monitor and help if necessary as students continue individually. Students compare in pairs before you go through the answers as a class.

1 lost 2 've had 3 hasn't drunk 4 Have/ever lived
5 Did/watch

Extra plus

In pairs, students ask the questions in exercise 7 again. They start with a present perfect question and use the past simple to ask for details.

C Listen and follow a conversation

In this section, students listen and follow detail in a short conversation and then order information using a conversation map.

11 4D.2 Read through the instructions and questions 1–3. Play the audio. Students answer the questions and compare in pairs.

1 James 2 in 2001 3 fell downstairs

12 Direct students to the conversation map and the small letters at the beginning of each turn. Tell students that each row is a new turn. Talk through the options at each turn and see if students can remember which conversation route Alice and James took. Play the audio a second time for students to check answers. Students can check with audioscript 4D.2 on >> p.152.

2 b 3 d 4 g

13 In pairs, students practise the conversation. Encourage them to refer to the conversation map if necessary. Ask for volunteers to have their conversations for the class.

ABC Put it all together

14 To introduce the activity, tell students to ask you a *Have you ever ...?* question, e.g. met a famous person. Tell students to ask you *Wh ...* questions to see if you are telling the truth or not and warn them that you might not answer their questions honestly. After five or six questions, ask students if they think you really have met ...

Tell students to turn to >> p.127. Go through the instructions as a class and make sure students write six *Have you ever ...?* questions. Direct them to *How Independent Are You?* for ideas. Ask for two volunteers to have the conversation and put students into small groups of three or four to play the game. At the end, ask students to tell the class about interesting experiences others have had.

Student performance

Students should be able to start and maintain a short conversation.

Use this checklist for monitoring and feedback or to assess students' performance.

Interaction	Do students respond to questions appropriately? exercise 12
Fluency	Do students ask *Have you ever ...?* without a lot of hesitation? exercise 8
Coherence	Do students ask appropriate questions about the experience? exercise 12

I can talk about experiences.

Students tick *on my own* if they can ask *Have you ever ...?* questions without using their notes. They tick *with some help* if they need to read some of their questions.

Early finishers

Students write different questions and repeat the activity with a different group.

Additional material

www.oup.com/elt/result for extra practice material
www.oup.com/elt/teacher/result for extra teacher resources

How to talk about experiences

G present perfect with *ever*; past simple

A Read a questionnaire and respond

1 Work in small groups. Complete the sentences below and compare your answers.

Example In my country, most people ...

1 leave school at about _____ (age).
2 leave home at about _____.
3 rent or buy their first home at about _____.
4 get married at about _____.
5 have children at about _____.

2 Read the first paragraph of **How Independent Are You?** opposite. What's the topic?
a foreign languages b leaving home c the family

3 Read and complete the **Glossary** opposite.

4 Do the test with a partner and count your score.

5 **4D.1▶** Listen to Callum's answers to questions 1–7 opposite. Is he more or less independent than you?

B Grammar present perfect with *ever*; past simple

6 Match these pictures with the sentences.

1 Have you broken your arm?
2 Have you ever broken your arm?
(In this question, *ever* means 'at any time in your life before now'.)

7 Write *Have you ever ... ?* questions with these words.
1 sleep/boat *Have you ever slept on a boat?*
2 steal/hotel towel
3 lose/your house keys
4 pay a bill/credit card
5 buy something/Internet

8 Ask your questions to a partner. Answer your partner's questions. Use the expressions from the box below.

Yes,	I have.	No,	I haven't.
	once.		never.
	twice.		
	a few times.		
	lots of times.		

Example Have you ever slept on a boat?
    Yes, a few times.

9 Read the grammar box and answer the questions below.

present perfect	past simple
I've broken my arm once (before now). now	I broke my arm last summer. now
before now (unfinished time)	last summer (finished time)

unfinished times	finished times
before now today	last summer yesterday
this week in my life	last week in 2001
this month this year	when I was five

1 'I've broken my arm.' Do we know when?
2 'I broke my arm last summer.' Do we know when?
3 'I've had a coffee today.' Is today finished?
4 'I had a coffee yesterday.' Is yesterday finished?
5 For unfinished times, what tense do we use?

10 Underline the correct words.
1 I've lost/lost my car keys last week.
2 I've had/had the flu three times this year.
3 She hasn't drunk/didn't drink any coffee today.
4 Have/Did you ever lived/live in another country?
5 Have/Did you watched/watch TV last night?

More practice? **Grammar Bank** ≫ p.139.

C Listen and follow a conversation

11 **4D.2▶** Listen to a short conversation between Alice and James and answer the questions.
1 Who has broken their arm - Alice or James?
2 When did it happen?
3 How did it happen?

12 Follow the conversation in exercise 11 on this conversation map. Listen again to check.

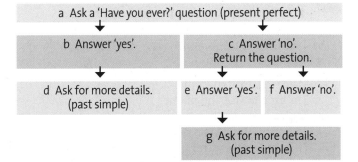

13 Practise the conversation with a partner.

ABC Put it all together

14 Work in groups. Play the *Liar!* game on ≫ p.127.

I can talk about experiences.

Tick ✓ the line.   with a lot of help   with some help   on my own   very easily

43

Writing A thank you note

A Read and understand the writer's aim

1 Read the note and answer the questions.
1 Where is it?
2 Who wrote it?
3 Why did she write it?

> Hi Ana!
>
> Sorry I'm not here to welcome you!
>
> Make yourself at home.
>
> Help yourself to anything in the fridge.
>
> There's tea and coffee in the cupboard above the cooker.
>
> I've made the bed for you in the end room.
>
> Feel free to have a shower and turn the heating on.
>
> Back from work @ 6.30.
>
> Phillipa

2 Detective work. What can you guess from the note? Write *yes*, *no* or *perhaps*.
1 Ana is a guest in Phillipa's house. *Yes*
2 Ana got the key from Phillipa's neighbour.
3 Phillipa's at work.
4 The weather's hot.
5 There's milk in the fridge.
6 Ana's going to stay for the night.

B Vocabulary welcome and thanking phrases

3 Write *W* or *T* after these phrases.

W = from a welcome note
T = from a thank you note

1 Make yourself at home. *W*
2 Feel free to use the phone.
3 You've been really kind.
4 I'm sorry I broke the plate.
5 Thanks for everything.
6 Help yourself to a drink.
7 I've had a great time.

C Imagine your reader's questions

4 Read the situation. Work with a partner and write Ana's thank you note.

Situation

It's two days later, and Ana's leaving Phillipa's flat. Phillipa is at work again. Ana writes a thank you note to Phillipa. She imagines Phillipa's possible questions:

Did Ana have a good time?
Did Ana feed the cat?
Where are the keys?
Why is there a new box of eggs in the fridge?
Where's Ana's towel?

> Hi Phillipa
> I've had a great time!
> I've fed . . .

5 **4E.1▶** Listen. How is this text different from your thank you note?

6 Read the audio script on ›› p.152 and check.

ABC Put it all together

7 Work with a partner. Imagine you have stayed for a weekend in a friend's home while he or she was away. You've had lots of small accidents. Write a list.

broken a glass	dropped an egg
cut your hand	burnt a hole

8 Imagine your friend's questions when he/she comes home.

Why is there a black hole in the sofa?
Why is the bin full of broken glass?

9 Write a thank you note. Answer the questions you imagined in exercise 8.

I can write a thank you note. ▮▮▮▮▮▮▮▮▮▮▮▮▮▮

Tick ✓ the line.   with a lot of help   with some help   on my own   very easily

Orientation

Context and Language

In this lesson, students will think about a readers and writer's purpose for writing thank you notes.

New language	*Feel free to ..., Help yourself to ..., Make yourself at home.*, etc.
Recycled language	words: *things and actions around the house* grammar: *present perfect*

End product

In *Put it all together,* students write a short note (about 70 words) based on audio script 4E.1 on >> p.152–53.

Warmer

Ask students to imagine they stayed at a friend's house and left before the friend arrived home. Ask for a show of hands to see how many would leave a thank you note. Write *How to write a thank you note* on the board.

A Read and understand the writer's aim

In this section, students analyse a note to determine why it has been written.

1 Check students understand the title of the section. Go through the instructions and the questions. Direct students to the note. Set a short time limit for students to skim and scan to answer the questions. Go over answers as a class.

> 1 Phillipa's house (maybe in the kitchen)
> 2 Phillipa   3 She's not home to welcome Ana.

2 Ask students to read items 1–6 and check vocabulary. Do the example to make sure students understand the activity. They compare in pairs before you go over answers as a class.

> 2 perhaps   3 yes   4 no   5 perhaps   6 yes

Extra activity

Ask students for examples from Phillipa's letter which indicate that it's an informal note to a friend, e.g. *Hi!, use of short sentences – one on each line, imperatives, contracted forms.*

B Vocabulary welcome and thanking phrases

3 Direct students to the title and ask *When?* to elicit the situations in which the two things are done. Go through the example as a class and put students in pairs to think about the function of each phrase. Monitor and help as necessary. Nominate pairs to give answers and ask students to find examples of welcome phrases in Phillipa's note.

> 2 W   3 T   4 T   5 T   6 W   7 T

C Imagine your reader's questions

In this section, students are introduced to a strategy which they can use to help make the content of their writing appropriate.

4 Read the instructions. Go through the situation and the questions as a class and elicit possible answers. Write notes on the board, encouraging students to use their imagination and give some background detail. Point out that if a writer imagines a reader's questions it can help decide what to include in the note.

Ask students to write the answers to Phillipa's questions, and to look again at the phrases for thank you notes in exercise 3 for help. Monitor and check correct use of the present perfect. Give positive feedback for ideas.

5 4E.1 Go through the instructions and check students understand the activity. Tell students to put a tick by any information which is the same, and write key words to note any differences. Play the audio and give students the option of listening a second time if necessary.

6 Direct students to audio script 4E.1 on >> p.152–53 to check. Ask for volunteers to give similarities and differences. Explain that students' texts are not wrong if there are differences, but that they should check they have answered the questions in exercise 4.

Extra help

Go through the questions in exercise 4 and ask students for the answers in the audio script.

ABC Put it all together

7 Read through the instructions with the class and check students understand the activity. Put students in pairs to share ideas. Monitor and refer students to the note in exercise 1 and lesson 4B for more ideas if necessary. Elicit a couple more small accidents around the class.

8 Go through the instructions and elicit some explanations around the class. In pairs, students think about the questions their friend might ask about the accidents they have had in the home. If necessary, direct students back to the questions in exercise 4. Encourage students to use their dictionaries.

9 Ask for an example of a greeting and a closing, and remind them to use both. Tell students to look at audio script 4E.1 on >> p.152–53 for help if necessary. Students should review their writing for short forms for the present perfect, and make corrections if necessary. Ask pairs to swap notes and to check they have answered the questions in exercise 8.

Student performance

Students should be able to write a thank you note (about 70 words) using simple sentences. Their writing might contain occasional errors if they try to express the connection between an event and its consequences.

Use this checklist for monitoring and feedback or to assess students' performance.

Content	Have students given explanations for two or more accidents?
Organization	Have students used greetings and closings? Have students thanked and apologized?

I can write a thank you note.

Students tick *on my own* if they have explained each mishap. They tick *with some help* if they need to include more information.

Early finishers

In small groups, students tell others what happened during their stay and then read their notes. The group decides if the note explained the situations.

Additional material

www.oup.com/elt/result for extra practice material
www.oup.com/elt/teacher/result for extra teacher resources

Warmer

Remember who

Write sentences 1–10 below on the board. In small groups, students write down who said or wrote them. They check answers by looking back through the unit.

1 Could I have an alarm call at 7.30 a.m., please? 2 I haven't watered the cactus. 3 Have you ever broken your arm? 4 Have you fed Toby? 5 I've made the bed for you in the end room. 6 Just for one night? 7 I haven't started on the kitchen yet. 8 I've fed the cat. 9 I've cleaned the floor. 10 We've decided to come home early.

1 the guest	4 Lisa's mum	7 Frank	10 Lisa's mum
2 Lisa	5 Phillipa	8 Ana	
3 James	6 the receptionist	9 Lisa	

A Grammar

1   can/could (requests) 4A exercise 14

Warm-up: Write these words on the board for students to make a hotel request: *please, TV, work, send, could, someone doesn't, the, you, to, it, at, look, ?*

> The TV doesn't work. Could you send someone to look at it, please?

Set-up: Go through the example with the class.

> 2 Could I have a cup of tea, please?
> 3 Could you send me some new towels, please?
> 4 Could I have an alarm call at seven, please?
> 5 Could you tell me how to turn the heating off, please?

Follow-up: Students write translations of the questions and compare ways of making polite requests in their language.

2   Present perfect for recent events 4B exercises 4–5

Warm-up: Direct students to look at *Bingo!* on **» p.38**. Say a picture number for students to say what's happened.

Set-up: Ask students to read the text and check any vocabulary problems. Go through the example as a class.

> 2 He's dropped the milk.   3 He's burnt the toast.
> 4 He's broken the plate.   5 He's cut his finger.

Follow-up: Students say past actions from exercise 4 on **» p.39** or invent their own. A partner says the present result.

3   Present perfect for recent events 4C exercise 4

Warm-up: Remind students about Lisa. Ask *What hasn't she done?* and elicit ideas around the class.

Set-up: Use the example and tell students to make sentences by moving from left to right, right to left, up and down but not diagonally. The first word of each sentence is numbered.

> 2 Has she cleaned the floor?
> 3 Lisa has invited her friends for a party.
> 4 Has she washed up?
> 5 Lisa has turned on the heating.
> 6 Lisa has dropped food on the floor.
> 7 Lisa hasn't kept the kitchen clean.
> 8 Her parents have decided to come home early.
> 9 Has she fed the dog?

Follow-up: Students tell a partner about the things they've done and not done before they came to class.

4   Present perfect questions with *ever* 4D exercise 7

Warm-up: Nominate students and ask a few questions in *How independent are you?* on **» p.42**.

Set-up: Ask students to read the text and check vocabulary. Do the example as a class.

> Have you ever ...
> paid for the shopping? paid rent?
> cooked for your family? cooked for guests?
> put soap in the washing machine? put a shelf on the wall?

Follow-up: Students role play the conversation and then ask each other the questions.

B Vocabulary

5   Hotels 4A exercise 11

Warm-up: Ask students for three things a hotel receptionist and a guest might say.

Set-up: Tell students to read the conversation. Ask *How long is the guest staying? (One night.) What's the hotel room number? (224.)*

2 room	5 included	8 key
3 night	6 May	9 second
4 with	7 passport	

Follow-up: In pairs, students write their own gapped conversation for another pair to complete. They check each other's answers at the end.

6   Around the house 4A exercise 3, 4C exercise 1

Warm-up: Write *bedroom, bathroom, living room* on the board. Set a short time limit for students to write a list of the things they might find in each room.

Set-up: Go through the instructions and the example as a class.

2 blanket	6 towel	10 heating
3 pillow	7 toilet roll	11 gas
4 tap	8 ashtray	12 electricity
5 soap	9 lamp	

Follow-up: Students choose ten things around the house from unit 4 and write their own anagrams. They swap lists and find the words. Students check their partner's answers and spelling.

7   Irregular past participles 4B exercise 6

Warm up: Write some of the past participles from the word pool on the board. Ask students for the infinitive and the past tense.

Set up: Go through the instructions and the example as a class.

2 burnt	5 done	8 paid	11 stolen
3 bought	6 fallen	9 put	12 taken
4 cut	7 kept	10 seen	

Follow up: Students choose three past participles they want to remember and write a sentence for each one.

8   Time phrases 4D exercise 9

Warm-up: Draw two columns on the board entitled *finished time* and *unfinished time*. Elicit time phrases and write them on the board. Direct students to **» p.43**, exercise 9 to check.

Set-up: Ask students to read conversations 1–3 and check any vocabulary.

> 1 never, once   2 last, this   3 times, twice

Follow-up: Students ask each other two questions using *Have you ever ...?* and *How many times have you ...?*

Early finishers

Students review the unit and choose ten verbs. They draw three columns and write the verb, past tense and participle. They check with a dictionary.

Unit 4 Review

A Grammar

1 *can / could* (requests) You are staying at a hotel. Write requests with *can* or *could*.

1 You want a taxi.
   Could you call a taxi for me, please?
2 You want a cup of tea.
   _____
3 You want new towels.
   _____
4 You want an alarm call at seven.
   _____
5 It's hot and you don't know how to turn the heating off.
   _____

2 **Present perfect for recent events** Write four more sentences about little Steven.

Little Steven is five years old. He's standing in the kitchen and there is a jam sandwich on the floor. There is a carton of milk on the floor. There is toast in the toaster and it's black and smoking. There are pieces of broken plate on the floor. There's a cut on his hand and he's crying.

1 *He's dropped a jam sandwich* _____ .
2 _____ .
3 _____ .
4 _____ .
5 _____ .

3 **Present perfect for recent events** Find nine sentences about Lisa.

1 Lisa	**2** Has	**3** Lisa	has	invited	her
hasn't	she	cleaned	**4** Has	she	friends
watered	the	the	floor?	washed	for
5 Lisa	plants.	**6** Lisa	has	up?	a
has	**7** Lisa	hasn't	dropped	food	party.
turned	**8** Her	kept	the	on	the
on	parents	have	kitchen	clean.	floor.
the	heating.	decided	to	come	home
9 Has	she	fed	the	dog?	early.

4 **Present perfect questions with *ever*** Write questions and Callum's answers.

Callum's 24 years old and he's never lived alone. He's paid for the shopping but he's never paid rent. He's cooked for his family but he's never cooked for guests. He's put soap in the washing machine but he's never put a shelf on the wall.

You Have you ever lived alone, Callum?
Callum No, I haven't.
You Have you ever ...

B Vocabulary

5 **Hotels** Complete the conversation with these words.

with ~~help~~ included key may
night passport room second

A Can I [1] *help* _____ you?
B Yes, I'd like a [2] _____ please.
A Just for one [3] _____?
B Yes. How much is it?
A It's €80, [4] _____ breakfast [5] _____.
   [6] _____ I see your [7] _____, please?
B Yes, here you are.
A Thanks. Here's your [8] _____. It's room 224 on the
   [9] _____ floor.

6 **Around the house** Find the words in these anagrams.

On the bed
1 these _____ *sheet*
2 kneblat _____
3 wipoll _____

In the bathroom
4 pat _____
5 paso _____
6 wetol _____
7 littoe lorl _____

In the living room
8 rasthay _____
9 plam _____

Services
10 gethain _____
11 sag _____
12 cletticeriy _____

7 **Irregular past participles** Find the past participles of these verbs. Some letters are used twice.

~~break~~ burn buy cut do fall
keep pay put see steal take

B	U	R	N	T	T	P
R	O	C	E	N	S	A
O	P	U	T	E	P	I
K	S	T	G	D	I	D
E	E	T	T	H	L	T
N	E	P	O	E	T	A
K	N	O	T	L	N	K
E	L	D	O	N	E	E
N	F	A	L	L	E	N

1 *broken*
2 _____
3 _____
4 _____
5 _____
6 _____
7 _____
8 _____
9 _____
10 _____
11 _____
12 _____

8 **Time phrases** Complete the conversations with these words.

~~ever~~ last never once this times twice

1 **A** Have you *ever* broken your leg?
   B No, I've _____ broken my leg, but I broke my arm _____.
2 I broke a glass _____ night and I cut my foot on a piece of it _____ morning.
3 **A** How many _____ have you been in hospital?
   B Only _____ – once when I was five and again two years ago.

Clothes

dress sandals shorts socks
suit /suːt/ sweatshirt tights /taɪts/
top tracksuit trainers underwear

WINDOW SHOPPING

How to **talk about clothes**

Orientation

Context

In this lesson, students will focus on using adverbs and adjectives to give their opinions on clothes.

Window Shopping is a cartoon strip which features two shop dummies, Gavin and Jeff, who 'come alive' in a shop window. Gavin, who is outside the picture, tells Jeff his clothes have attracted the attention of a female passer-by. Jeff thinks the woman is looking at Gavin, who is shocked because he isn't dressed for the window display.

Photos 1–11 illustrate the vocabulary in *Clothes*.

Language

Focus grammar	adverbs of degree: *a bit, a little, enough, quite, really, too, very*
Focus words	clothes: *socks, top, tights, tracksuit, trainers, underwear* adjectives: *bright, dark, nice, tight*
Focus phrases	*What do you think of my ...?, It's/They're really nice!, It suits you.*, etc.
Recognition vocabulary	*half-price, perhaps, sales*
Recycled language	clothes: *dress, sandals, shorts, suit, sweatshirt, trousers* adjectives: *big, casual, comfortable, long, short, small, smart,* etc.
Pronunciation	intonation in opinions 5A.2
Discourse	object pronoun substitution *it, they*

Language note

In spoken English, speakers tend to give negative opinions with rising intonation. This gives the impression that the opinion is tentative, so the hearer is less likely to be upset by it. For example, *They're a bit unusual.* said with rising-falling intonation sounds positive, while the same words said with falling-rising intonation sounds negative. Euphemism, for example, saying *It's a bit expensive.* rather than *It's very expensive.* is also a convention in spoken English, used to avoid giving displeasure.

End product

In *Put it all together*, students exchange opinions on what people are wearing in pictures in *Pairwork* on >> p.127 and >> p.133.

Warmer

Review colours and test students' recognition of clothes words by asking *Who's wearing something pink today? Who's wearing brown trousers? Who's wearing a white shirt? Who's wearing smart clothes? Who's wearing a green jacket? Is anyone wearing red socks? Is anyone wearing a blue T-shirt?*

Write *How to talk about clothes* on the board.

A Vocabulary clothes

1   Check students have covered >> p.46. Put students into pairs or small groups and give them three to four minutes for the brainstorming activity. Elicit vocabulary around the class. Ask for spellings as you write words on the board and check students understand the meaning of any new vocabulary.

2   Students work individually, then in pairs to match the words to the photos. Check answers by saying a photo number for the class to say the word. Monitor for pronunciation and direct students to the pronunciation of *suit* and *tights* in *Clothes*.

> 1 suit 2 sandals 3 top 4 socks 5 trainers 6 shorts
> 7 tracksuit 8 underwear 9 sweatshirt 10 tights 11 dress

3   Give students time to read questions 1–4 and check any vocabulary. Do the first item as a class before students continue individually and then compare answers in pairs. Monitor for pronunciation of the final /s/ and give positive feedback when students pronounce words correctly.

> 1 women's clothes: dress, tights, top   men's clothes: suit
> 2 smart clothes: suit   casual clothes: shorts,
>   sweatshirt   sportswear: tracksuit, trainers, sweatshirt
> 3 plural words: sandals, shorts, socks, tights, trainers
>   singular words: dress, suit, sweatshirt, top, tracksuit,
>   underwear
> 4 Students' own answers.

4   Go through the instructions and check students understand the adjectives. Read the examples and give one or two strange combinations, e.g. *long trainers, smart socks* to help students understand the activity. Tell them to think of two combinations for each adjective. Monitor and help as necessary. To check answers, go through each adjective in turn and elicit suggestions from the class. Encourage students to use *a* with singular clothes words and *some* with plural clothes words.

> **Suggested answers**
> **big** sweatshirt, sandals   **casual** top, dress
> **comfortable** sweatshirt, sandals   **long** socks, top
> **nice** suit, dress   **small** sweatshirt, trainers
> **short** socks, dress   **smart** top, suit, dress
> **tight** top, shorts   **warm** sweatshirt, tights

Language note

Comfortable has only three syllables. The 'or' in the middle is not pronounced. The 'gh' in *tight* is not pronounced and in British English the 'r' in *warm* is silent.

Extra help

Students test each other on the opposite adjectives, e.g. **A** *long socks* **B** *short socks* **B** *tight trainers* **A** *comfortable trainers*, etc.

B Listen for key words

In this section, students listen to a dialogue to recognize key words and for detail.

5   Direct students to *Window Shopping*. Ask them to look at the pictures and say who the people are *(two shop window dummies, and a woman in the street)*. Set a short time limit to name all the clothes vocabulary in the story. Check answers, encouraging students to use the collocations from exercise 4.

The Story of Jeans

The first jeans came from Genoa in Italy. The name *jeans* comes from the French name for Genoa, *Gênes*. Sailors in the Genoese navy wore jeans because they're strong and you can wear them wet or dry. The sailors washed their jeans by putting them in a large bag and dropping them in the sea.

Modern jeans were invented by Levi Strauss. Strauss moved to America from Germany, and he started making jeans in the 1870s. He originally made them for miners in California. He made them blue so they wouldn't look dirty.

In the 1950s, pop and movie stars like James Dean and Elvis Presley wore jeans, and they became fashionable with teenagers and young adults. At that time, wearing jeans was a symbol of independence for young people. However, in the 60s and 70s, jeans became a fashion for all ages. Today, the average American person owns seven pairs of jeans.

Dean's jeans!

Clean jeans, neat jeans
Sitting on your seat jeans
Dear jeans, cheap jeans
Wear them on the beach jeans
Wear them with a sweater
Great in any weather
Dirty jeans, clean jeans
The trousers of your dreams
Dean's jeans!

Buying Jeans

a

Shop assistant Do you like these ones?
Customer Yes. How much are they?
S £54.99.

b

C I'm not sure.
S OK, try this pair on. The changing room's over there.

c

S What do you think?
C Yes, they're fine. I'll take them.

d

S How would you like to pay?
C I'll pay in cash.

e

S How are they?
C They're a bit small.

f

S OK, try the next size. Here you are.
C Thanks.

g

S Can I help you?
C Yes, I'm looking for a pair of jeans.

h

C Can I try a pair on?
S Yes, of course. What size are you?

How to ask for things in shops

Orientation

Context

In this lesson, students will practise using shopping phrases.

The Story of Jeans describes the origin of jeans and their modern-day equivalent.

The verse *Dean's Jeans* is an advertising jingle, with 'ea' spellings, which are also stressed syllables, highlighted.

Buying Jeans is a photo story where we see a customer and a shop assistant in a typical clothes shopping situation. The pictures are not in the correct order.

Language

Focus grammar	phrasal verbs: *put … on, take … off, turn … off, turn … on, try … on*
Preview grammar	past passive
Focus words	*changing room, fine, jeans, a pair of jeans, pair, size*
Focus phrases	shopping phrases: *Can I try it/them on?, I'll pay in cash., I'll take them., I'm not sure.*
Recognition vocabulary	*cowboys, dear, dry, fashionable, independence, miners, neat, symbol, wet*
Recycled language	words: *cheap, favourite, invent, sailor, trousers* phrases: *a bit small, how much,* grammar: *how much, how many*
Pronunciation	sounds spelt with *ea* 5C.1
Discourse	substituting pronouns: *this one/these ones*

End product

In *Put it all together*, students role play a conversation in a clothes shop, based on the dialogue *Buying Jeans*. They talk about three or four situations, and can look at the pictures to help them remember. Students have rehearsed similar conversations with a different partner.

Preparation

Write the words *try, on, them* and *these jeans* on pieces of different coloured cards. You should be able to make all the sentences in exercise 15 at the same time. Take these and some blu-tack to class if you want to demonstrate how particles in phrasal verbs can change position (see exercise 15, *Teaching tip*).

Warmer

If you have room, put students into groups of five. Ask them to line up according to the following criteria: *who is wearing the biggest shoes to who is wearing the smallest shoes; who went shopping for clothes most recently to who went shopping for clothes least recently; who is wearing the oldest top to who is wearing the newest top; who spends the most money on clothes to who spends the least money on clothes.* Alternatively, run the activity as a seated discussion, with students numbering themselves from 1 to 5. Get some brief feedback from the groups after each line-up.

Write *How to ask for things in shops* on the board.

A Think about the topic before you read

In this section, students read a factual article for specific information and practise giving personal responses to the content.

1   Put students in groups of three to four to discuss the questions and monitor and help as necessary. Listen for interesting comments and contribute to students' discussion if possible. After about five minutes, go through the questions and ask for a volunteer to report back the group's answers. Tell the class any interesting facts or comments.

2   Write *The Story of Jeans* on the board. Tell students that they will think about what they already know first, to help them with their reading. Ask students to read questions 1–3 and check any vocabulary. Students continue individually and then compare their answers in pairs or groups.

3   Direct students to *The Story of Jeans* on >> p.50 to check their answers. Monitor and help with vocabulary as necessary. Go over answers as a class and ask students if the text was easy or difficult to understand. Give students time to read again and answer any vocabulary questions.

> 1 b   2 a   3 c

4   Explain to students that when we read factual texts, we often find out something new or interesting and tell a friend about it. Give or elicit the responses from the example and write them on the board. Go through the example as a class. Read A's part and nominate different students to respond. Encourage students to sound interested in the conversation but don't focus too long on this.

Ask students to underline four examples of new or interesting information. Monitor and help as necessary. Put students in pairs to do the activity and give positive feedback when students sound convincing in their response.

Extra activity

In pairs, students write their own interesting facts about any topic. Students read one sentence each to the class, and nominate another student to respond.

B Pronunciation sounds spelt with *ea*

5   5C.1 Direct students to the title of the section. Ask *Can you tell the pronunciation of words in English from spelling? (Not always.)* Tell students that one difficult area is knowing how to pronounce words with 'ea'. Direct students to the table and copy the five symbols on the board. Elicit a word for each sound and write it on the board.

Go through the instructions and tell the class that they are going to hear an advert for jeans in the form of a poem. Point out that the 'ea' sounds are highlighted. Play the audio twice, and ask students to compare answers between each play. Give them time to write the words before going over answers as a class. Ask the class to read the words and check pronunciation.

> /iː/ jeans, clean, neat, cheap, beach, dreams
> /e/ sweater, weather   /eɪ/ great   /ɪər/ dear   /eər/ wear

6   Put students in small groups to think of more words. Tell them to look in their dictionaries if they need to check.

> ### Suggested answers
> /iː/ team, eat, meal, reach, tea, pea, leave, peace
> /e/ breakfast, dead   /eɪ/ steak   /ɪər/ ear, hear   /eər/ bear

7 Play the audio and pause after each line for students to repeat. Play it a second time, but stop after every two lines for students to repeat. Finally, play it all the way through for students to read quietly with the audio. Students practise reading the poem aloud in pairs.

C Vocabulary shopping phrases

8 5C.2 Introduce the topic by asking the class when they last bought a pair of jeans and about their experience. Tell students they will listen to a conversation in a shop and ask them to cover the picture page.

Students read questions 1–4. Ask them to look at question 1 and write *How much are the jeans?* on the board, underlining *are* and *jeans* to show the grammatical connection. Contrast this with question 3. Write *How many pairs of jeans ...?* and underline *many* and the *s* in *pairs*. Play the audio and go over answers as a class.

> 1 £54.99   2 No   3 two   4 cash

9 Encourage students to think more about the context of shopping. Direct them to *Buying Jeans* and set a short time limit for them to put the pictures in order. Ask students to compare in pairs but do not give answers yet.

10 Play the audio for students to check and go over answers as a class. Go through the conversation again and ask about the highlighted words and phrases Ask *Are they singular or plural? What do they refer to, jeans or a pair of jeans?* Divide the class into A/B groups to read the conversation.

> 1 g   2 a   3 h   4 b   5 e   6 f   7 c   8 d

Extra activity
Books closed. Write the words *customer* and *shop assistant* on the board. Say some of the phrases from the dialogue, for students to say who says each one. Add *Thanks, I'm just looking.* and *I'm fine, thanks.* as customer phrases on the board.

11 Go through the instructions and the example. Do one or two more examples to demonstrate the activity. Students continue in pairs.

12 5C.3 Play the audio for students to check. Go over any problems as a class. Play the audio a second time, pausing after each item for students to repeat.

13 Put students in pairs to practise the conversation and check they swap roles. As students go through the conversation, monitor and encourage them to read, look up from the page, make eye contact with their partner and say some phrases from memory. Give positive feedback for all attempts.

Extra help
Students repeat the exercise with another clothes item from 5A.

D Grammar phrasal verbs with *on* and *off*

14 Direct students to the dictionary entry and go through the question as a class. Ask *What kind of word is try on? (A phrasal verb.)* Explain that the position of *sth* in the dictionary tells us that the noun can be placed between the verb and the preposition. Tell students that this is not the same for all phrasal verbs, and that they can use their dictionary to help.

15 Go through the example sentences as a class and put students in pairs to work out the rules. As you go over each rule, give cues to elicit more sentences, e.g. *trousers, sweater.*

> 1 can   2 can   3 can   4 can't

Teaching tip
Stick the different coloured cards to the wall to demonstrate how the noun can move (see *Preparation*).

16 Go through the instructions and check students understand the activity. Ask students to read items 1–8 to find examples of other phrasal verbs *(turn on/off, take off)*. Explain that these phrasal verbs follow the same rules as *turn on*. In pairs, students do the exercise. Monitor and help as necessary. Check answers as a class.

> 2 ✓   3 ✓   4 ✗ I'm going to take it off.   5 ✓
> 6 ✗ Take them off.   7 ✓   8 ✗ ... try it on?

Extra help
Activate phrasal verbs with this TPR (Total Physical Response) activity. Students give each other instructions to perform in small groups or as a whole class. Do some examples as a class. Say *Take your ring off. Put it on again. Turn the lights off.*

17 Go through the instructions and the example. Put students in pairs to practise a few times and do the exercise as a group drill. Say the prompts for students to respond as a class. Point out that these are very short exchanges, similar to the ones in the *Buying Jeans* dialogue.

> **Suggested answers**
> 2 Turn the heating off.   4 Turn the lights on.
> 3 Take them off.   5 Try it on.

ABCD Put it all together

18 Read through the instructions and put students in pairs to practise the conversation. Remind them to look at the pictures and say phrases from memory. Check they swap roles.

19 Books closed. Put students with a different partner to have the conversation from memory.

Student performance
Students should be able to have a short transactional conversation.

Use this checklist for monitoring and feedback or to assess students' performance.

Content	Do students role play three or four shopping situations? exercise 11
Interaction	Do students make suggestions? exercise 17
Coherence	Do students sometimes use pronouns in place of a noun? exercise 11

I can **ask for things in shops.**

Students tick *on my own* if they can role play three or four shopping situations from memory. They tick *with some help* if they look at the highlighted phrases in *Buying Jeans* once or twice.

Early finishers
Students write another shopping dialogue, with a very difficult customer. They say their conversations for another pair, who count how many problems the customer has.

Additional material

www.oup.com/elt/result for extra practice material
www.oup.com/elt/teacher/result for extra teacher resources

How to ask for things in shops

G phrasal verbs with *on* and *off* V shopping phrases P sounds spelt with *ea*

A Think about the topic before you read

1 Work in small groups. Ask and answer the questions.
   1 How many people in the class are wearing jeans?
   2 Have you got many pairs of jeans?
   3 When do you wear them?
   4 What colour jeans do you prefer?
   5 Have you got a favourite pair of jeans?

2 Guess the correct answers.
   1 Who first wore jeans?
      a American cowboys
      b Italian sailors
      c Chinese miners
   2 Where does the word *jeans* come from?
      a the French name for the city Genoa
      b a short form of the name James Dean
      c an Arabic word meaning *trousers*
   3 Who invented modern jeans?
      a Lee Wrangler b Elvis Presley c Levi Strauss

3 Now read **The Story of Jeans** opposite. Check your answers in exercise 2.

4 Work with a partner. Read four sentences from the text and respond.
   Example **A** The first jeans came from Genoa in Italy.
             B I didn't know that / I knew that already /
             That's really interesting.

B Pronunciation sounds spelt with *ea*

5 5C.1▶ Listen to the **Dean's Jeans** advert opposite. Notice the pronunciation of *ea*. Then write the *ea* words from the advert in the box.

ea /iː/ *most common*	ea /e/ *also common*	ea /eɪ/	ear /ɪər/	ear /eər/
teach	head	break	near	bear

6 Can you add any more words to the spelling box?

7 Practise saying the advert.

C Vocabulary shopping phrases

8 5C.2▶ Listen to a conversation in a jeans shop, and answer the questions.
   1 How much are the jeans?
   2 Does the customer know his size?
   3 How many pairs does the customer try on?
   4 Does the customer pay in cash or by credit card?

9 Look at **Buying Jeans** opposite. Put the pictures in order.
   Example 1 = g

10 Listen again and check.

11 Work with a partner. This time the customer is buying a sweater, not jeans. Change the phrases in orange.
   Example Do you like these ones? *Do you like this one?*

12 5C.3▶ Listen and check.

13 Act the **Buying Jeans** conversation with a partner.

D Grammar phrasal verbs with *on* and *off*

14 Look at this dictionary entry. What do you think *sth* means?

> **PHRASAL VERBS** try sth on felpróbál: *Can I try these jeans on, please?*

Extract from *Oxford Wordpower: angol-magyar szótár nyelvtanulóknak*

15 Look at the example sentences and complete the rules with *can* or *can't*.
   Try these **jeans** on. ✓   Try on these **jeans**. ✓
   Try **them** on. ✓   Try on **them**. ✗
   1 You _____ put a noun between *try* and *on*.
   2 You _____ put a pronoun between *try* and *on*.
   3 You _____ put a noun after *on*.
   4 You _____ put a pronoun after *on*.

16 Which sentences are correct? Write ✓ or ✗. Correct the mistakes.
   1 I like these jeans, but ~~I tried on them~~ and they were too small. ✗ *I tried them on*
   2 I'm hot. Can you turn the heating off?
   3 It's dark. Can you turn on the light?
   4 This sweater's too warm. I'm going to take off it.
   5 Put your coat on before you go outside.
   6 Those sunglasses are too dark. Take off them.
   7 You can't wear shoes in here. Please take them off.
   8 If you like this shirt, why don't you try on it?

17 Work with a partner. Take turns to be A and B.
   A Say a problem.
   B Make a suggestion with a phrasal verb.
   1 I'm a bit cold. *Turn the heating on.*
   2 It's too hot in here.
   3 These shoes are uncomfortable.
   4 It's too dark in here.
   5 I like this shirt but I don't know if it's my size.

More practice? **Grammar Bank** ≫ p.140.

ABCD Put it all together

18 Act the conversation in **Buying Jeans** with a partner, but for a shirt, not jeans. Take turns to be **A** and **B**.

19 Close your book. Work with a different partner. Role play a conversation in a clothes shop.

I can ask for things in shops.

Signs

Please keep off the grass

Skateboards Bicycles and Rollerblades **PROHIBITED**

NO HOODIES NO BASEBALL CAPS

THANKYOU

LOUNGE NO ADMISSION TO PERSONS WEARING WET SHOES OR WET CLOTHING

Welsh mall says NO to wheels in heels

A new kind of training shoe, with wheels in the heel, are in fashion in Wales. Many teenagers asked for them at Christmas. But the manager of the St Elli Shopping Centre in Llanelli says the shoes, called 'Heelies', are dangerous. He says kids in 'Heelies' can't enter the mall. They must take them off and walk around in their socks.

The manager, Gilmour Jones, thinks there is a safety problem. Teenagers with these shoes could break a shop window or knock down an older customer. Mr Jones says that the rule against wheels is not new. 'For many years we have had rules against using rollerblades or skateboards in the centre.'

Many other malls also have specific dress rules for teenagers. In the USA, some malls have rules about wearing baseball caps. You mustn't wear your cap to the side – the cap must be straight, and you mustn't wear it low over your face. Many shops in Britain now have rules about tops with hoods, or 'hoodies'. You mustn't enter the shop with the hood up. The security camera must be able to see your face.

Many of these rules are to stop big groups of teenagers getting in the way of shoppers. Groups of kids sometimes stand on the stairs or in doors and customers can't pass. Some shoppers are afraid of large groups of noisy teenagers. One mall manager said, 'We are here to sell. If you don't want to buy, we don't want you here.' However, the problem with 'Heely' shoes is not just the feelings of the other shoppers. There is a real safety problem – these shoes can be dangerous. The company that makes them tells users not to wear them in crowded places.

baseball cap

hoodie

hood

rollerblade

wheel

How to **talk about rules** (1)

Orientation

Context

In this lesson, students will practise using *must* and *mustn't* to talk about rules in public places.

Signs depicts four common rules and regulations found in public places.

Welsh mall ... is a newspaper-style article which deals with the topic of teenagers wearing heelies in a shopping centre in Wales. The text contains examples of different types of rules in shopping centres.

The small labelled photos below the text illustrate key vocabulary.

Culture note

Using modal verbs *must* and *mustn't* implies authority over someone else. In British culture, it is natural for a teacher, parent, doctor or boss to use them with their student, child, patient or employee because the hierarchical relationship between them is clear. *Must* and *mustn't* are often used in written rules.

Language

Focus grammar	*must, mustn't*
Focus phrases	*Can you repeat that?, Ehm, let's see ..., Sorry?*
Recognition vocabulary	words: *crowded, heels, hoods, mall, roller blades, skateboards, wheel* phrases: *a safe place, be careful*
Recycled language	everyday topics: *behaviour, documents, dress, drink, equipment, food, time* prepositions of place
Pronunciation	*must, mustn't* 5D.1

Language note

The final 't' in *must* and *mustn't* is only fully audible if it comes before a word with an initial vowel sound, e.g. in *must enter*. The final 't' in the middle of *mustn't* is always silent /'mʌsnt/.

End product

In *Put it all together,* students have conversations about different rules of a place, using their notes to help. Their conversation is based on the listening in 5D.2. They try and use phrases to help manage the conversation.

Preparation

Make a list of rules for a place students know, e.g. the library at your school or a form of public transport.

Warmer

Write the name of a place on the board. Set a three-minute time limit and put students into small groups to brainstorm the rules. Go round each group and ask for a rule. Ask the other groups if they agree and award a point if the rule is correct. Monitor and see how well students use *must* and *mustn't* but do not overcorrect for accuracy at this stage.

Write *How to talk about rules* on the board.

A Read a news article

In this section, students use visual clues and a title to anticipate the content of a news article. They also read for gist and detail.

1   Students engage with the theme of the text by matching signs and rules. Ask students to read items 1–4 and check any vocabulary. Direct students to *Signs* on **>> p.52** and set a short time limit for them to do the activity individually. Check answers as a class.

> 1 Skateboards, bicycles, and rollerblades prohibited
> 2 Please keep off the grass
> 3 No admission to persons wearing wet shoes or wet clothing
> 4 No hoodies, no baseball caps

2   Put students into pairs. Set a time limit of about two minutes for them to read the title and look at the pictures to think about the content of the article. Elicit answers around the class and write key words on the board.

3   Go through the instructions and read items a–d and check any vocabulary. Students work individually and match topics a–d with a paragraph. Monitor and help as necessary. In pairs, students compare answers. Go over answers as a class, eliciting examples of words and phrases in the paragraphs which helped students decide.

> a paragraph 3 (other malls)   c paragraph 1 (new, fashion)
> b paragraph 2 (safety, break,   d paragraph 4 (shoppers)
>   knock down)

4   Focus students' attention further on key factual information through closer reading of the text. Read the instructions and ask students to read items 1–6. Check vocabulary and go through the example as a class. Ask students why the first statement is false *(Teenagers mustn't enter the mall if they are wearing a new kind of training shoe, Heelies)*. As students continue individually, monitor and help as necessary. Go over answers as a class and, if a sentence is false, ask students to explain why. Do not overcorrect for accuracy at this point.

> 2 True
> 3 False. They can walk around in their socks.
> 4 False. They mustn't wear baseball caps.
> 5 True
> 6 False. The mall manager doesn't want large groups of teenagers standing on the stairs.

B Grammar *must, mustn't*

5   Students think about the meaning of the target grammar in the context of rules for shoppers. Read the instructions and write *You mustn't use rollerblades in the centre.* on the board. Ask students to decide individually which sentence a, b, or c, best explains the meaning. Take a class vote. Go through each one and ask *Why?* or *Why not?*

> Option a is wrong because it means that people can wear rollerblades if they want to.
> Option c is wrong because we use *should* or *shouldn't* for opinions.
> Option b is the correct answer.

Warmer

Remember the situations

Write lessons A–D *How to* titles on the board: *A ... talk about clothes, B ... make promises and offers, C ... ask for things in shops, D ... talk about rules.* Say phrases 1–10 below for students to call out the lesson.

1 You mustn't use rollerblades in the centre. 2 I'll lend you my jacket. 3 It really suits you. 4 It isn't warm enough to wear shorts. 5 How much are they? 6 You mustn't cycle here. 7 Shall I carry it? 8 We'll call you later. 9 Can I try a pair on? 10 I love your shirt.

> 1 D   2 B   3 A   4 A   5 C   6 D   7 B   8 B   9 C   10 A

A Grammar

1   Adverbs of degree 5A exercise 11

Warm-up: Choose five clothes words from *Clothes* on **>> p.46**. Students say adjectives which can be used to describe them.

Set-up: Ask students to read items 1–8 and point out the two parts of the exercise.

> 2 too   3 a bit   4 enough   5 too   6 quite   7 a little   8 enough

Follow-up: Direct students to exercise 13, **>> p.47**. In pairs, students write five similar sentences and swap with another pair. They swap back and check each other's answers.

2   *will* (offers and promises) 5B exercises 9, 12

Warm-up: See what students remember about Sadie and Vic. Ask *Who phoned who to invite them to go shopping? (Vic.) Who bought lots of things? (Vic.) Who didn't have enough money to buy a scarf? (Vic.).* Direct students to look at **>> p.48** to remember the story.

Set-up: Ask students to read items 1–8 and check vocabulary.

> 1 Shall   2 'll   3 won't   4 'll   5 Shall   6 won't   7 'll   8 won't

Follow-up: Students use audio script **5B.2** and mark the sentences in exercise 9 on **>> p.49** for stress. They say the sentences to a partner, who says *offer* or *promise*.

3   Phrasal verbs with *on* and *off* 5C exercises 14–17

Warm-up: Write the following words on the board, for students to make a sentence: *I, jeans, on, but, them, too, like, small, they, these, I, tried, and, were.* Students revise the grammar section on **>> p.51**, if necessary.

> I like these jeans, but I tried them on and they were too small.

Set-up: Go through the first item as a class.

> 1 Turn the computer off .../Turn off the computer ...
> 2 Can I try it on?
> 3 Put your coat on .../Put on your coat ...
> 4 You must take off .../You must take your shoes off ...
> 5 Can you turn on the lights?/Can you turn the lights on?
> 6 Turn them off.

Follow-up: Students choose a sentence containing a phrasal verb with *on* or *off* in lesson 5C. They write a jumbled sentence for a partner and check answers at the end.

4   *must* and *mustn't* 5D exercise 7

Warm-up: Ask students, in small groups, to write some tips for travellers. Set a two-minute time limit and ask for suggestions around the class.

Set-up: Ask students to read items 1–6 and see how many of their tips are the same.

> 2 must tell   3 mustn't take   4 mustn't leave   5 must arrive   6 mustn't smoke

Follow-up: Ask students to put the tips in order of importance for them. They compare with a partner.

B Vocabulary

5   Clothes 5A exercise 2

Warm-up: Ask students to turn to **>> p.46** and look at the pictures in *Clothes*. Ask them to cover the words. Say the numbers in random order for the class to say the name and spell the word.

Set-up: Do one or two items as a class.

> **Across:** 1 trousers   3 sweatshirt   5 dress   7 tights   8 suit   9 scarf
> **Down:** 1 tracksuit   2 shirt   3 sandals   4 trainers   6 hats   7 tie

Follow-up: Ask students to work in pairs and write *M* (man), *W* (woman) or *M/W* (both) next to the clothes.

6   Shopping phrases 5C exercise 8

Warm-up: Put students in pairs to write two shopping phrases for a shop assistant and two for a customer.

Set-up: Ask students to read the conversation and say what the shopper buys.

> 2 ones   3 try   4 size   5 fine   6 take   7 pay   8 cash

Follow-up: Students write a similar conversation but for a shopper who decides not to buy anything. They act their conversations out for another pair.

7   Favours 5B exercise 13

Warm-up: Direct students to the shopping maze on **>> p.127** and elicit favours for a couple of the situations.

Set-up: Go through the instructions and example to check students understand the activity.

> I'll pay your telephone bill.
> I'll water your plants and feed the cat.
> I'll lend you my camera.
> I'll lend you a warm coat.
> I'll meet you at the airport.

Follow-up: In pairs, students role play the conversation.

Early finishers

Students choose and copy three useful phrases from lessons A–D. They write a brief conversation using each one, and a translation in their language.

Unit 5 Review

A Grammar

1 Adverbs of degree Put the best word in each gap.

too   enough   a bit   ~~really~~

1 I love your suit. It's _really_ nice.
2 I hate white chocolate. It's _____ sweet.
3 The shirt's _____ big, but it's not a problem.
4 These shoes aren't big _____. They don't fit.

quite   enough   too   a little

5 I can't see anything – it's _____ dark.
6 This shirt's _____ nice, but I prefer the other one.
7 The colour's _____ bright, but I like bright clothes.
8 This coat isn't warm _____ in winter.

2 will (offers and promises) Complete these promises and offers with 'll, won't or shall.

1 _____ I put these in a bag for you?
2 I _____ lend you five pounds.
3 I _____ tell anybody your secret.
4 I _____ pay you back tomorrow, I promise!
5 _____ I open the door for you?
6 You _____ find better prices anywhere.
7 We _____ replace any broken parts.
8 I _____ forget.

3 Phrasal verbs with on and off Write the word in the sentence. There may be two possible places.

1 Turn the computer and go to bed! (off)
2 I like this shirt. Can I try it? (on)
3 Put your coat, it's cold outside. (on)
4 You must take your shoes when you go into the house. (off)
5 It's dark. Can you turn the lights, please? (on)
6 These lights use a lot of electricity. Turn them. (off)

4 must and mustn't Complete the sentences with must or mustn't and one of these verbs.

take   smoke   arrive   ~~keep~~   leave   tell

Tips for travellers

1 You _must keep_ your money in a safe place.
2 If anything is stolen, you _____ the police.
3 You _____ bags on the plane for strangers.
4 You _____ cameras, phones, or money in your hotel room.
5 You _____ at the airport 2 hours before your flight.
6 You _____ on the plane.

B Vocabulary

5 Clothes Do this crossword.

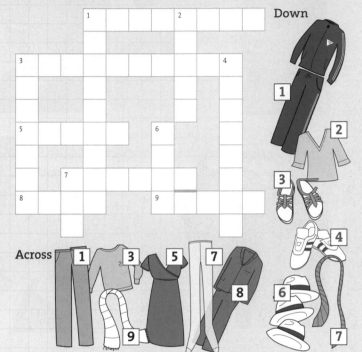

Down

Across

6 Shopping phrases Complete the conversation in a shoe shop with these words.

fine   cash   ones   size   pay   ~~help~~   take   try

A Can I ¹ _help_ you?
B Yes, I'm looking for some trainers.
A Do you like these ² _____?
B Yes. Can I ³ _____ a pair on?
A Of course. What ⁴ _____ are you?
B 38 … They're ⁵ _____. How much are they?
A €35.
B OK, I'll ⁶ _____ them.
A How would you like to ⁷ _____?
B I'll pay in ⁸ _____.

7 Favours Read about your friend's holiday problems. Write seven offers with these verbs.

~~take~~   pay   water   feed   lend (x2)   meet

Your friend is going away on holiday.

– She's got heavy bags and she hasn't got a car to go to the airport.
– Who's going to pay her telephone bill?
– What about her plants and her cat?
– She wants to take photos but she hasn't got a camera.
– She's going to a cold place but she hasn't got a warm coat.
– She's going to arrive back at the airport really late next Sunday night and she thinks there won't be any taxis.

Help her!

Example   1 I'll take you to the airport.

Paola phones the college

a Hello, Central College? — Yes, can I speak to Mr Hardy please?

b Yes, who's calling? *CLICK* — Paola Nesta ...

c Hello, Kwikfix Motors. — Kwikfix Motors? Oops, sorry, wrong number!

d Hello, Central College? — Yes, can I speak to Mr Hardy please?

e Did you say Mr Ardy? — No, Mr Hardy – with an *H*.

f Ah, Mr Hardy, OK. Who's calling? — Paola Nesta. I called a moment ago but I got cut off.

g Oh, yes. Just a moment ... I'm sorry, he's busy at the moment. Would you like to leave a message? — No thanks. I'll call back later. Thanks.

h Hello, Central College? — Yes, can I speak to Mr Hardy please? This is Paola Nesta. I called earlier. — Oh, yes. Hold the line, Ms Nesta. Don't hang up. I'll put you through ...

i Hello ... — Oh hi, is that Mike Hardy? This is Paola Nesta speaking. — Hi Paola! I can't speak now. Can you call back later?

Automated Message

Sometimes when you phone a bank or a big company, you speak to a machine, not a person. These are some of the things you hear ...

Thank you for calling, hold the line
Please press **1** and we'll waste your time
Press **2** and we'll put ^{1}_____
^{2}_____ up, you're in a queue
Hello, my name's Caroline
Please press **3** and hold ^{3}_____
If you want some music, just press **4**
Then press **5** and hear some more

Press **6** to speak to an operator
Sorry, she's ^{4}_____, ^{5}_____ later
Press **7** for an answer-phone
And leave ^{6}_____ after the tone
Press **8** and wait and then press **9**
If no one answers, just hold the line
If you're calling from abroad, press **10**
Get ^{7}_____ off and dial again

How to talk on the phone

Orientation

Context

In this lesson, students will practise using telephone phrases to get put through to someone.

Paola phones the college is a picture story which shows Paola becoming more frustrated as she tries to speak to her college tutor on the phone. She gets cut off, gets the wrong number, and isn't understood by an operator. The conversations are fairly formal so all speakers use polite expressions such as *Can I ...?, please, thank you,* and *sorry* and limit their conversational turns to a minimum.

Automated Message takes a light-hearted look at recorded telephone messages.

Culture note

Different languages and cultures have different telephone conventions. For example, a Brazilian answering the phone might ask *Where are you calling from?*, whereas European Spanish speakers might say *Yes, tell me.* British people tend to say *Who's calling?* or *Who's speaking?* or say the telephone number or name of the company. If a person answering the phone doesn't meet a caller's expectations then it can disturb the flow of conversation and take time before the speakers adjust to each other.

Language

Preview grammar	*if* + imperative
Focus words	*answer-phone, busy, earlier, later, operator, press, tone*
Focus phrases	telephone phrases: *busy at the moment, call back later, get cut off, hang up, hold the line, leave a message, put you through, wrong number*
Recognition vocabulary	words: *landline, queue* phrases: *waste your time*
Recycled language	words: *abroad* phrases: *Can I ...?, I'll ..., Just a moment, Sorry, can you repeat that?, Would you like ...?*
Pronunciation	stress in corrections 6A.5

End product

In *Put it all together*, students take turns making and answering telephone calls using the role cards in *Pairwork* >> **p.128**. Students have conversations from memory, checking, confirming and clarifying information as necessary.

Preparation

Think about how you will organize the classroom for the telephone role plays in *Put it all together* (ideally the students should be sitting back-to-back). Tell students to bring bilingual dictionaries for the next class (lesson 6B).

Warmer

Write *Communication* on the board and elicit and write different ways of communicating, e.g. *letters, emails, text messages,* etc. Students rank them in the order of frequency they use them, (1 for the least and 5 for the most frequently used). Students discuss their order in pairs or small groups. Ask each group to report back on whether their answers were very similar or different.

Write *How to talk on the phone* on the board.

A Read and follow a conversation

In this section, students skim short telephone conversations before reading and inferring for detail.

1   Go through the questions with the class and check vocabulary. Put students in pairs to discuss their answers briefly and ask for volunteers to report back on what their partner said.

2   6A.1 Direct students to the pictures and focus on the scenario. Ask *Is Paola happy?* (No, she seems to be getting more and more unhappy as the situation continues.) Read the instructions and elicit or explain that *How many phone calls does she make?* means how many times does she dial the number. Play the audio and go over answers as a class.

> Paola makes four calls: to the college, to Kwikfix Motors, to the college, to the college.

3   Prepare students to read for detail and infer by pointing out that they will need to read carefully. They will also need to think about the situations as the answers are not always written in the texts. Demonstrate by focussing on the first question together as a class. Ask students to look at the first two pictures and read the conversations. Elicit the problem and write *Paola gets cut off* on the board and tell students to continue in pairs. Ask for volunteers to give answers and explain why. See if the class agrees.

> 1 phones (or dials) the wrong number; Mr Hardy's busy
> 2 Central College   3 Yes, she's his student.

Extra activity

Ask for four volunteers to role play the conversations.

B Vocabulary telephone phrases

4   Check students cover >> **p.56** and ask *Who calls?* and *Who answers?* Direct students to typical phrases used in polite telephone conversations in the columns in the box. Use the example to demonstrate the activity and put students in pairs or small groups to continue from memory. Monitor and give the first letter or syllable of words to help jog students' memory, and tell them to leave any problem phrases for the moment. Ask for full phrases as you elicit answers around the class. Do not say if answers are correct at this stage.

5   6A.2 Play the audio while students listen and read to check their answers. Play the audio a second time as a model, pausing after each key phrase. Students repeat chorally, then nominate individual students to repeat. Listen carefully and praise and correct pronunciation as appropriate.

> 2 number   3 cut   4 back   5 busy   6 leave   7 line   8 hang
> 9 put

Extra help

Backchain drill. Help students remember difficult phrases by getting them to repeat starting with the final word. Add one word at a time until students can say the whole phrase from memory. Play the audio again for students to repeat the phrases and check intonation. The phrases sound most polite when rising and falling intonation is used, with the most important voice movement on the stressed word. Check students make their voices start a little higher on these words, and then fall.

Warmer

Remember the sentences

Team game. Write these words on the board: *I, can, Mr, to, the, speak, wrong, Perry, no, later, did, Berry, you, off, call, hold, sorry, number, cut, say, line, got, back.*

Give students three minutes to make sentences in small teams. Tell them they can reuse words. Ask each team in turn to say a sentence. Ask the class *Is it correct?* If it is (and they're correct) give two points to the team who wrote the sentence. If it isn't, give two points to the first team to correct the sentence.

> **Possible answers**
> Can I speak to Mr Perry? Did you say Mr Berry? No, Mr Perry.
> Hold the line. Can you call back later? Sorry, wrong number.
> I got cut off.

A Grammar

1 *have to, don't have to, mustn't* 6B exercise 5

Warm-up: Say some sentences from **>> p.59**, exercise 9. Students repeat the sentences if they are correct for where you are.

Set-up: Tell students all the sentences are about rules in Britain. Ask them to read items 1–7 and check vocabulary.

> 2 don't have to   3 mustn't   4 don't have to   5 have to
> 6 mustn't   7 don't have to

Follow-up: Students decide if the sentences in items 1–7 are true in their country.

2 Past of irregular verbs 6C exercise 12

Warm-up: Do a quick review of past tense verbs on **>> p.61**. Say a sentence in the present for students to transform into the past.

Set-up: Tell students to look horizontally, vertically and diagonally to find the verbs.

> **Across:** told found saw bought sent left drove got
> **Down:** came broke put went lost wrote stole

Follow-up: In pairs, students design their own irregular verbs word search with eight columns and rows. Pairs swap word searches.

3 Past simple or continuous 6D exercise 8

Warm-up: Say a period of time, e.g. *from 10 o'clock to 10.30 last night*. Ask students what they were doing. Ask if anything else happened at the same time.

Set-up: Go through the example with the class.

2 was walking	6 stopped	10 phoned
3 was crossing	7 was lying	11 was leaving
4 knocked	8 was coming	12 said
5 was going	9 put	

Follow-up: Sentence completion game. Put students into groups of three or four and tell them to think of a past continuous clause beginning with *when*. Each student says their sentence opener, for others in the group to complete it in a different way. The student who said the sentence decides which ending is the most interesting.

B Vocabulary

4 Telephone phrases 6A exercise 4

Warm-up: Read some of the telephone phrases from **>> p.57**, exercise 4 for the class to say *caller* or *answerer*.

Set-up: Go through the example as a class, pointing out that the first letter of the missing word is given.

> 2 calling   3 cut   4 line   5 through   6 message   7 back

Follow-up: Put students in pairs to act out a conversation using the phrases on **>> p.57**, exercise 4.

5 On the road 6B exercise 2

Warm-up: Ask students to look again at exercise 1 and find *On the road* words (*drivers, cyclists, pedestrians, bus, train, driving, fare*).

Set-up: Go through the example with the class.

> 2 helmet   3 seat-belt   4 accident   5 pavement   6 licence
> 7 motorway   8 pedestrian crossing

Follow-up: Set a three-minute time limit for students, in small groups, to write the story of an accident. They try to use as many of the words in exercise 6 as possible.

6 Bank and post office 6C exercise 2

Warm-up: Write the names *Barry Lyn Stoller* and *Gennifer Robinson* on the board. Ask students to choose one of the characters and to see how many facts they can remember from their true story. Direct students to *True Crimes* on **>> p.60** to check.

Set-up: Go through the example and point out that there are two blanks for each item.

> 2 traveller's cheques   3 credit card   4 insurance details
> 5 bank account

Follow-up: Students write gap-fill sentences with anagrams of *Bank and post office* vocabulary on **>> p.61**. They swap with a partner and find the words. At the end they check with the students who wrote the anagrams.

Early finishers

Direct students to read the audio scripts on **>> p.153** for lesson 6A. They copy five phrases they think are useful and write a translation in their language.

Unit 6 Review

A Grammar

1 *have to, don't have to, mustn't* Complete the sentences with *have to*, *don't have to* or *mustn't*.

1 Drivers in Britain _have to__ have insurance.
2 Cyclists _____ wear bright coloured clothes, but it's a good idea.
3 Pedestrians _____ cross the road when the red light is on.
4 If you take the bus, you _____ worry about parking your car.
5 When you're travelling by train, you sometimes _____ show your ticket.
6 You _____ use your mobile phone when you're driving.
7 Students _____ pay the full train fare – there is a special students' fare.

2 **Past of irregular verbs** Find the past forms of 16 more verbs. Some letters are used twice.

T	O O K	T	O	L	D
C	F	O	U	N	D O S
A	A	P	S	A	W S T
M	B	U	G	N	E T O
E	R	T	G	O	N W L
B	O	U	G	H	T R E
H	K	S	E	N	T O G
R	E	N	L	E	F T E
A	R	D	R	O	V E T

3 **Past simple or continuous** Put the verb in the correct tense – past simple or past continuous.

I ¹ _saw__ (see) an accident when I ² _____ (walk) along Baker Street. A woman ³ _____ (cross) the road and a cyclist ⁴ _____ (knock) her down.
I ⁵ _____ (go) to work and I was late, but I ⁶ _____ (stop) to help. The woman ⁷ _____ (lie) on the floor and blood ⁸ _____ (come) from a cut on her head. I ⁹ _____ (put) my coat under her head and then I ¹⁰ _____ (phone) an ambulance.
Later that day, when I ¹¹ _____ (leave) the office for lunch, a colleague ¹² _____ (say), 'Are you OK?' 'Yes', I said, 'Why?' 'Because there's blood on the back of your coat,' she said.

B Vocabulary

4 **Telephone phrases** Complete the telephone conversation.

Jim Hello, can I ¹speak____ to Mr Perez, please?
Lil Yes, who's ²c_____?
J It's his student, Jim. I called a moment ago but I got ³c_____ off.
L Hold the ⁴l_____ please. I'll put you ⁵t_____.
ring ring
L I'm sorry. Mr Perez is not in his office at the moment. Would you like to leave a ⁶m_____?
J Yes please, could you tell him Jim phoned and I'll call ⁷b_____ later? Thanks.
L OK. Thank you. Goodbye.

5 **On the road** Solve the anagrams at the end of the sentences to find the words.

1 You have to stop at these when they are on red.
fftarci hglist _traffic lights___
2 You don't have to wear this if you are on a bicycle.
melhet h_____
3 Passengers don't have to wear these in some countries.
teas-slebt s_____-b_____
4 You have to wait for the police if you have one of these.
tednccia a_____
5 You mustn't drive your car on this - it's where people walk.
nepavemt p_____
6 You have to have one of these to drive a car.
cliecen l_____
7 In some countries, you have to pay to drive on one of these.
towmayor m_____
8 Everyone has to stop at these when people are walking across the road.
destinaper grossinc p_____ c_____

6 **Bank and post office** Complete the sentences with these words.

account bank card ~~cash~~ cheques credit details insurance ~~machine~~ traveller's

1 You can take money out of a *cash machine.*
2 You can normally cash _____ in banks and hotels.
3 You normally use a _____ to buy things on the Internet.
4 If you have a crash, you have to give the other driver your _____ _____.
5 When you phone the bank, you have to tell them your _____ _____ number.

Job Advertisements

1 Wanted
Telephone sales staff

for a company selling holiday apartments on the Mediterranean coast

- Attractive salary plus commission
- Flexible working hours
- Excellent opportunity

Call 071 882 7720 for interview

2 Native Spanish & Italian teachers

wanted for city centre language school

- Evening classes
- 2 years' experience
- £10/hr
- 1-year contract

Fax CV to 071 883 2765 or email paul@newlang.com

3 POWER GYM

We are looking for fitness instructors

**Must be fit and friendly
Evenings and weekends
Competitive salary**

info@powergym.com
Contact Rob on 071 882 6653

4 Age Care

WANTED

Experienced, qualified nurses to visit old people in their homes

- Car provided
- Must have a valid driving licence
- Salary £1,000 /month

CALL 071 637 4463

5 Drivers wanted

for a luxury limousine company to meet VIPs at airport, etc.

– Clean driving licence
– Must have good appearance
– Uniform provided
– Flexible hours
– Good salary

Contact Stewart on 071 539 6209

6 ZedBeds

We are looking for bed testers

- No experience necessary
- Must enjoy sleeping
- Pyjamas provided
- Work hours: nights

Call 071 558 3865 for interview

7 Want to travel, have fun, and get paid for it?

We are looking for entertainers to work on cruise ships – musicians, actors, magicians, comedians

- Must be fun, friendly, and work well in a team
- 2 weeks on, 2 weeks off
- All expenses paid
- Attractive pay

Call 081 773 6635 for interview

Dictionary

staff /stɑːf; USA stæf/ nombre, verbo
▸ n [v sing o pl] personal, plantilla: *The staff are all working long hours.* Todo el personal está trabajando hasta tarde.

flexible /ˈfleksəbl/ adj. **1** hajlékony **2** rugalmas: *flexible working hours*

uniform /ˈjuːnɪfɔːm/ ▸ agg uniforme
▸ s divisa, uniforme LOC **in uniform** in divisa

salary /ˈsæləri/ n (pl -ies) salaire

magic /ˈmædʒɪk/ s magia: *like ~* como que por magia ● adj mági-co magical adj mágico /məˈdʒɪʃn/ s mágico/a

Extracts from *Diccionario Oxford Pocket para estudiantes de inglés*, *Oxford Wordpower: anglo-magyar szótár nyelvtanulóknak*, *Dictionnaire Oxford Poche pour apprendre l'anglais*, *Dizionario Oxford Study per studenti d'inglese*, *Oxford Pocket Dicionário Bilíngüe para brasileiros*

How to have a conversation about work

Orientation

Context

In this lesson, students will focus on asking questions to keep a conversation about work going.

The job advertisements are typical of those found in the general employment section of a newspaper. The advertisement for bed testers, for a company called Zed Beds, is a joke.

The bilingual dictionary extracts for various languages show the different type of information given.

Culture note

Contrastive stress is often used to manage a conversation and turn-taking. In some speaking cultures, it is normal for conversations to be animated, with the loudest speaker often taking the floor. For speakers of English, it is normal to invite a listener to join the conversation.

Language

Focus words	jobs: *company, expenses, experience, fax, flexible, qualified, responsibilities, salary, staff, time off, well-paid,* etc.
Focus phrases	job conditions: *long hours, travel a lot, wear a uniform, work in a team,* etc.
Recognition vocabulary	*commission, contract, cruise ship, entertainer, luxury, provided, valid, VIP,* etc.
Recycled language	words: *address, email, look smart, name, phone number* grammar: *present simple; Wh- questions; have to; don't have to; must*
Pronunciation	contrastive stress: returning questions 7A.1–3

End product

In *Put it all together*, students have short conversations about their real jobs or jobs they would like to have. The conversation is based on the listening in exercise 13 and students can refer to cues in exercise 14 for help.

Preparation

Consider how to organize classroom space for the *Put it all together* activity.

Warmer

Ask students how people find jobs and write ideas on the board (newspaper adverts, job centres or agencies, through friends, on the Internet, etc.). Put students into small groups to brainstorm questions they would ask about a job and write key words on the board, e.g. pay, hours, experience, travel. Take a class vote on the most important aspect of a job.

Write *How to have a conversation about work* on the board.

A Read for information

In this section, students practise skimming, scanning and reading advertisements for detail.

1 Activate students' background knowledge about job advertisements. Go through the type of information using examples from the *Warmer* to help students understand the vocabulary. In pairs, students put a number by each item, 1 = essential, 2 = not necessary. Go through each item and ask for a show of hands to see how important students think the information is.

2 See if students understand the main points in the job advertisements. Set a short time limit for students to skim and scan the texts to find one which isn't real. Ask about each advertisement with the class, and for students to say why it is or isn't a joke. See if they would like the job or not.

> Advertisement 6 is the joke.
> **Clues:** sleeping, and working hours are nights

3 Direct students to items 1–8 and check any vocabulary before they read the texts in more detail. Use the example to show them that there might be more than one job for each description. Monitor and help as students continue individually.

> 2 Job 2   3 Job 7   4 Job 1   5 Job 5   6 Jobs 3, 7   7 Job 3
> 8 Jobs 2, 4

4 Tell students to think about the job and the reasons, using ideas from exercises 1 and 3. Put students in pairs or small groups to discuss. Monitor and give feedback for the correct use and pronunciation of *have to.* For feedback, nominate students and ask questions, e.g. *What job did ... choose? Would anyone in your group like to be a ...? Why? Why not?*

Extra plus

Students evaluate each advert according to the information given, e.g. specific or general information about salary, number of hours work, etc.

Extra activity

Students think about the job they would least like and compare their reasons in small groups. Take a class vote on the worst job and elicit reasons around the class.

B Use a dictionary

5 Direct students to the dictionary extracts at the bottom of >> p.66 and tell them they will use the information after each blank to guess the missing word. Do the first one together and see if students can guess from the pronunciation. Ask them to look for a word they think will sound similar. If they can't guess, see if they can use other clues. In pairs, students continue the activity. Monitor and help as necessary. Go through the answers with the class and ask students which advertisement the word appears in.

Office Life

Episode two

1
Holly Boss-alarm!

2
Anna Justin, this is Joan. She's new. Can you show her around and tell her the office rules?

3
Justin OK, let's start with coffee. The rules say you can't have more than four cups a day. So I've started drinking tea.

4
Justin This is the smoking room. Nobody can go in there because smoking isn't allowed.
Joan So why is there a smoking room?

5
Justin Don't ask. Now, this is the office supplies cupboard. You can take anything you want, if you can find the key.

6
Joan Are there any dress rules?
Justin Yes, but they're quite flexible. You aren't allowed to wear jeans but you can wear any colour socks you want.

7
Joan Hmm. Can you send personal emails?
Justin Yes, but not before 6.00.
Joan But the office closes at 6.00!

8
Justin True. Now, we also have our own office rules. You can't arrive early, you can't leave late and you can't work in the lunch hour.

9
Justin And finally, this is the boss-alarm. If you see her coming, you have to ring this bell. That gives us time to start working.
Joan Ahem …

How to talk about rules (2)

Orientation

Context
In this lesson, students will practise using *can* and *can't* to talk about permission.

In this episode of the comedy sketch, *Office Life,* a new employee called Joan joins the staff. Justin is asked by his boss, Anna, to explain the office rules. He is in the middle of explaining how to use the boss-alarm when she appears behind him.

Culture note
Justin's ironic comments are typical of English humour, of which irony is a central feature. He makes statements which appear on the surface to be serious, but which are actually ridiculous, e.g. *you can wear any colour socks you like, you can't send personal emails before 6pm* (when the office closes), etc. Irony also often plays on the use of opposites or paradoxes, as in *You can't arrive early, you can't leave late and you can't work in the lunch hour.*

Language

Focus grammar	*can / can't* (permission)
Focus phrases	*not allowed to ..., take time off, wear (jeans)*
Recognition vocabulary	words: *dress rules, forbidden, hit, miss* phrases: *show somebody around*
Recycled language	office words: *cupboard, emails, mobile phones, office, supplies,* etc. clothes: *jeans, skirt, socks, suit, trousers,* etc. everyday routines: *eat, run, smoke, speak, talk, wear,* etc. preposition of place: *in the classroom, in the corridor, in the office* *can* (polite request): *Can you show her ...?*
Pronunciation	short and long o /ɒ/ and /əʊ/ **7C.2–3**

Language note
The position of the mouth shape is fixed for the short *o*, but opens a bit then rounds with the long *o*.

End product
In pairs, students describe the rules in a place they know using their notes to help.

Preparation
Check the difference between pictures A and B in *Pairwork* on **» p.129** and **» p.134** so you can help students with exercise 11 if necessary.

Warmer
Brainstorm places where there are rules, e.g. at school, at work, around town, on the road, in airports, in games, in sports, etc. and write these on the board. Ask students *Have you ever broken a rule in one of these places or situations? Is it important for people to obey (or keep) the rules?*

Write *How to talk about rules* on the board.

A Read a comedy sketch

In this section, students scan a dialogue for gist and detail.

1 Direct students to *Office Life* on **» p.70**. Put students into pairs or small groups and set a short time limit for them to say what they remember about the people. Ask *Is Justin a good employee? (Not very.) Is he a good colleague? (Yes.)* to remind them of his character. Students can look again at 1C if necessary.

2 Go through the instructions and titles a–d. Set a short time limit for students to skim the text for gist. Put students in pairs to compare ideas and ask for suggestions around the class.

> *Office Rules* is the best title as this is the topic Justin talks about the most.

3 Go through the instructions as a class before students work individually and compare in pairs. Nominate students to answer the questions at the feedback stage.

> 1 No more than four cups of coffee a day; no smoking; you can take any office supplies from the cupboard; no jeans; no personal emails.
> 2 No, because he adds ironic comments to each rule as he describes it.

4 Students engage more closely with the language to predict how a TV audience will react to the comedy sketch. In pairs, students read and decide.

5 7C.1 Play the audio for students to confirm their answers.

> Audience laughter occurs after the lines: *I've started drinking tea, Don't ask, ... if you can find the key, any colour socks you want, True, That gives us time to start working* and *Ehm ...*

Extra activity
Nominate or ask for four volunteers to take the parts of Holly, Anna, Justin, and Joan to read the sketch for the rest of the class to mimic audience laughter.

6 Go through the instructions and items 1–5. Students find and underline the sentences in the text individually. They compare with a partner. Nominate students to say the phrases. Do not explain the grammar at this point as it is the focus of section B.

> 2 Smoking isn't allowed.   3 You aren't allowed to wear jeans.
> 4 You can wear any colour socks you want.   5 Can you send personal emails?

7 Discuss this question with the whole class. Ask *Would you like to work with Justin? Why? Why not?* Help students express ideas.

> *You* is used generally in the sentences to talk about anyone who works in the office.

B Grammar *can/can't* (permission)

8 Write *can/can't permission* on the board, and elicit or give a sentence with each for the rules in *Office Life*, e.g. *You can wear coloured socks. You can't wear jeans.* Write the sentences on the board and direct students to the grammar box. Elicit the other sentences to complete the box and write them on the board for students to copy. To reinforce the concept, ask *Are these sentences about permission or ability? (Permission.)*

A day in the life of **a postman in India**

1 Rajendra gets on his _bicycle_ and starts _work_.

2 Geeta gets a _____ from her _____ in Bangalore.

3 The news is _____ so Geeta's _____.

4 Today, Sua gets her _____.

5 Sua can't _____ her name, so she gives her fingerprint. Rajendra has to _____ her.

6 Rajendra _____ a number for Samundar.

7 At the _____ of the day, Rajendra does the _____.

Six mornings a week, Rajendra Prasad gets on his bicycle and starts work. He puts on his postman's uniform, and takes mail to the desert villages of Rajasthan. He wears a turban on his head because the desert sun is very hot. When he arrives in a village, he rings the bell on his bike and everybody runs out. They don't get many visitors so they're excited. Today, Rajendra's first stop is Geeta's house. She's got a postcard from her cousin in Bangalore. Rajendra has to read it out because Geeta can't read. The news is good, so she's happy.

Rajendra doesn't only take the mail. He also has to take the pension money for the old people. Today Sua gets her pension. She can't sign her name, so she has to give her fingerprint instead. Rajendra has to help her because she's very old. "I don't know how old I am," says Sua. "Maybe 50 or 60?" Her neighbours think she's about 75.

Rajendra also carries a telephone because many of the villages don't have phones. It's good for Rajendra because he can earn 1,000 rupees a month as commission from the telephone calls. His salary is only 3,000 rupees a month (under €50). Today, Samundar wants to make a call. She shows Rajendra the number in her notebook and he dials for her. She speaks to her son Vishnu. "I told him to come home because I need some money," she says.

At the end of the day, Rajendra does the paperwork and thinks about his job. He knows the problems well because he's been a postman for 22 years. The big problem is transport. Sometimes there are no roads. Sometimes he has problems with his bike so he has to push it. "But on the whole, it's a good job," he says.

Adapted from a text by Geeta Pandey on http://news.bbc.co.uk

How to describe a typical day

Orientation

Context

In this lesson, students will practise using *because* and *so* to give details about factual information.

A day in the life of ... is a magazine article which gives a description of the job of a postman in India. As well as delivering mail, he helps local villagers in many different ways. The photos which decorate the article show different aspects of his work.

Language

Focus grammar	*because, so*
Focus words	*bring, postman, mail, neighbour*
Recognition vocabulary	*caption, commission, fingerprint, paperwork, pension, turban*
Recycled language	words: *bicycle, customers, desert, dial, excited, postcard, switch on, telephone, uniform, village* grammar: *present simple for repeated actions* prepositions of place: *in India, on his bicycle, on his head,* etc. discourse: *using pronouns to substitute for names of people*
Pronunciation	grouping words **7D.1–2**
Discourse	joining sentences with *because* and *so*

End product

In *Put it all together,* students give, follow and respond to a mini-presentation about a typical day. Students use their notes, which are organized chronologically, to help.

Preparation

Plan your own simple personal pie chart for the *Warmer*.

Warmer

Draw a circle on the board and tell students it represents a typical day in your life. Divide the circle up into sections, e.g. with about a third marked *sleeping,* a third *working,* and the rest in smaller sections marked *shopping, watching TV, talking with friends, doing sports,* etc. Now tell students about your typical day. Ask students to draw their own charts, and put them in small groups to explain a typical day to each other. Ask for volunteers to tell the class anything interesting they found out about their classmates.

Write *How to describe a typical day* on the board.

A Read and identify the people

In this section, students use pictures to predict content before reading a magazine article for gist and detail.

1 Write *A day in the life of ...* on the board. Ask students to cover the text and look at the photos. Elicit ideas about the person's daily life and write some key words on the board. Students read *A day in the life of ...* quickly to see if their ideas are in the text.

2 Direct students to the caption for the first photo and ask students where they see these types of captions *(in newspapers, on the Internet).* Ask students to read captions 2–7 and explain or demonstrate *fingerprint.* Put students into pairs and set a short time limit for them to complete the captions. Monitor and help them locate information if necessary. Nominate pairs to read their captions and check students understand *pension.* Elicit or point out that the captions are in the present simple.

> 2 postcard/cousin   3 good/happy   4 pension   5 sign/help
> 6 dials   7 end/paperwork

3 Students work individually and check in pairs. Don't worry about pronunciation of the names but ask students for spellings if clarification is needed.

> 2 Rajendra, Geeta   3 Geeta   4 Rajendra, Sua   5 Sua
> 6 Rajendra, Samundar   7 Rajendra

4 Go through the instructions and ask students to read questions 1–9 to check vocabulary. Write the example question on the board and circle *he.* Ask students *Who is 'he'? (Rajendra.)* and *What kind of word is 'he'? (A pronoun.)* Ask students to circle the pronouns in the questions, and continue the activity individually. Monitor and help as necessary and ask students to compare in pairs before nominating students to give answers.

> 2 they – everybody in the village   3 he – Rajendra, it – the postcard   4 she – Geeta   5 she – Sua   6 he – Rajendra, her – Sua   7 he – Rajendra   8 she – Samundar, him – Vishnu   9 he – Rajendra

5 Do the example as a class and point out or elicit that the questions begin with *Why* so the answers in notes begin with *because.* Put students in pairs to continue and tell them to guess any new vocabulary and then check in their dictionaries. Check answers with the whole class.

> 2 because they don't get many visitors.   3 because Geeta can't read.   4 because the news on the postcard is good.   5 because she can't sign her name.   6 because she's very old.   7 because many of the villages don't have phones.   8 because she needs some money.   9 because he's been a postman for 22 years.

B Grammar *because, so*

6 Write *She's happy because the news is good.* on the board. Ask *Who is she? (Geeta.)* Ask *Why is she happy?* to elicit *Because the news is good.* Now say *The news is good.* and ask *What's the result?* to elicit *She's happy.* Direct the students to the grammar box and go through the rule together as a class.

> *Because* comes **after** the result. *So* comes **before** the result.

7 Go through the instructions and the example to demonstrate. In pairs, students write the sentences. Monitor and help as necessary. Nominate students to read out the answers.

Material and shape

wood
metal
cloth
plastic
glass
cardboard
china

round round round round round round

square square square square square square

long and thin

flat

Making pencils

- [ ] The pencil sandwich is cut into separate pencils.
- [ ] The blocks are cut into flat pieces.
- [1] The wood is cut into square blocks.
- [ ] An eraser is fitted on the end of the pencil.
- [ ] The information about the pencil is printed on the side.
- [ ] Lines are cut in one side of each flat piece.
- [ ] A second flat piece is stuck on top of the first to make a pencil sandwich.
- [ ] The pencil leads are put in the cut lines.
- [ ] The pencils are shaped and painted.

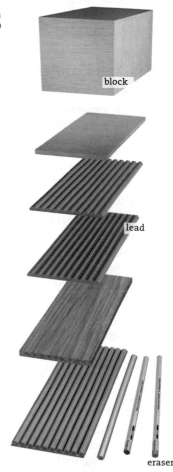

block

lead

eraser

PENCILS TRIVIA

On left-handed pencils, the printed text goes in the other direction.

Carpenters use flat pencils. They are flat so they don't roll.

Most pencils sold in the USA have erasers on the end. Many pencils without erasers are sold in Europe.

You can draw a 50-kilometre line with an average pencil.

You can write under water with a pencil.

75% of wooden pencils sold in the USA are painted yellow.

Over 10 billion pencils are made every year.

carpenter's pencil

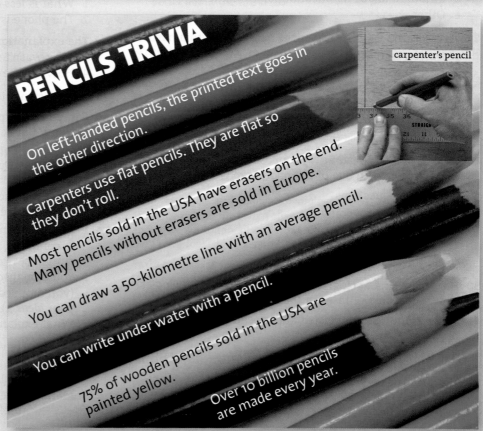

How to describe things

Orientation

Context

In this lesson, students will practise using passive forms to describe the shape and material of objects.

Material and shape shows photos of common objects and gives the words to describe what they are made of and their shape.

Making pencils is a text about the manufacturing process for making pencils. It is in jumbled order.

Pencils trivia provides information that students may not know about pencils.

Language

Focus grammar	present passive
Focus words	material: *cardboard, china, cloth, glass, metal, plastic, wood* shape: *flat, long, round, square, thin*
Focus phrases	*it's got ..., it's made of ..., it's put in ..., it's used for ...,* *it works by ...*
Recognition vocabulary	*billion, block, carpenter, eraser, front, lead, left- right-handed,* *roll, roll off, trivia*
Recycled language	household items: *coffee table, pan, plate, spoon, toothbrush,* etc. verbs: *leave, move, paint, wash, wear,* etc.
Pronunciation	passive or active? auxiliary *be: 's, 're* in passives 8B.1

Language notes

In passive sentences, the person or people involved in the process can be added at the end of the sentence by adding ... *by someone,* e.g. *Pencils are used by people all over the world.* This part of the sentence is called the *agent* and will be dealt with in the next level. Note the pronunciation of *lead* is /led/.

End product

Students work in small groups, taking turns to describe everyday household objects in *Pairwork* on >> **p.129** for a partner to guess what is being described. The descriptions are based on audio scripts 8B.2-3 on >> **p.155–56**, and students use key words to help.

Preparation

Take a bag of simple man-made objects for the *Warmer*, e.g. a paper clip, a coin, a pencil sharpener, a marble, a small toy, a scarf, a dice, and a traditional wooden pencil. Students must not be able to see into the bag.

Take enough pencils to class so pairs can look at one for exercise 5.

Warmer

Hold out the bag of objects and invite different students to put their hand in, choose an object, and try to guess what it is without looking. Ask *What's it made of? What shape is it?* to see how much vocabulary students know, but do not teach any new vocabulary at this stage.

Write *How to describe things* on the board.

A Vocabulary material and shape

1 Direct students to *Material and shape* vocabulary on >> **p.78**. Point to different things in the classroom and ask yes/no questions, e.g. *Is this made of cardboard? Is this round?* Tell students to do the matching activity using the vocabulary panel as a visual dictionary. Check answers as a class. Monitor for /ə/ in the second syllable of *china* and *metal*, the /θ/ sound in *cloth*, and the /kw/ sound in *square*.

> 2 plate   3 pan   4 coffee table

2 Use the example to introduce the activity. Copy the sentence on the board and circle *long, thin,* and *plastic*. Ask *What kinds of words are these?* and write *shape, shape, material* above them. Monitor and help with vocabulary and pronunciation as necessary while students continue in pairs. Do not focus on the passive structure here as students will study this in section C.

B Read for interest

In this section, students read for gist and follow the logical sequencing of a text.

3 To introduce the topic, ask students what they usually write with *(a pencil, biro, fountain pen, felt tip pen)* and why. Ask *Does anyone know how pencils are made?* Help students express their ideas but do not correct for accuracy at this stage.

Direct students to *Making pencils* and the picture on >> **p.78**. Tell students not to worry about new vocabulary and to work in pairs to put the text in order. Find the first sentence with the class. Monitor and help if necessary. Go over answers as a class.

> 2 The blocks ...   3 Lines are cut ...   4 The pencil leads ...
5 A second flat piece ...   6 The pencil sandwich ...
7 The pencils are ...   8 The information ...   9 An eraser ...

4 Ask *What colour are most pencils in the USA? What distance can an average pencil draw?* and elicit suggestions. Go through the instructions and direct students to *Pencils trivia* on >> **p.78**. Students read the text and underline new or interesting information.

Nominate students to tell others about new or interesting information and help them get their ideas across. Demonstrate the meaning of information in the text using a pencil, e.g. show students how well/badly you write with your right/left hand. Direct students back to the title and elicit or give the meaning of *trivia (small facts or details that aren't important).*

5 Put students in pairs and check they can see a pencil. Go through the instructions and ask them to read questions 1–7, explaining any vocabulary. As students discuss the questions, monitor and respond to interesting comments. Nominate a few students, and ask for volunteers to tell the rest of the class if anything surprised them.

C Grammar present passive

6 Do the activity as a class. Read the instructions and the two possible titles. Ask for a show of hands for each title. Copy title 2 on the board and ask students why this is better.

> 2 The text doesn't say anything about the people.

7 Read the instructions and ask *Which sentence is better, a or b?*

> b The focus of the text is on the materials and the process of making pencils not the people.

8 Direct students to the grammar box, and go through the questions with the class. Underline the beginning of each sentence on the board from exercise 2 to highlight *It's* + shape, and *It's made of* + material.

> 1 The words *a person.*   2 The object moves and becomes the subject of the sentence.   3 *cuts* becomes *is cut.*

9 Ask students to underline the verbs in the passive in *Making pencils*. Nominate students to read them out. Use the second example in *Making pencils* and ask about the form of the passive. Ask *What starts the sentence? (A noun.)* and *The second word? (The verb be.)* and *The next word? (The past participle.) What tense is the verb? (Present simple.) Why is it the present simple here? (Because the pencil making process is always the same.)*

> 1 is cut   2 are cut   3 are cut   4 are put   5 is stuck   6 is cut
> 7 are shaped   8 is printed   9 is fitted

Extra help

Transformation drill: active to passive. *T Someone cuts the blocks. SS The blocks are cut. T A person cuts the leads. SS The leads are cut. T Someone puts the leads into the wood. SS The leads are put into the wood. T A person prints information on the pencils. SS Information is printed on the pencils.* etc.

10 Go through the example with the class. Ask students to read items 2–6 and check vocabulary before they complete the exercise individually. Monitor and check for singular/plural agreement between nouns and verbs. Ask students to compare in pairs before going over answers.

> 2 The pencils are painted yellow.
> 3 Tuna fish is sold in cans.
> 4 The plates are washed and put away.
> 5 The ties are made from the best cloth.
> 6 Toothbrushes are made of plastic.

Extra plus

In pairs, students make some sentences about what they think happens before and after the pencil-making process. Write answers on the board at the checking stage.

> **Possible answers**
> **before:** Trees are cut down. The wood is brought to the factory.
> **after:** The pencils are put in boxes. The pencils are sent to shops. The pencils are bought by different people.

D Pronunciation passive or active?

11 8B.1 Direct students to the pronunciation box and ask *What's the difference between the sentences in the first and second row? (Singular/plural.)* Play the audio, pausing after each sentence for students to say active or passive. Play the audio a second time, pausing for students to repeat. Monitor and encourage students to pronounce the /s/ if it isn't clear. The answers are given on the audio, so pause the audio just before the answer each time.

12 In pairs, students test each other. Monitor and give positive feedback. Ask for volunteers to test themselves against the class.

E Listen for key words

In this section, students listen for key words in order to answer short quiz questions.

13 8B.2 Books closed. Students listen and write down the object *(a hairdryer)*. Play the audio twice before asking for suggestions.

14 Give students the opportunity to understand and reflect on how they listen. Go through the instructions. When they have marked their text, ask *How many words did you underline? How many words didn't you underline?* to show how effective this strategy is. Write *plastic, metal, electricity, handle, drying, hair* on the board. Elicit or explain that if students understood these words, they should be able to guess the object.

15 8B.3 Tell students they will listen to descriptions of three more objects and that they must listen carefully for key words. Play the audio. Students compare answers in pairs. Play the audio a second time if necessary. Check answers. Ask students to use audio script 8B.3 on >> p.156 to underline key words. Write the key words on the board and see if students agree.

> 1 dishwasher (key words: metal, plastic, big, square, electricity, washing, dishes, plates, spoons, pans)
> 2 paint brush (key words: wood, hair, handle, long, thin, painting, artists)
> 3 sunglasses (key words: glass, plastic, metal, two pieces, dark, glass, round, sunny, eye)

Extra help

Elicit or give useful phrases for describing objects *(it's made of ..., it's got ..., it's used for ..., it's put in ...)* and write them on the board. In pairs, students choose one of the items from audio scripts 8B.2–3 and describe it for their partner to guess.

ABCDE Put it all together

16 Put students into small groups and go through the instructions. Ask students to choose two items and to make notes of useful size and shape vocabulary from the lesson and audio scripts 8B.2-3 on >> p.155–6. Tell students to listen to the complete description before they reveal their guesses. Groups choose a description to tell the class and the class guesses the object.

Student performance

Students should be able to give a short description.

Use this checklist for monitoring and feedback or to assess students' performance.

Content	Do students describe three or more properties of an object? exercise 2
Vocabulary	Do students use different size and shape words? exercise 1
Pronunciation	Do students pronounce *be* in the passive clearly? exercise 12

I can **describe things.**

Students tick *on my own* if they can describe an object without looking at the vocabulary panel on >> p.78. They tick *with some help* if they looked at the vocabulary panel on >> p.78 once or twice.

Early finishers

Students work with a new partner and describe an object from *Material and shape*, giving information about what it's used for and where it's found.

Additional material

www.oup.com/elt/result for extra practice material
www.oup.com/elt/teacher/result for extra teacher resources

How to describe things

G present passive   V material and shape   P passive or active?

A Vocabulary material and shape

1 Look at **Material and shape** opposite. Match these descriptions with things in the photos.
   1 It's made of wood. It's long and thin. *Spoon*
   2 It's round and flat. It's made of china.
   3 It's made of metal. It's round and it's got a handle.
   4 The top is round and flat. It's made of glass and metal.

2 Describe and guess the other things in the picture.
   Example   A It's long and thin. It's made of plastic.
               B Toothbrush!

B Read for interest

3 Read **Making pencils** opposite. Put the text in order.

4 Read **Pencils trivia** opposite. What new information did you find out about pencils?

5 Work with a partner. Read the texts again. Now find a wooden pencil and answer these questions.
   1 Can you see that it is made of two pieces of wood?
   2 What information is printed on the side?
   3 Is there an eraser fitted on the end?
   4 Does it roll off your desk easily?
   5 Do you think it is a left-handed pencil?
   6 How many kilometres are left in it?
   7 Is it painted the same colour as most American pencils?

C Grammar present passive

6 Here are two possible alternative titles for the **Making pencils** text. Which one do you think is best? Why?
   1 The people who make pencils
   2 How pencils are made

7 Why is sentence b better for **Making pencils**? What is more important, the person or the wood?
   a **active**   A person cuts the wood into square blocks.
   b **passive** The wood is cut into square blocks.

8 Look at the grammar box and answer the questions.

	subject	verb	object
active	A person	cuts	the wood ...
passive	The wood	is cut ...	

To make the passive:
1 Which words are taken out of the sentence?
2 Which words are moved?
3 How does the verb change?

9 Underline the examples of verbs in the passive in **Making pencils**.

10 Make these sentences passive.
   1 People sell CDs in plastic boxes.
      CDs are sold in plastic boxes.
   2 A person paints the pencils yellow.
   3 People sell tuna fish in cans.
   4 A person washes the plates and puts them away.
   5 A person makes the ties from the best cloth.
   6 People make toothbrushes of plastic.

More practice? **Grammar Bank** >> p.143.

D Pronunciation passive or active?

11 **8B.1▶** Listen and say active or passive. Then listen and repeat.

active	passive
He watched.	He's watched.
They painted.	They're painted.

12 Test a partner.
   Example   A He's watched.   B Passive!

E Listen for key words

13 **8B.2▶** Listen and guess the object.

14 Read the text. When did you first guess the object? Which words helped you? Underline them.

   It's made of plastic and metal, and ehm, it works by electricity. It's got a handle, and it's used for drying hair. It has two words, and the first word is *hair*, and the second word begins with the letter *d*. And the answer is ... It's a hair-dryer!

15 **8B.3▶** Listen and guess three more objects.

ABCDE Put it all together

16 Work in small groups. Look at the objects on >> p.129. Take turns to describe an object. Guess the object.
   Example   It's made of metal. It's used for cutting things ...

I can describe things.
Tick ✓ the line.   with a lot of help   with some help   on my own   very easily

ADULTS OF THE FUTURE

Britain's kids predict how lives will change in the next 1,000 years

'Mobile phones will be everywhere. Everyone will have one in their pocket. And they will be amazing. They will control everything – TV, car, even Mum! And everyone will eat food out of packets – plastic food or something like that.'
James Williams, 11, Bristol | 1

'We'll have time machines, so instead of going on holiday to Spain we'll go to another time. But we won't go to the future because that will ruin everything. I'd like to go to the past and meet my great grandma.'
Jessica Potter, 8, Wallasey | 2

'All our pets will have computers so we can talk to them and understand them. They'll be able to talk to us, so they won't just be pets anymore they'll be more like friends. Perhaps they'll even be able to get jobs.'
Kelly Graham, 7, Liverpool | 3

'You won't have to get dressed. You'll just put this thing around your neck, press a button and your clothes will drop down. It'll save a lot of time in the morning and my mum won't shout at me so much.'
Nicholas Paolozzi, 9, Monkseaton, North Tyneside | 4

'We will live in tall buildings miles high.'

'Everybody will be dead in the next 1,000 years – or else they'll be really old. Most people will live in houses underground because they won't be able to live on top of the earth like we do now – the air and the land will be too horrible.'
Rachael Gadomski, 10, Newcastle | 5

'We will live in tall buildings miles high. But we won't have normal lifts. We will go up big tubes, but nobody will do any work because they will have too much fun going up and down the tubes.'
Rosie Smith, 7, Wirral | 6

'There will be lots of robots everywhere and they'll get really angry and eat us all – or most of us, anyway. Only a few people will live, and we'll be able to beat the robots in the end.'
Joseph Taylor, 7, Merseyside | 7

'We'll have houses made of chocolate because it's easy to work with, and if you get hungry you can eat it. You won't eat the floor though because you've walked on it.'
Paul Ashworth, 8, Anfield | 8

How to make predictions

Orientation

Context

In this lesson, students will focus on using *will* to talk about the future.

Adults of the future are abridged authentic newspaper texts reporting the views of British children, aged 7–11, on what they think life will be like in the next 1,000 years. The predictions concern typical child-like ideas, including innocent yet humorous comments. For example, one child says that mobile phones might control 'Mum', and another that pets will have learnt to talk and will have their own computers.

Language

Focus grammar	*will, won't* (predictions)
Focus words	*amazing, control, environment, optimist, optimistic, pessimist, pessimistic, pocket,* etc.
Focus phrases	*I hope so, I think so, I've no idea,* etc.
Recognition vocabulary	*economics, politics, robot, ruin, tubes, underground*
Recycled language	*education, food, science, telephones, travel, TV, weather* linkers: *and, because, but, or, so* indefinite pronouns
Pronunciation	pronoun + *'ll* 8C.1–2

End product

In *Put it all together*, students exchange ideas on how things will change in the future; agreeing, disagreeing and commenting on a partner's suggestion. Students can use their notes during the activity, and check and clarify as necessary during the conversation.

Warmer

Write the figure 3008 on the board and ask what it could refer to *(a date about 1000 years from now)*. Write *The future?* and the following topics on the board: *politics, robots, pets, health, clothes, the environment, mobile phones, economics.* Check vocabulary and ask students to put them into two lists: *topics children might talk about* and *topics adults might talk about*. Politics, healthcare, the environment and economics are unlikely topics for children to think about, as they usually think about things close to their own lives.

Write *How to make predictions* on the board.

A Read for general meaning

In this section, students read several short texts for gist and detail.

1 Having raised interest in the topic of the lesson with the *Warmer*, direct students to the titles and the quote *'We will live in …'*. Ask *Do you think these texts will be serious or not?* Help students express their ideas, encouraging them to give reasons.

Go through the instructions and set a short time limit to encourage students to skim the texts quickly for gist. Students work individually before comparing answers in pairs. Ask for volunteers to give answers.

8 Chocolate houses	4 Clothes	5 Environment
1 Mobile phones	3 Pets	7 Robots
6 Tall buildings	2 Time travel	

2 Read through the instructions with the class. Direct students to the first text and ask *Optimist or pessimist? (optimist)* to check students understand the activity. Ask students for examples of words and phrases which helped them decide *(amazing, even mum!)*. Students continue individually before comparing with a partner. Go over answers as a class.

5 dead, really old, horrible; 7 really angry, eat us all

Extra activity

Ask students to read the texts again and circle these words: *and, or, but, so* and *because*. Ask *Which child gives the most detail? (James Williams.) Which children don't give any explanation? (James Williams, Nicholas Paolozzi.)*

3 Ask students to read questions 1–3. Check any vocabulary and put students in pairs or small groups to continue. Encourage them to use their dictionaries and to underline the parts of the text which supports their answers. Monitor and help as necessary, and join in where you can. Go through each question, nominating students to report back on what they talked about. Ask students about things children in their country might say about the future.

Teaching tip

To maximize student-talking time, ask students to stand up and mingle. They compare answers with at least three others.

B Grammar *will* (predictions)

4 Help students think about the meaning of *will*. Copy the example sentence on the board. Go through questions 1–3.

1 The future. (next 1,000 years) 2 She is guessing.
3 c (She's expressing an opinion but she does say that everybody will have fun, which suggests she thinks it's a good idea.)

5 Point to the sentence on the board and ask students if they agree. Nominate a student who doesn't agree to make the negative and ask him or her to write it on the board. Write ? and elicit and write the question. Direct students to the grammar box and ask them to complete it individually. Monitor and help as necessary and go over answers as a class.

+ Robots **will do** all the work. Our pets **will be able** to talk.
– We **won't live** underground. Our pets **won't be able** to talk.
? **Will** robots **do** all the work?

6 Tell students to underline examples of *will* in the text. Monitor to ensure they are underlining a variety of structures, e.g. *won't*, *will be able to, will have to* and ask them to compare in pairs.

7 Point again to the question *Will we live in tall buildings miles high?* on the board and ask *Is this question asking for a fact or an opinion? (An opinion.)* Direct students to the example question in the exercise and elicit or explain that we use *Do you think we will ...?* to ask for an opinion. Model and drill the question, making sure students are pronouncing *Do you think* as /dju:θɪŋk/ or /djəθɪŋk/. Elicit some possible answers, e.g. *Yes, I think so, I don't know,* then drill the answers. Point out that it's not possible to answer *Yes, I think.*

Ask students to read the question and answer columns and go over any vocabulary as a class. Ask for two volunteers to have the example conversation to demonstrate the activity. In pairs, students do the controlled practice activity. Monitor for word order in questions. If students say *Do you think will it happen?* use a swapping gesture to indicate a word order error and encourage self-correction. Get feedback by asking *Is your partner an optimist or a pessimist? Why?*

Teaching tip

Many students use *will* for talking about the future when they should be using *going to* or the present continuous. Emphasize that *will* is used for talking about things which we *think, believe,* or *imagine* will happen but which we can't control.

Extra help

Transformation drill for question forms. *T We will live in houses underground. SS Do you think we will live in houses underground? T We will live in tall buildings. SS Do you think we will live in tall buildings? T We'll have time machines. SS Do you think we'll have time machines? T There will be lots of robots. SS Do you think there will be a lot of robots? T Everybody will be dead in 1,000 years. SS Do you think everybody will be dead in 1,000 years?*

C Pronunciation pronoun + 'll

8 8C.1 Write /ju:l/ on the board and see if students can read and pronounce it naturally as *you'll.* Check they pronounce this contracted form as one syllable. Ask students to spell the words and write *you'll* on the board. Circle *'ll* and ask *What is this short for? (Will.)* Show them that *you'll* is the example in item 1. Check students understand the activity and point out that the phonetic script indicates that the words are said together so they sound like one word.

Play the audio, pausing after each item for students to write their answers.

9 8C.2 To check answers, play the audio a second time, pausing after each item for students to repeat. Give extra pronunciation practice as necessary.

> 2 she'll   3 they'll   4 we'll   5 he'll   6 I'll   7 it'll

10 8C.3 Direct students to the sentences in both columns in the box. Point out that they are the same in each column, except for *'ll.* Play the audio and pause for students to repeat each pair of sentences. Play the audio a second time if students need more practice pronouncing the contracted words in context.

11 8C.4 Play the audio to give students practice in distinguishing the difference by saying *present* or *future.* The answers are given on the audio, so pause the audio just before the answer is given each time to allow the students to give their answers

12 In pairs, students test each other. Monitor and check they are pronouncing *'ll* audibly. At the end, ask for volunteers to test themselves against you. Give fair and honest feedback about whether you hear *'ll* clearly.

D Listen for general meaning

In this section, students listen to a short monologue for gist and detail.

13 8C.5 Tell the students they will hear a boy making a prediction and they must identify the topic. Give students time to read the word pool and elicit a few key words associated with each of the topics to help prepare students for the listening. Play the audio and ask students to compare their answer in pairs. Play the audio a second time if students want to listen again. Nominate a student to give the answer *(telephones),* and cross-check to see if everyone agrees.

14 Read the question and tell students to listen again carefully. Play the audio and give students time to note some key words to express their own opinion. Put them into pairs to have a short discussion and remind them to use answers from the table in exercise 7. Set up an open class discussion by asking *Who agrees with Jon? Why?* and then ask for a student who doesn't agree to add a comment. Elicit a couple of reasons from students who agree and students who don't.

ABCD Put it all together

15 Read through the instructions with the class and check students understand the activity. Give students time to find useful vocabulary in their dictionaries. Direct them to the example and nominate or ask for two volunteers to read the conversation. Remind students to give extra information after they have agreed or disagreed. In pairs, students continue.

16 Put students into small groups to compare their opinions and decide who is the most optimistic and pessimistic. Ask for a volunteer from each group to report to the class and give examples of what others said.

Student performance

Students should be able to exchange points of view and indicate if they agree or disagree.

Use this checklist for monitoring and feedback or to assess students' performance.

Content	Do students give reasons for agreeing or disagreeing with an opinion? exercise 14 Do students talk about what will and won't happen? exercise 14
Pronunciation	Do students mostly use the short form *'ll*? exercise 10

I can make predictions.

Students tick *on my own* if they can say what they think and respond to their partner's ideas without looking at exercise 5. They tick *with some help* if they have looked at exercise 5 more than twice.

Early finishers

Students choose one topic and mingle to find others who share their predictions.

Additional material

www.oup.com/elt/result for extra practice material
www.oup.com/elt/teacher/result for extra teacher resources

How to make predictions

G *will* (predictions)   P pronoun + *'ll*

A Read for general meaning

1 Read **Adults of the future** opposite quickly. Match the texts with these topics.

- [1] Chocolate houses
- [ ] Mobile phones
- [ ] Tall buildings
- [ ] Clothes
- [ ] Pets
- [ ] Time travel
- [ ] Environment
- [ ] Robots

2 Most of the children are optimists 😊. Read the texts again and find the pessimist(s) 😟. Underline the words that helped you. Compare with a partner.

3 What do you think of the texts? Answer these questions and tell your partner.

1 Do you agree with any of the predictions?
2 Which text is funniest?
3 Which text has the most interesting ideas?

B Grammar *will* (predictions)

4 Read the sentence and answer the questions.
'We will live in tall buildings miles high.' (Rosie Smith)

1 Is Rosie talking about the past, present, or future?
2 Does Rosie know this is true, or is she guessing?
3 Does Rosie want this to happen?
   a yes   b no   c doesn't say

5 Complete the table.

+	We'll live underground.	Robots _____ _____ all the work.	Our pets _____ _____ _____ to talk.
–	We _____ _____ underground.	Robots won't do all the work.	Our pets _____ _____ to talk.
?	Will we live underground?	_____ robots _____ all the work?	Will our pets be able to talk?

6 Underline examples of *will* for prediction in **Adults of the future**.
More practice? **Grammar Bank** >> p.143.

7 Ask and answer with a partner.
Example
A Do you think Italy will win the next World Cup?
B I hope so!

question	answer
Do you think Italy will win the next World Cup?	Yes, I think so.
Do you think the world will run out of oil?	No, I don't think so.
Do you think we will have flying cars?	I hope so!*
Do you think ... *add your own questions!*	I hope not!
	I've no idea!

*I hope so. = I want this to happen.
I hope not. = I don't want this to happen.

C Pronunciation
pronoun + *'ll*

8 8C.1▶ Listen and match the words and their pronunciations.

I'll   ~~you'll~~   he'll   she'll   it'll   we'll   they'll

1 /juːl/ *you'll*_____
2 /ʃiːl/ _____
3 /ðeɪl/ _____
4 /wiːl/ _____
5 /hiːl/ _____
6 /aɪl/ _____
7 /ɪtl/ _____

9 8C.2▶ Listen, check and repeat.

10 8C.3▶ Listen and repeat.

present	future
We go to Spain.	We'll go to Spain.
They live in boxes.	They'll live in boxes.
I have lunch at 2.00.	I'll have lunch at 2.00.
They talk to us.	They'll talk to us.

11 8C.4▶ Listen and say *present* or *future*.

12 Test a partner.
Example   A We'll go to Spain.   B Future!

D Listen for general meaning

13 8C.5▶ Listen to Jon (age 12) talking about the future. Which topic is he talking about?
TV   travel   weather   telephones   education
food   world politics   science

14 Listen again. Do you agree with Jon's prediction? Tell a partner and say why or why not.

ABCD Put it all together

15 Work with a partner. Talk about the topics in exercise 13. How do you think these things will change in the future?
Example   A I think TVs will be bigger.
            B Yes, and there will be thousands of channels.

16 Compare your ideas in small groups. Who is the most optimistic? And the most pessimistic?

I can make predictions.
Tick ✓ the line.   with a lot of help   with some help   on my own   very easily

It's your lucky day!

My documents

CD burner

Security Scan

✉ Inbox

— ☐ ✕

File Edit View Go Tools Help

✉ New | ✕ Delete ✉← Reply ✉→ Forward ✉→ Send 📎 Attachment

Inbox   ✉ **icon**

✉	Jeff Rodriguez	cheap medicines from Canada!
✉📎	f27dc9the3	Re: Good News!
✉	Hugo Pinta	It's your lucky day!
✉	customer service	important account information

It's your lucky day!

— ☐ ✕

File Edit View Go Tools Help

✉ New | ✕ Delete ✉← Reply ✉→ Forward ✉→ Send

From: Hugo Pinta   **window**
To: BAYES, Tim
Subject: It's your lucky day!

Dear Friend

1 My name is Hugo Pinta. I'm the accounts manager at the Columbus Bank in Fairbanks, Alaska. Four years ago, a man from your country opened an account at my bank and put $14,920,000 into it. I will call the man Adam, but that is not his real name. Adam worked for a big oil company in the Arctic.

2 After Adam opened his account, I never saw him again. Nobody moved any money in or out of his account. Finally, I decided to contact his company. They told me he was dead. He died in an accident near Prudhoe Bay. The money is still in his account and nobody from his family has claimed it.

3 If nobody claims the money within 5 years, the government will take it. I think that is a terrible waste of money – I'm sure you agree. So I would like to make a suggestion. Will you take the money? You simply send me your full name, date of birth, and address. I will fill in a document to confirm that you are a member of Adam's family. Then, if you send me your bank account details, I will send the money to your account. We can share the money: 55% for me, 40% for you and 5% for expenses. If you reply, I will send more details about how this will work.

4 Don't worry, there is no risk to you. If anything goes wrong, it will be my problem, not yours. If you are interested, please reply quickly. If you don't reply within 48 hours, I will find another person.

Best Regards

Hugo Pinta

Recycle bin

▌ Start   ▶ Media Player   **Ws** WordSoft   ✉ Email

How to talk about results of future actions

Orientation

Context

In this lesson, students will practise using *will* clauses to talk about future results.

The picture shows the various stages of a computer screen when an email programme is opened. Some of the items are labelled.

It's your lucky day! is a junk email with the opening salutation *Dear Friend*. In the email, a bank manager is trying to trick somebody into giving their bank details so he can gain access to their bank account and money. This is called a scam (trick) and the email is junk (something people usually delete without reading).

Language

Focus grammar	1st conditional
Focus words	email: *attachment, click, delete, desktop, download, icon, laptop, online, scan,* etc.
Recognition vocabulary	*Alaska, CD burner, government, media, online, recycle bin, security, someone else*
Recycled language	*claim, desktop, junk, laptop, open, reply, send, will*
Pronunciation	intonation in conditional clauses 8D.2

Language note

As is the case with many words, *download* can operate both as a verb and a noun. When it is a verb the stress is on the second syllable, but when it is a noun the stress is on the first syllable. Other words which follow this rule include *record, research, produce,* and *import.*

End product

In *Put it all together*, students talk about what their future actions might be, based on the pictures in *Pairwork* on >> p.129. They are given time to read, think and make notes before exchanging ideas.

Warmer

Write *Computers: the good, the bad, the future?* on the board. Put students into small groups and set a short time limit for them to talk about the three aspects of computers. Draw three columns on the board and ask one person from each group to report back, writing key words in the columns.

Write *How to talk about results of future actions* on the board.

A Vocabulary email

1 Read the instructions and set a short time limit. In pairs, students show what they already know about the topic vocabulary. Ask around the class and write any new words on the board.

2 Direct students to *Computer words* at the top of >> p.82. Tell students to use their dictionaries to check meaning and to write the words in two lists: *verbs* and *nouns*. To go over answers, draw two columns on the board and invite students to call out the words. Ask for spelling if students' pronunciation isn't clear and give help as necessary. Tell students to look at >> p.82 and ask some concept questions to check understanding, e.g. *Are* icons *words or pictures? (Pictures.) Do you* download *messages when sending or receiving emails? (Receiving.) Do you* delete *things you want to keep? (No.)*

> **verbs:** click, delete, download, receive, send
> **nouns:** attachment, button, icon, message, virus, window

3 Direct students to *Receiving* and *Sending emails* and ask *Which is easier to do?* If students don't use computers regularly, ask them to think about letters. Students read the texts to answer the question *(Receiving emails)*. Read the first part of the sentence to the class and demonstrate the activity. Do one or two more examples together and then ask students to continue individually. Monitor and help as necessary and ask students to compare in pairs. Do not give answers at this stage.

4 8D.1 Play the audio for students to confirm their answers. Pause the audio just before each answer and ask students to call out what they think it is before you play it. Give extra help with pronunciation if necessary. Ask *Which words are verbs? (download, delete, double-click). Where's the stress? (On the final syllable.) Where's the stress on the nouns* icon, subject *and* window? *(On the first syllable.) Where's the stress on* attachment *and* online? *(The second syllable.)* Ask students to mark word stress in their books. Play the audio a second time.

> 2 icon   3 click   4 download   5 Delete   6 attachment
> 7 window   8 subject   9 Send   10 online

Extra help

Test students by saying the beginning of a phrase for them to finish. *T receive ... SS ... an email T click on ... SS ... an icon* (or *an attachment*) *T download ... SS ... an attachment.* etc.

B Read and interpret

In this section, students read an email for gist, specific information and 'between the lines'.

5 Go through the pre-reading questions to raise interest in *It's your lucky day!* on >> p.82. Ask students to read questions 1–3 and check any vocabulary before putting students into small groups to talk about the questions. Monitor and join in the conversations but do not overcorrect for accuracy.

Go through the questions, asking for volunteers to report back. Ask follow-up questions if students answered yes to questions 1 and 3, e.g. *How did the virus affect your computer? What did you do? Who do you send money to? Do you think it's safe?*

6 Refer students back to the *Warmer* and ask them (again) whether they would read Hugo Pinta's email or not. What do they think it might be about? Give a three-minute limit to ensure that students skim the text quickly for gist. Students work individually then compare answers in pairs before checking with the whole class.

> b to steal money from the reader

7 Go through the questions as a class and tell students to read the email again carefully. Put students into pairs to compare answers before going over them as a class. When checking, ask students to explain their answers. At the end ask *Does Adam exist? And his money?* to check students have understood that the email is a scam (or a trick). Ask if anyone has ever received an email like this.

> 1 We don't know, but probably not in Alaska.
> 2 Probably not.
> 3 If it is not claimed within five years, the state will take it.
> 4 He wants the reader's bank account details.
> 5 Probably not.

C Grammar 1st conditional

8 Copy the sentence on the board and ask *True or false?* (True.) and do the concept checking questions as a class. After you have checked answers, highlight the form of the sentence by writing *possible future action* on the *If* clause and *future result* on the result clause. Point to the *possible future action* clause and ask *What tense is the verb? (Present simple.)* Point to the *future result* clause and ask *What do we need here? (will + bare infinitive.)*

Ask students to make the *If clause* negative, and write *If you don't*. Repeat for the *result* clause and write *Hugo Pinta won't ...* Underline *don't* and *won't* and remind students that we use *don't* to make present simple sentences negative.

> 1 Hugo Pinta will steal your money.
> 2 Hugo Pinta will steal your money.
> 3 Hugo Pinta won't steal your money.
> 4 ... you send him your bank details.

9 Read the instruction with the class and direct students to the grammar box. Point out the headings in the two columns, and read the two clauses of the sentence across the columns. Monitor and help as students continue individually, checking they write the correct form of the verbs in both clauses.

Students compare in pairs before you check with the whole class. Read out the *If* clause of each sentence and encourage students to respond with the future result clause. Then read out each future result clause for students to respond with the appropriate *If* clause.

> 2 If you **open** that attachment, you'**ll get** a virus.
> 3 If nobody **claims** the money, the government **will take** it.
> 4 If you don't **reply**, Hugo **will look** for another person.

10 Go through the instructions and the example as a class. Students do the controlled practice exercise in writing individually. Monitor and check they are using the auxiliary *do* in the *if clause* and *won't* in the result clause for negative sentences. Ask students to compare in pairs before checking answers as a class.

> 2 If you click on this icon, a new window will open.
> 3 If you give them your address, you'll get lots of junk mail.
> 4 If we don't open the attachment, we won't get the virus.
> 5 If you don't watch your bag, somebody will steal it.
> 6 If Hugo gets your bank details, he'll steal your money.
> 7 If you don't want the money, I'll give it to someone else.

11 8D.2 Read the instruction and information with the class. Play the first sentence on the audio, pausing at the end of the *If* clause. Ask *Did the voice go up or down? (Up.)* Play the result clause and ask *Did the voice go up or down? (Down.)* Play the audio for students to listen and repeat, breaking the sentences up into the two clauses if necessary. Monitor and check students are saying the contracted form *'ll*. Play the audio a second time for students to repeat if necessary.

ABC Put it all together

12 Read the instructions and direct students to *Pairwork* on ›› **p.129**. Ask students to look at number 1 and check vocabulary. Elicit or give *If you buy a desktop computer ...* and write this on the board. Ask around the class for positive and negative options for the action. Repeat with *If you buy a laptop computer.* Put students in pairs to make notes on the good and bad points for each of the situations and options.

13 Go through the instructions as a class and ask for two volunteers to have the conversation to demonstrate. Put students into different pairs to continue. At the end, ask students to share any interesting or useful advice with the class.

Student performance
Students should be able to respond to indirect requests.

Use this checklist for monitoring and feedback or to assess students' performance.

Content	Do students give positive and negative future results? exercise 10
Pronunciation	Do students mostly use the short form *'ll*? exercise 11 Do students try to use rise/fall intonation? exercise 11

I can talk about results of future actions.

Students tick *on my own* if they talk about the possible results of future actions using their notes. They tick *with some help* if they need to look at the grammar box up to three times.

Additional material

www.oup.com/elt/result for extra practice material
www.oup.com/elt/teacher/result for extra teacher resources

A Vocabulary email

1 Work with a partner. Make a list of English words you know connected with email, internet, and computers.

2 Look at **Computer words** opposite. Which ones are nouns and which ones are verbs? Check in your dictionary.

3 Underline the correct word.
   Receiving emails
   If you ¹double-click / send on the *Email* ²click / icon, the email Inbox will open. Now ³delete / click on the *Send and Receive* button to ⁴download / delete your messages. If it's junk mail, highlight it and click on the ⁵Send / Delete button. Be careful – if the message has an ⁶icon / attachment, don't open it. It could be a virus.

   Sending emails
   If you click on the *New Message* button, an email ⁷window / icon will open. Write the email address and the ⁸attachment / subject at the top. Write your message and click on the ⁹Send / Delete button. The message will go the next time you are ¹⁰online / send.

4 **8D.1▶** Listen and check.

B Read and interpret

5 Work with a partner. Answer these questions together.
   1 Have you ever had a computer virus?
   2 What is junk email? Is it a problem for you?
   3 Do you ever buy things online?

6 Read **It's your lucky day!** opposite. Why did Hugo Pinta write it?
   a to steal money from the reader
   b to give the reader some money

7 Read the email again and answer the questions.
   1 Where do you think Hugo lives?
   2 Is Hugo his real name?
   3 What does Hugo say will happen to Adam's money?
   4 What does Hugo want?
   5 Is any part of the story true?

C Grammar 1st conditional

8 Read the sentence and answer the questions.
   'If you send your bank details, Hugo Pinta will steal your money.'
   1 What are the two possible future actions?
      You send your bank details or ...
   2 Imagine you send your details. What will happen?
   3 Imagine you don't send your details. What will happen?
   4 Will Hugo Pinta steal your money? *Yes, but only if ...*

9 Complete the grammar box with the correct form of these verbs.
   claim reply get (x2) open look take (x2)
   Use present simple tense for the possible future action. Use *will* + infinitive for the future result.

possible future action	future result
1 If Hugo _gets_ your bank details,	he'_ll take_ money from your account.
2 If you _____ that attachment,	you _____ a virus.
3 If nobody _____ the money,	the government _____ it.
4 If you don't _____,	Hugo _____ for another person.

   If you put the future result first, you don't need a comma:
   He'll take money from your account if you send your bank details.

10 Write sentences.
   1 you open the attachment / you get a virus
      If you open the attachment, you'll get a virus.
   2 you click on this icon / new window open
   3 you give them your address / you get lots of junk mail
   4 we not open the attachment / we not get the virus
   5 you not watch your bag / somebody steal it
   6 Hugo get your bank details / steal your money
   7 you not want the money / I give it to someone else

11 **8D.2▶** Pronunciation The intonation goes up at the end of the *action* part and down at the end of the *result* part. Listen and repeat the sentences from exercise 10.

   If you open the at^tach_me^nt, you'll get a ^virus.

   More practice? **Grammar Bank** ≫ p.143.

ABC Put it all together

12 Work with a partner. Look at **Options** on ≫ p.129. Think about the good and bad points of the different options.

13 Change partner and do a role play.
   Student A Choose one of the options and tell your partner.
   Student B Give your partner advice about which option to choose.

   Example A I want a new computer – maybe a laptop, but I can't decide.

           B Well, if you get a desktop, it'll be cheaper ...

Writing A message of apology

A Read for the main idea

1   Which is the worst mistake? Decide with a partner. Compare with the class.
1   I forgot to reply to your last email.
2   I forgot to send you a message on your birthday.
3   I sent you a virus by mistake.
4   I thought your email was junk mail and I deleted it.
5   I wrote an email to someone else and I sent it to you by mistake.

2   Read this email. How well does Paul know Jen?

> Hi Jen, I'm sorry but I think I've sent you a virus by mistake. because I opened an email this morning, and I didn't know who sent it but the subject was just 'Good News!', and It had an attachment called 'Message from a Friend' and I opened it without thinking and It was a virus and I think it went into my address book and sent an email to all my contacts so if you got an email from me, DON'T open the attachment because If the virus gets into your computer, it will go to all the people in your address book and I'm really sorry about this, all the best from Paul. : (

3   When we apologize, we often give details to explain what happened. What details does Paul give?

4   Work with a partner. How would you apologize for the other mistakes in exercise 1?

B Check the style

5   **8E.1▶** Read the email again and listen. Answer the questions.
1   Is it easy to understand? Why?/Why not?
2   How many sentences are there?
3   How could you make it better?

6   Use these symbols to edit the email, and change the punctuation if you want.
//   new line
/   new sentence
~~and~~   delete word

Example   Hi Jen,// I'm sorry but I think I've sent you a virus by mistake./ ~~because~~ I opened an ...

7   **8E.2▶** Listen. Does the speaker pause in the same places where you put // and /? Now check the audio script on >> p.156.

C Organizing an apology message

8   Put this email in order.
a   ☐ All the best, Jen
b   ☐ Could you send it again?
c   ☐ 1 Hi Paul
d   ☐ It came together with a lot of junk emails and I deleted them all.
e   ☐ Sorry, I've deleted the email you just sent by mistake.
f   ☐ Sorry about that!
g   ☐ Then I remembered there was a message from you, but it was too late.

9   Match parts of the message with the sentences in exercise 8.
1   Greeting = ☐ c
2   Why I am sorry. = ☐
3   What happened. = ☐ and ☐
4   What to do (or not to do) next. = ☐
5   Final apology. = ☐
6   Goodbye. = ☐

10   Work with a partner. Find the same parts of the message in Paul's email in exercise 2.

ABC Put it all together

11   Think of a situation where you did something bad to someone by mistake. Answer the questions.
1   What did you do?
2   Why did you do it?
3   What did the other person do/say?

12   Write an email message to apologize. Remember to include the parts of the message in exercise 9.

13   Check your partner's message.
Are the sentences too long?
Do they give details to explain what happened?

I can write a message of apology.

Tick ✓ the line.   with a lot of help   with some help   on my own   very easily

Orientation

Context and Language

In this lesson, students will focus on writing an email apology.

New language	*by mistake, without thinking*
Recycled language	words: *address book, attachment, computer, contacts, virus* grammar: *past tense*

End product

In *Put it all together*, students write a paragraph (about 75 words) describing a mistake and offering an explanation and apology. Their message is based on the model text in exercise 2.

Warmer

Write the following on the board: *not replying to a letter or email, forgetting someone's birthday, losing someone's book.* In small groups, students put the mistakes in order of seriousness and report to the class. Write *How to write a message of apology* on the board.

A Read for the main idea

In this section, students read an email for gist and detail.

1 Go through items 1-5 and check vocabulary. Put students in pairs to grade the mistakes as 1 not a big problem, 2 quite a big problem, or 3 a really big mistake. Monitor and help students express their ideas. Ask for volunteers to tell the class.

2 Set a short time limit for students to read the email for gist. Go over the answer as a class, asking students to give reasons.

> Paul knows Jen quite well. He uses an informal greeting, he has her address in his address book, he uses an emoticon to sign off.

3 Ask students to underline the details. Elicit answers.

> He opened an email this morning ... he didn't know who sent it ... it had an attachment ... he opened the attachment ... it was a virus ... it went into his address book ... it sent an email to all his contacts ...

4 Ask students to circle expressions for apologizing or talking about mistakes in Paul's email. Write them on the board. *(I'm sorry ... (I sent it) by mistake... (I opened it) without thinking ... I'm really sorry about this.)* In pairs, students talk about the mistakes in exercise 1. Monitor and encourage them to use the expressions on the board, or other apologizing language from lesson 8A. Nominate different students to give answers.

B Check the style

5 8E.1 Go through the instructions and questions 1–3 and tell students to read and listen. Play the audio for students to listen and decide how clear the message is. Check answers as a class.

> 1 The message isn't clear. It's read out in a rushed manner, without any pausing.
> 2 One.
> 3 It needs to be read more slowly, with pauses to indicate where sentences begin and end.

6 Tell students that punctuation and pronunciation are connected. Copy the symbols on the board. Go through the example as a class and check students understaånd the activity. Ask students to continue individually and to compare in pairs.

7 8E.2 Play the audio for students to listen and identify the pauses. Check answers as a class and play the audio a second time.

Extra activity

Put students in pairs to practise reading the email aloud. Monitor and give feedback on effective use of pausing.

C Organizing an apology message

8 Ask students to read items a–g. Check any vocabulary. Students continue individually and compare in pairs. Check answers.

> 1c 2e 3d 4g 5b 6f 7a

9 Go through the instructions and do the activity as a class. Check answers and point out that the order is typical of the way an apology would be sequenced. Ask students if they would use the same order in their language.

> 2e 3d,g 4b 5f 6a

10 Put students in pairs to find the parts of the message in the email in exercise 2. Monitor and help as necessary.

ABC Put it all together

11 Read through the instructions and check ståudents understand.

12 Tell students to use the sequence in exercise 9 as a plan for their email. Remind them to write legibly, as they will give their email to their partner to read.

13 Ask students to swap messages. Tell them to look at their partner's message and use the symbols in exercise 6 to check each other's work. Students tell each other how they could change the style to make it clearer. Point out that they can use these symbols when they review their own writing.

Student performance

Students should be able to write a short and clear description using simple compound sentences.

Use this checklist for monitoring and feedback or to assess students' performance.

Content	Have students given sufficient detail to explain the mistake?
Organization	Have students followed the plan in exercise 9?
Punctuation	Have students used capital letters and full stops appropriately?

I can **write a message of apology.**

Students tick *on my own* if their partner finds the apology acceptable. They tick *with some help* if they have to shorten some sentences or give extra details about what happened.

Early finishers

In small groups, students read their letters aloud and vote for the one with themost convincing details.

Additional material

www.oup.com/elt/result for extra practice material
www.oup.com/elt/teacher/result for extra teacher resources

Warmer

Remember what

Read phrases 1–10 below for students to write the name of the items. Students answer in pairs or small groups.

1 It's made of wood. It's long and thin. 2 It's used to send emails. 3 It's made of plastic and metal. It's use to take photos. 4 It's often lost. 5 It's long and thin. It's made of plastic. 6 It's made of metal. It's round and it's got a handle. 7 It's round and flat. It's made of china. 8 It's made of cloth. It's long and thin. 9 The top is round and flat. It's made of glass and metal. 10 It's made of plastic and metal. It's got a handle.

Possible answers		
1 a spoon, a pencil	5 a toothbrush	8 a tie
2 a computer	6 a pan	9 a table
3 a camera	7 a plate	10 a hairdryer
4 an umbrella		

A Grammar

1 Possessive pronouns 8A exercises 12, 13

Warm-up: Write the following words on the board: *phone's, so, they, her, broken, hers, used.* Ask students, individually, to make the sentence. *(Her phone's broken so they used hers.)* Review possessive pronouns if necessary.

Set-up: Go through the example with the class.

> 2 Which seat is mine?   3 That's ours!   4 Is that hers?
> 5 It isn't theirs.   6 Are these his?

Follow-up: In pairs, students write a conversation similar to >> p.76, *Sorry!* without naming the article. They read their conversation for another pair, who guesses the article.

2 Present passive 8B exercises 8, 10

Warm-up: Give students two minutes to look at the picture on >> p.78, *Making pencils.* Books closed. In pairs, students write the nine stages of pencil making. Elicit answers around the class and make notes on the board. Direct students back to >> p.78 to check answers.

Set-up: Tell students to read items 1–7 and say what is being made *(doors).* Go through the example as a class and do the second item together if necessary. Point out that *the trees* can be replaced by *them* in the second sentence.

> 2 Then the trees/they're put on a lorry.
> 3 The wood is taken to a factory.
> 4 The wood/It is cut into flat pieces.
> 5 The pieces/They are made into doors.
> 6 The doors/They are painted.
> 7 The doors/They are sold.

Follow-up: In pairs, students write five sentences for another pair to change into the passive. They can use >> p.79 exercise 10 for ideas and also prepare an answer key.

3 *will* (prediction) 8C exercise 5

Warm-up: Ask the example question around the class. Take a class vote for the most interesting or amusing suggestion.

Set-up: Do the example on the board with the class. Ask students to read through the conversation and ask *Who wants to live to be 100? (A.)*

> 2 will live longer; people will live   3 you will see
> 5 will be   7 you will live   9 I'll leave; I'll have

Follow-up: In small groups, set a three-minute time limit for students to brainstorm answers to the question *What do you think life will be like in the future?* Ask for suggestions and the

class to decide if the sentences are grammatically correct or not. Give two points for grammatically correct answers, and award an extra point to a team who corrects any mistakes.

4 1st conditional 8D exercises 9, 10

Warm-up: Say a conditional part of a sentence using a local situation, e.g. about the weather or sport. Elicit result clauses around the class and correct as necessary.

Set-up: Go through the example with the class.

> 2 leave; 'll call   3 'll get; rains   4 will steal; leave
> 5 drinks; 'll be

Follow-up: In pairs, students write three conditional clauses. They swap with another pair and complete the sentences. Students correct answers.

B Vocabulary

5 Apology phrases 8A exercise 10

Warm-up: See what students remember about Tina and Bill from lesson 8A. Ask *Who, What, How* questions.

Set-up: Tell students to read the conversation, ignoring the gaps. Ask *What happened?*

> 2 mistake 3 all right   4 worry   5 really   6 mind

Follow-up: Students choose an object and an event for another pair to write and act an apology conversation.

6 Material and shape 8B exercise 2

Warm-up: Books closed. Write *material* and *shape* on the board. Set a two-minute time limit for students to write as many associated words as they can. Direct students to the vocabulary panel on >> p.78 to check.

Set-up: Point out or elicit that students could use *It's used for ..., It works by ..., It's got ... .*

> **Suggested answers**
> 2 It's made of cardboard. It's got food inside.
> 3 It's made of wood. It's long and thin.
> 4 It's round. It's made of metal. It's got a handle. It's used for cooking.
> 5 It's made of glass. People look into it.
> 6 It's made of cotton. It's flat. It's used for drying things.

Follow-up: Students use dictionaries to prepare descriptions of two or three objects in the classroom. In small groups, they take turns to read a description. The first person to recognize the object gets one point for pointing to it, and three points if they can name it.

7 Email 8D exercise 2

Warm-up: Write *email* on the board. Set a two-minute time limit for students to write words connected to the topic. Go through suggestions as a class, and nominate different students to spell the words.

Set-up: Ask students to read the clues. Check vocabulary.

> 2 icon 3 attachment   4 junk mail   5 button   6 virus
> 7 click   8 delete

Follow-up: Students use dictionaries to write three clues for other email or computer-related words from lesson 8D and swap with a partner.

Early finishers

Students look through the unit a make a list of words which are the same or similar in their own language. They use dictionaries and make a note of any pronunciation differences.

Unit 8 Review

A Grammar

1 Possessive pronouns Write sentences with possessive pronouns.

1 Is this your bag?   *Is this yours*   ?
2 Which is my seat?   _____?
3 That's our camera!   _____!
4 Is that her bike?   _____?
5 It isn't their car.   _____.
6 Are these his glasses? _____?

2 Present passive Write the sentences in the passive.

1 First, a person cuts the trees down.
   First, the trees are cut down   .
2 Then, a person puts the trees on a lorry.
   _____.
3 A person takes the wood to a factory.
   _____.
4 A person cuts the wood into flat pieces.
   _____.
5 A person makes the flat pieces into doors.
   _____.
6 A person paints the doors.
   _____.
7 Finally, a person sells them.
   _____.

3 will (prediction) Correct the conversation. Eight of the verbs are in the present simple when they should be in the *will* form.

1 **A** What do you think life ~~is~~ ^(will be) like in the future?
2 **B** I think people live longer. More people live to be 100.
3 **A** Do you think you see your 100th birthday?
4 **B** I hope not! I don't want to be really old!
5 **A** Yes, but maybe there are new body parts – a new
6   heart, new eyes …
7 **B** Yuk! I don't think so. Do you think you live to be
8   100?
9 **A** I hope so. I leave work at 60 and then I have a 40
10   year holiday!

4 1st conditional Put these verbs in the correct tense in the sentences.

steal   call   ~~win~~   leave (x2)   get   be (x2)   rain   drink

1 If he *wins*_____ this race, he *'ll be*_____ the world champion!
2 If you _____ your telephone number, she _____ you back later.
3 You _____ wet if it _____.
4 Someone _____ your car if you _____ the door open.
5 If she _____ any more coffee, she _____ awake all night.

B Vocabulary

5 Apology phrases Complete the conversation with these words.

mistake   mind   really   all right   ~~sorry~~   worry

A I'm ¹ *sorry*_____. I took your bag by ²_____.
B That's ³_____. Don't ⁴_____ about it.
A I'm ⁵_____ sorry. My bag is very similar, you see.
B Never ⁶_____. It's an easy mistake to make.

6 Material and shape Describe these things. Use *material* and *shape* words.

1 A CD
   It's flat and round.
   It's made of plastic.

4 A pan
   _____
   _____

2 A cereal packet
   _____
   _____

5 A mirror
   _____
   _____

3 A brush handle
   _____
   _____

6 A towel
   _____
   _____

7 Email Solve these computer anagrams.

1 nilone   Connected to the Internet.   *online*
2 noic   A small picture.
3 themactant   A file sent with an email.
4 njuk alim   Mail you don't want and didn't ask for.
5 totbun   You press this.
6 ruvis   This is dangerous for your computer.
7 ilkcc   You do this with the mouse.
8 tdeele   To cut and remove a file.

Prepared food

a baked potato   some frozen peas   some grated cheese   a boiled egg
some grilled fish   some mashed potato   a fried egg   some scrambled egg
a roast chicken   some sliced bread

Healthy, tasty, or easy?

Do you like your food healthy, tasty, or easy? Do this quiz and find out!

1 Which of these is most important to you?
  a Vitamin pills.
  b My recipe books.
  c The microwave.

2 What's the most difficult part of a meal?
  a Choosing what to have.
  b Opening the tin or packet.
  c Washing the vegetables.

3 How do you usually eat potatoes?
  a In a bag of crisps.
  b Boiled.
  c Baked.

4 How do you like your bread?
  a Fresh.
  b Wholemeal.
  c Sliced.

5 Which question do you ask most often?
  a What's in it?
  b How long does it take to make?
  c How do you make it?

6 Which sounds best to you?
  a Healthy!
  b Delicious!
  c Ready to eat!

7 In a competition, you win one of these free for a year. Which do you choose?
  a Takeaway pizzas.
  b Meals in a good restaurant.
  c Fresh farm vegetables.

8 You read about a man who lived for a year eating only hot dogs. What do you say?
  a That's so boring!
  b That's so bad for his health!
  c I think I'll try it!

9 You buy a cheese sandwich and it's a bit dry. What do you say?
  a Oh well, it will fill me up!
  b Oh well, it won't kill me.
  c I can't eat that!

10 You're eating fish in a restaurant and you send it back. Why?
  a It isn't fresh.
  b It's overcooked.
  c It's got bones in it.

Now check your score on page 135.

How to **talk about food**

Orientation

Context

In this lesson, students will practise talking about food and meals they like and dislike.

Healthy, tasty, or easy? is a personality quiz typical of those found in magazines about healthy living. It takes a light-hearted look at the types of food people eat and invites the reader to answer questions to find out about their 'food personality'. The scores are on **» p.135**.

Photos a–j illustrate the vocabulary items in *Prepared food*.

Language

Focus grammar	countable / uncountable
Focus words	food: *baked, boiled, fresh, frozen, grated, grilled, mashed, scrambled,* etc.
Focus phrases	*Do you like ...?, Is there anything...?, What about you?, What ... do you like?*
Recognition vocabulary	words: *bones, fish, microwave, overcooked, pie, serve, sushi, vitamin pills, wholemeal* phrases: *fill up, ready to eat, takeaway, won't kill me*
Recycled language	*don't like, favourite, hate, like*
Pronunciation	linking consonant-vowel 9A.1

Language note

Although peas are small and, in practical terms, uncountable, grammatically they are countable. This can be seen in the sentence *These frozen peas are delicious.* in contrast to *This grated cheese is delicious. Some* is used because peas are almost always talked about in the plural form. This is also true for food words such as *grapes* and *beans*.

End product

In *Put it all together*, students exchange opinions on food and meals in small groups. They decide who they would most like to have dinner with. Students can refer to their notes for exercise 10 for help.

Preparation

Take in some magazine pictures of food. Check students have dictionaries. If you want to do exercise 6, *Extra activity*, write the following words on an OHT: *sausage, pineapple, tomato, fish, lettuce, orange, carrot, mushroom, egg, yoghurt, cheese, ham.*

Warmer

Show magazine pictures of food to the class and elicit the names of some of the food in the pictures. Write the following categories on the board: *fruit, vegetables, meat, dairy* and brainstorm a few foods for each category. Put students into small groups. Pass the magazine pictures around and ask students to discuss what kinds of food they like and don't like.

Write *How to talk about food* on the board.

A Vocabulary prepared food

1 Put students into pairs or small groups to talk about the questions. Monitor and listen for interesting comments and join in the conversations where you can. React to any unusual answers and ask some follow-up questions, e.g. *What kind of meat was it? What did it taste like? Uncooked egg – yuk! Why did you eat that?* Go over the questions with the class and nominate students to comment. Do not correct for accuracy at this stage but help students get their ideas across. Share interesting comments with the class.

2 Students activate vocabulary on the topic of food. Direct students to *Prepared food* on **» p.86** and elicit or give the meaning of *prepared*. Go through the example and set a short time limit for students to continue individually. Students compare in pairs before you go over answers as a class. Check answers by saying the picture letters for students to call out the answers. Monitor and help with pronunciation as necessary.

> b some scrambled egg e a baked potato   h some frozen peas
> c a boiled egg   f some mashed potato i some sliced bread
> d a roast chicken   g some grated cheese j some grilled fish

Extra help

Direct students to the adjective *grated* and ask *One syllable or two? (Two.)* In pairs, students continue with the other words in *Prepared food*. Check pronunciation and give help as necessary.

> **one syllable:** boiled /bɔɪld/   roast /rəʊst/   baked /beɪkt/
> mashed /mæʃt/   sliced /slaɪst/   grilled /grɪld/
> **two syllables:** scrambled /skræmbəld/   grated /greɪtɪd/
> frozen /frəʊzn/

3 Go through the instructions and questions 1–3 with the class. Demonstrate the activity using the word *grated,* pointing out that both apple and carrots *can* be grated. Ask students to choose three adjectives and continue individually. Monitor and help students use their dictionaries if necessary.

4 Use the example to demonstrate the activity, and put students in pairs to continue. Monitor and help by saying the different combinations for students to hear the words together. Check answers by asking students to give possible combinations.

> 2 bread   3 yoghurt   4 milk   5 oil   6 ice-cream   7 soup

5 9A.1 Go through the instructions and use the example to demonstrate the activity. Write *a norange* on the board and ask students to say it aloud. Then write *an orange* and show how the consonant 'n' links to the vowel 'o' in *an͜orange.* Play the audio and pause for students to listen and then write the phrase. Write the answers on the board as you go along. Play the audio a second time, pausing after each item, for students to repeat.

> 2 a sliced apple   3 a boiled egg   4 some grilled onion
> 5 some scrambled egg   6 an uncooked egg

Extra plus

Write *Which do you like best, baked or mashed potatoes?* and *Which do you like best, boiled or scrambled eggs?* on the board. In pairs, students prepare more questions with new vocabulary from the section. Monitor and help as necessary. Put pairs together to ask each other the questions.

B Grammar countable/uncountable

6 Point to picture a in *Prepared food* and ask *How many fried eggs are there? (One.)* Now point to picture b and ask *How many scrambled eggs are there? (We don't know. We can't count them.)* Write *a fried egg* and *some scrambled egg* on the board, and underline *egg* in both phrases and ask *What kind of words are these? (Nouns.)* Point to the first phrase and ask *What kind of noun is* egg *here? (Countable.)* Point to the second phrase and ask *Is* egg *always countable? (No, it depends how it's prepared.)* Go through the instructions and the table. Do a few more examples as a class before students continue in pairs.

Nominate students to give answers, and encourage them to say the whole phrase. Monitor for pronunciation, and check they pronounce *a* and *an* as /ə/ and /ən/ and *some* as /səm/. Underline *some* and the 's' at the end of *peas* to highlight the fact that *peas* is a plural countable noun.

> **countable:** a fried egg, a boiled egg, some frozen peas, a roast chicken
> **uncountable:** some mashed potato, some scrambled egg, some grated cheese, some sliced bread, some grilled fish

Extra activity
Use the OHP or write the words in *Preparation* on the board. Write these questions and ask students to write at least four answers for each one: *What do you like in a salad? What do you like on a pizza? What do you like for breakfast?* Monitor and check students are using *a, an,* and *some* correctly and encourage them to include adjectives from *Prepared food*. Put students into small groups to discuss their answers and find someone with the same or similar tastes.

C Read and respond

In this section, students scan a text to find vocabulary before reading for detail to complete a questionnaire about food.

7 Write *Healthy, tasty, or easy?* on the board. Elicit or give a couple of examples of words for students to classify, e.g. *vegetables, brown bread, pizza, ice-cream, a boiled egg, a tin of soup.* Talk about the text as a class. Direct students to look at the quiz on **>> p.86** quickly. Ask about options a–c, one at a time, checking students understand vocabulary. Ask them which option they think is the correct one *(c).*

8 Go through the instructions with the class and use the example to demonstrate the activity. Ask students to read items 2–5 and check any vocabulary problems before they continue individually. Monitor and help by directing students to the question number in *Healthy, tasty, or easy?* if necessary. Students compare in pairs before you go over answers as a class. Check students pronounce *recipe* with three syllables /ˈresəpi/ or /ˈresɪpi/. Point out that the 'w' in *wholemeal* is silent.

> 2 recipe book (question 1)   3 wholemeal (question 4)
> 4 fresh (questions 4 and 10)   5 overcooked (question 10)

9 Put students into pairs to do the quiz. Monitor and help with vocabulary as necessary. Direct students to **>> p.135** to calculate their score and read their result. Students decide if they agree with their result or not and compare answers. Ask for a show of hands for the *healthy, tasty,* and *easy* scorers.

D Listen for detail

In this section, students listen and follow a conversation about food to identify topics talked about.

10 9A.2 Read the instructions to the class. Ask students to read questions 1–4 in *Conversation A* and check vocabulary. For each question, elicit words students expect to hear when people talk about the topic and write them on the board. Repeat the procedure for *Conversation B.* Warn students that the speakers do not use exactly the same questions, so they will need to listen for the general meaning of the conversations. Play the audio, and ask students to compare in pairs. Play the audio a second time and ask students to raise their hands when they hear the words on the board.

> Conversation A

11 Go through the instructions and direct students to the pictures. Nominate individuals and ask them if they like the foods or not. Play the audio again for students to complete the table with the details of the conversations. Students check answers in pairs before you check with the whole class.

> **Jon:** fish pie   **Kate:** spaghetti, olives, cooked fish

Extra activity
Direct students to audio script 9A.2 on **>> p.156**. Go through the conversation and show how the speakers collaborate with each other: by giving details *(fish pie ingredients)*, returning the question *(What about you?)*, responding to the other's opinion *(either agreeing or disagreeing)*, using back-channelling responses, and having short turns. Put students in pairs to practise reading the conversation.

ABCD Put it all together

12 Go through the instructions and give students time to make notes to answer the questions in exercise 10. Put students into small groups and tell them to try and ask and answer three or four questions each. At the end of the activity ask students who they would like to have dinner with and why.

Student performance
Students should be able to describe and give supporting detail on personal preferences.

Use this checklist for monitoring and feedback or to assess students' performance.

Fluency	Do students join some consonant-vowel phrases? exercise 5
Accuracy	Do students use adjectives before nouns? exercise 4
Vocabulary	Do students use different food vocabulary to give details? exercise 4

I can talk about food.

Students tick *on my own* if they have asked and answered three questions, using their notes. They tick *with some help* if they have looked at *Prepared food* once or twice for vocabulary.

Early finishers
Students work in different groups to find another person to have dinner with.

Additional material

www.oup.com/elt/result for extra practice material
www.oup.com/elt/teacher/result for extra teacher resources

How to talk about food

G countable / uncountable   V prepared food   P linking consonant-vowel

A   Vocabulary prepared food

1   Do you like cooking? Why? / Why not? What type of food do you ususaly cook? Tell a partner.
    cabbage   carrot   egg   fish   fruit   meat   peas

2   Look at **Prepared food** opposite. Match the phrases with photos a–j.
    Example   a = a fried egg

3   Choose three adjectives from **Prepared food**. Answer the questions.
    1   Can you find this adjective in the dictionary?
    2   Can you find a similar verb in the dictionary?
    3   Can you guess the meaning of the adjective from the meaning of the verb?

4   ~~Cross out~~ the wrong word.
    1   some grated carrot / ~~orange~~ / apple
    2   some boiled bread / cabbage / rice
    3   some sliced tomato / onion / yoghurt
    4   some roast milk / beef / lamb
    5   some fried onion / oil / rice
    6   some grilled pork / tomatoes / ice-cream
    7   some mashed soup / banana / potato

5   **9A.1▶ Pronunciation** Listen and complete the phrases. Then listen and repeat.

    When a word ends with a consonant and the next word begins with a vowel, it often sounds like the consonant is part of the second word. For example:

these phrases	)) sound like ...
1 *an orange*	'a norange'
2 _____	'a slice tapple'
3 _____	'a boil degg'
4 _____	'some grill donion'
5 _____	'some scramble degg'
6 _____	'a nuncook tegg'

B   Grammar countable / uncountable

6   Which foods in photos a–j opposite are countable? Which are uncountable? Complete the table. What do you notice about egg and potato?

countable	uncountable
a *baked* potato	some _____ potato
a _____ egg	some _____ egg
a _____ egg	some _____ cheese
some _____ peas	some _____
a _____	some _____

More practice? **Grammar Bank** >> p.144.

C   Read and respond

7   Look at **Healthy, tasty, or easy?** opposite. Where do you think the text is from?
    a   a text book for students of medicine
    b   a general interest magazine
    c   a public health poster

8   Read the text again but don't answer the questions. Find words with these meanings.
    1   An adjective for something which has a nice taste.
        tasty
    2   A book which tells you how to cook different meals.
    3   A natural, brown bread.
    4   An adjective meaning the opposite of *old*, for food.
    5   An adjective meaning *cooked too much*.

9   Work with a partner. Read the quiz and choose the best answers for you. Count and compare your scores on page 135. Do you think your scores are correct?

D   Listen for detail

10   **9A.2▶** You will hear two friends, Jon and Kate, having one of these conversations. Read the questions. Then listen and decide if it is conversation A or B.

    Conversation A
    1   What are your favourite dishes?
    2   What's in them? / How are they prepared?
    3   Are there any foods you really hate or can't eat?
    4   Is there anything you've never tried?

    Conversation B
    1   Can you recommend any good restaurants?
    2   What country or region does the cooking come from?
    3   What did you have last time you went there?
    4   Describe some of the other dishes they serve.

11   Listen again to Jon and Kate. What do they like?.

Jon likes	Kate likes ...
	pizza

olives   sushi   fish   pie

ABCD   Put it all together

12   Look at the conversations in exercise 10. Think about your answers to the questions. Have the conversations with two or three other students. Who would you most like to have dinner with?

    Example   **A** What are your favourite dishes?
              B Well, I really like moussaka ...

Extra activity

Ask students to underline the word which comes before the place word in items 1–5. Ask what the three kinds of words can be (*a, an, the*) then ask for examples of phrases with *the* in items 1–5. Point out that the rules for the use of the definite article with places in English is difficult. A good strategy for students at this level is simply to remember the phrases.

5   Go through the instructions and the example to demonstrate the activity. Show students that sometimes they will need to change the journey times and the way of travelling (*thirty minutes = half-hour, by air = flight*). Do the activity together as a class and write the answers on the board. Underline stresses in the phrases and tell students that the stress is always on the number and the form of transport (e.g. *a **thirty**-minute **drive**, a **twenty**-minute **bus** ride*).

> 2 a thirty-minute drive   3 a ten-minute walk   4 a twenty-minute bus ride   5 a four or five-hour drive

6   Direct students to *Journey times* at the top of **» p.96**. Ask *Which journey times are short? (not far, a thirty-minute drive, a half-hour flight, five minutes on foot, a short bus ride, a five-minute walk)* and *Which are long? (a two-day boat journey, four or five hours by car, six hours by train, a long way)*. Go through the example and check students understand that they should guess the answers. Students continue individually and compare in pairs or small groups. Monitor and check they are using singular time words, e.g. *minute* not *minutes*. Ask for suggestions around the class and see if students more or less agree.

7   Go through the instructions and elicit examples of local places nearby. Monitor for accuracy, and direct students to *Journey times* on **» p.96** to check if necessary. Nominate students to give one example and see if the class agrees.

Extra activity

Students write some true and false sentences about local places and test a partner.

C   Listen for general meaning

In this section, students use context to predict what people from different places say in similar conversations.

8   Go through the activity as a class. Nominate or ask for a student to read the conversation with you. Direct students to options a–c and check they understand *whereabouts (in which area of a place)*. Tell students to choose a response for Nick. Students can then compare in pairs.

9   **10A.1** Play the audio for students to check their prediction *(c)*. Ask or explain why options a and b aren't appropriate in this context *(a would be considered unfriendly and b is not logical)*.

10   **10A.2** Go through the instructions as a class. Write options a–c on the board in note form (e.g. *Cornwall* ✓, *Fowey* ✗). Tell students to focus on the person who asks *Where are you from?* and the follow-up questions as they listen. Play the audio and ask students to compare in pairs. Play the audio a second time if necessary. Check answers as a class.

> 1 c   2 a   3 b

11   Direct students to audio script **10A.2** on **» p.157** and do the activity as a class. Model and drill the two questions, making sure students put the stress on the final syllable in *where**abouts***. Put students in pairs to practise the conversation using the audio script.

> 2 *Whereabouts?* means *Where exactly?* within a specific location, while *Where?* asks about general location.

Extra help

Make the following prompts relevant to your teaching context to give students further practice with *Where?* and *Whereabouts?*: *? the college* SS *Where's the college?* T *In England. ? England* SS *Whereabouts in England?* T *On the south coast. ? south coast* SS *Whereabouts on the south coast?* T *In Brighton. ? Brighton* SS *Whereabouts in Brighton?* T *Near the Pavilion.* Write the prompts and question marks on the board. Point to the first place, and elicit the question. Answer and point to the next question prompt. Elicit a more exact location as a reply. Repeat until you've used all the prompts. In pairs, students practise the conversation a few times.

ABC   Put it all together

12   Go through the instructions together as a class. Read through the different suggestions for a place to choose and agree one as a class. Brainstorm more information about the place, and refer students to *Journey times* on **» p.96** for help. Draw three columns on the board and label them *from the same region, a different part of the country* and *a different country*. Elicit questions each of the people could ask and write students suggestions on the board in note form. Refer students to audio script **10A.2** on **» p.157** for help if necessary.

Encourage students to think of ideas for three places but help with ideas if necessary as they continue individually.

13   Put students in pairs and direct them to the example which shows them how to start of the conversation. Tell them to choose one of their places from exercise 12, and a person from the three columns on the board. Remind students to ask lots of questions to demonstrate they are interested in having the conversation. Check students swap roles.

Student performance

Students should be able to have a short social exchange giving factual information.

Use this checklist for monitoring and feedback or to assess students' performance.

Interaction	Do students respond to their partner's information appropriately? exercise 11
Politeness	Do students ask a few questions to show interest? exercise 11
Vocabulary	Do students use some places and journey times? exercise 11

I can ask and say where places are.

Students tick *on my own* if they can ask and answer three or more questions to keep each conversation going. They tick *with some help* if they have to look at the board two or three times for help.

Early finishers

Students work in groups of three. Pairs repeat exercise 13 using a different place. The third student acts as an observer, counting the number of questions. At the end, students decide who asked the most questions.

Additional material

www.oup.com/elt/result for extra practice material
www.oup.com/elt/teacher/result for extra teacher resources

A Read a description in a brochure

1 Read **Escape to Fowey!** opposite. Answer the questions with a partner.

1 How many places in the text have you heard of? What do you know about them?

2 What kind of people would like Fowey? People who:
  - [ ] like exciting nightlife?
  - [ ] like surfing?
  - [ ] like going to quiet places?
  - [ ] *others*?

3 Would you like to visit Fowey? Why? / Why not?

2 How near are these places to Fowey? Number them: 1 = nearest, 5 = furthest away.
  - [ ] London
  - [1] Polruan
  - [ ] Newquay
  - [ ] St Austell
  - [ ] Plymouth

3 Imagine you are planning a holiday in Fowey. Work with a partner. Decide how to get there from where you are now.

Example We could take a plane to ...

B Vocabulary places; journey times

4 Look at the box and complete the sentences below.

in	a country, a region, a town, a village, mountains, a forest, a desert ...
on	a river, a coast, a small island ...

1 I live _in_ a village _____ a small island _____ the south of Greece.
2 I live _____ Darwin, a town _____ the north coast of Australia.
3 I live _____ a small town _____ the desert _____ California.
4 I live _____ a town _____ the Danube in Hungary.
5 I live _____ a village _____ the Alps.

5 Read **Escape to Fowey!** again. Find phrases with these meanings.

1 thirty minutes by air *a half-hour flight*
2 half an hour by car
3 a short journey on foot
4 a short journey by bus
5 a few hours' drive

6 Look at **Journey times** opposite. Match them with the journeys in photos 2–4. Guess! There may be more than one correct answer. Compare with a partner.

1 Fowey to Newquay *a thirty-minute drive* or *half an hour by car*
2 London to Newquay
3 Place Road to the harbour
4 Plymouth to Glasgow
5 Plymouth to Santander
6 St Austell to Fowey

7 Look at **Journey times** again. Make sentences about five places that are near you with the times.

Examples The train station is a short bus ride from here. The museum's twenty minutes by bus.

Tell a partner. Do you agree?

C Listen for general meaning

8 Read this conversation. What do you think Nick will say next? Choose one option, a, b, or c.

Nick Hi, I'm Nick.
Wendy Hi Nick. I'm Wendy.
N Where are you from, Wendy?
W Cornwall.

  a OK, thanks. Goodbye.
  b Oh. I'm not from Cornwall.
  c Really? Whereabouts in Cornwall?

9 **10A.1▶** Listen to the start of the conversation and check.

10 **10A.2▶** You will hear Wendy telling three people where she's from. Match the three conversations with the people that Wendy's talking to.
  a someone from Cornwall, but not from Fowey
  b someone from another country, not from Britain
  c someone from a different part of Britain, not from Cornwall

11 Read the audio script on ≫ p.157. Answer the questions.
1 How did you know the answers to exercise 10? Underline the important phrases.
2 What's the difference between these two questions?
  a Whereabouts in Fowey?
  b Where's Fowey?

Act the conversations with a partner.

ABC Put it all together

12 Think of three interesting places you know and make notes about them. Use these ideas to help you.

The place
a place in your local town
another town or village in your area
a place in your region
a place in another part of your country
a place in another country

More information
– Where? Whereabouts?
– It's near / in / on ...
– Things to see and do

13 Ask and answer about your place with a partner.
Example **A** Have you ever been to Natal?
      B No. Where's that?

Warmer

Remember the places

Write the following places on the board: *A At the airport, B On the plane, C In and around Fowey, D Along the Silk Road.* Read out sentences 1–10 below for students to write the letter of the place.

1 *Fasten your seat-belts.*
2 *Go to the departure gate.*
3 *Walk to Readymoney beach.*
4 *Collect your bags.*
5 *Take a half-hour flight from London Gatwick.*
6 *Read the emergency instructions.*
7 *Shop at the duty-free shop.*
8 *Follow the camel caravan route.*
9 *Turn the intercom off.*
10 *Cross the border into Kyrgyzstan.*

> 1 B   2 A   3 C   4 A   5 C   6 B   7 A   8 D   9 B   10 D

A Grammar

1   Present perfect with *just, already* and *yet* 10B exercises 9, 10

Warm-up: Write these sentences on the board: *Ben's travelling to New York. Now he's in the departure lounge.* In pairs, students make a note of what Ben has and hasn't done, using *just, already* and *yet*. They check answers using audio script 10B.2 on >> **p.157**.

Set-up: Go through the example with the class. Explain that the extra word might be added to the question or the response.

> 2 Have you had breakfast yet?
> 3 I've already seen it.
> 4 No, I haven't finished it yet.
> 5 I've just turned it off.
> 6 No, I've already been there.
> 7 Has your brother left school yet?
> 8 No, I haven't read it yet.

Follow-up: Students choose a picture from *Ben's journey home* on >> **p.98**. A partner asks *Have you ... yet ?* to guess where they are.

2   Present perfect with *for* and *since* 10C exercise 6

Warm-up: Ask students to read the dialogue on >> **p.100**. Say some true/false sentences about Sandra and Beth using *for* and *since*. Students repeat any factually correct sentences as a class.

Set-up: Ask students to read items 1–8 and a–h. Check vocabulary as necessary.

> 2 h   3 g   4 f   5 a   6 b   7 d   8 e

Follow-up: In pairs, students prepare a similar exercise, using five sentence beginnings and endings. Pairs swap exercises.

3   *used to* 10D exercise 9

Warm-up: Write *New York used to be called ...?* on the board. Students say a complete sentence as they guess the answer.

Set-up: Go through the example and remind students of when to use *used to*.

> 2 built   3 travelled   4 used to go   5 wanted   6 used to be
> 7 used to sell   8 was

Follow-up: Individually, students choose a famous person and write five sentences, using *used to* or the simple past tense. In small groups, they read their sentences for others to guess who.

B Vocabulary

4   Journey times 10A exercise 6

Warm-up: See what students can remember about Fowey. Write notes on the board and direct students to read *Escape to Fowey!* again on >> **p.96** to check.

Set-up: Go through the example and show how the symbol shows the means of travel. Students write two sentences for each item.

> 2 thirty minutes by bus/a thirty-minute bus ride
> 3 six hours by train/a six-hour train ride
> 4 three days by camel/a three-day camel ride
> 5 a four hour ride by car/a four-hour car ride

Follow-up: In small groups, students tell each other how far their house is from the school, using different forms of transport.

5   Air travel 10B exercise 2

Warm-up: Write *Air travel* on the board. Set a two-minute time limit for students, individually, to write topically-related words.

Set-up: Ask students to read the clues on >> **p.131** and check vocabulary as necessary.

> **Across:** 3 land   5 fasten   6 belt   7 signs   8 through
> 10 departures   12 take off
> **Down:** 1 gate   2 passport   4 duty   6 board   9 seat   11 ask

Follow-up: Students choose one of the phrases in *Air travel* on >> **p.98** and make an anagram for a partner.

6   Prepositions of direction 10D exercise 1

Warm-up: Give students two minutes to read the text on p.103, exercise 1. Book closed. See how many places on the route they can remember.

Set-up: Ask *How long does it take to get to Angra?* Students read the text, ignoring the blanks *(about 5 hours)*.

> 2 along   3 through   4 past   5 follow   6 across   7 reach
> 8 across

Follow-up: In pairs, students write a short route plan for a well-known place near the school. They blank out the prepositions of direction and swap with another pair.

Early finishers

Students write a short description for a visitor coming to their house from the nearest airport.

Unit 10 Review

A Grammar

1 Present perfect with *just*, *already* and *yet* Add one of these words to the question or the response in each conversation.

already   yet   just

1   Why are your hands wet?
    I've washed them.   *I've just washed them.*

2   Have you had breakfast?
    No, I'll have it later.

3   Why don't you get this DVD?
    I've seen it.

4   Shall I check your homework?
    No, I haven't finished it.

5   Why is the TV warm?
    I've switched it off.

6   Let's go to Rome on holiday.
    No, I've been there.

7   Has your brother left school?
    Yes, he's at university now.

8   Can I borrow your newspaper?
    No, I haven't read it.

2 Present perfect with *for* and *since* Match the beginnings and ends of the sentences.

1   [c] Brasilia has been a capital city since
2   [ ] He's been asleep since
3   [ ] It's been dark for
4   [ ] I've had to wear glasses since
5   [ ] I've lived in London for
6   [ ] She's been off work with flu for
7   [ ] The USA has been independent for
8   [ ] They've been unemployed since

a   five years.
b   four days.
c   ~~1960.~~
d   over 230 years.
e   they left school.
f   I was a teenager.
g   three hours.
h   three o'clock.

3 *used to* Complete the sentences with *used to*. If *used to* is not possible, put the verb in the past simple tense.

1   New York _used to be_ (be) called New Amsterdam.
2   The emperor _____ (build) a great wall.
3   Marco Polo _____ (travel) to China.
4   The silk traders _____ (go) around the Taklimakan Desert.
5   Columbus _____ (want) to find a sea route to China.
6   The capital of Brazil _____ (be) Rio de Janeiro.
7   The traders _____ (sell) their silk in Europe.
8   Marco Polo _____ (be) in Venice.

B Vocabulary

4 Journey times Write two sentences for each sign.

1   🚶 **Metro** 5 minutes ❯
    The metro station is a five-minute walk from here .
    The metro station is five minutes on foot from here .

2   🚐 **Airport** 30 minutes ❯
    _____
    _____

3   🚂 **Scotland** 6 hours ❯
    _____
    _____

4   🐪 **Kashgar** 3 days ❯
    _____
    _____

5   🚗 **Coast** 4 hours ❯
    _____
    _____

5 Air travel Do the crossword. See clues on ❯❯ p.131.

6 Prepositions of direction Write the words in the gaps.

across (x2)   along   follow   ~~leave~~   past   reach   through

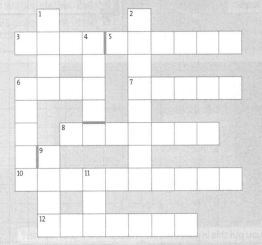

How to get to Ilha Grande

You ¹ _leave_ Rio de Janeiro and you go east ² _____ the coast. The road goes ³ _____ a short tunnel and ⁴ _____ Barra. After that, you ⁵ _____ the beach for half an hour. Then the road goes ⁶ _____ some hills to Campo Grande. After about five hours you ⁷ _____ Angra. Then you take a ferry ⁸ _____ to the island.

Portrait of a young woman

The artist's model in this painting is a young woman called Suzon. You are standing in front of her. She's looking straight at you, and she doesn't seem happy. She's working in a bar in Paris. There are lots of people in the bar – you can see them in the mirror. But she seems lonely. She doesn't really want to be there. Perhaps she hates the job. Perhaps she has problems in her life. We can see Suzon's back in the mirror, and the face of a man in front of her. The man doesn't seem friendly. You are standing in front of her, so of course, <u>you</u> are the man in the mirror.

1 *Girl With a Pearl Earring*, Jan Vermeer (c1665)

2 *Mona Lisa*, Leonardo da Vinci (14th Century)

3 *A Bar at the Folies-Bergère*, Edouard Manet (1882)

4 *The Shrimp Girl*, William Hogarth (c1745)

How to say how people appear

Orientation

Context

In this lesson, students will focus on describing scenes involving what people are doing and how they appear.

The four famous paintings of different young women are labelled with the name of the picture, the artist and the date the painting was done. *Portrait of a young woman* describes one of the paintings and includes the author's impressions on how the woman might be feeling and why.

Language

Focus grammar	action or state verbs: *hear, know, listen, look, seem, understand, etc.*
Focus words	*appear, model, perhaps, etc.*
Recognition vocabulary	words: *headscarf* phrases: *at this time, doing something funny, looking straight at you, etc.*
Recycled language	present simple; present continuous; prepositions of place: *behind, in a market, in front of, in Holland* articles: *a/the*
Pronunciation	unstressed words **11B.3**

Language note

The difference between *see* and *look at* and *hear* and *listen to* can often be confusing. *See* and *hear* are state verbs, but are usually prefaced by *can* rather than just used in the present simple. These describe abilities over which we don't have control. *Listen to* and *look at* are action verbs as they require more conscious effort. *look at* is used for things which are still, *watch* for things which are moving.

End product

In *Put it all together*, students describe a picture for others to listen for key words to identify the picture. Students can use their notes in exercise 12 for the descriptions.

Preparation

Think about how to organize your classroom to regroup students for *Put it all together*, exercise 13.

Warmer

Put students into pairs or small groups and direct them to the paintings on >> **p.108**. Tell them not to read the information next to each one, but to put the pictures in order according to when they were painted. Write these words on the board: *age, looking at, thinking, feeling* and ask for volunteers to tell the class which painting they think was the earliest and latest. See if students agree with each other. Ask *Were you talking about facts or appearance? (Appearance.)*

Write *How to say how people appear* on the board.

A Listen for key words

In this section, students practise using key words to identify the subject of short descriptions.

1 Direct students to the pictures on >> **p.108**. Ask *What kind of paintings are they all?* and elicit *portrait*. Then in pairs, students talk about the questions. If necessary, give students some topics to help them. Write the following on the board: *colours, clothes, eyes, smile, background, feeling*. Set a three-minute time limit for students, in pairs, to talk about the pictures. Monitor and join in with the conversations. Do not correct for accuracy at this stage. Ask around the class for suggestions and see which painting is the most popular.

2 **11B.1** Go through the instructions and check students understand the activity. Play the audio while students listen and check. Students compare their answers in pairs and then check as a class.

> Picture 3

3 Tell students to work individually and identify key words and phrases in *Portrait of a young woman*. Put students into pairs or small groups to compare ideas. Ask for suggestions around the class and write them on the board. Go over any vocabulary questions in the text at the end.

> **Suggested answers**
> looking straight at you; doesn't seem happy; in a bar; Paris; lots of people; lonely; back; in the mirror; face; man

4 **11B.2** Go through the instructions and play the audio for students to note the key words. Tell students not to worry about spelling, they should write what they hear. Put students in pairs to compare and play the audio a second time. Ask for suggestions around the class and write them on the board. Use the pictures to check students understand vocabulary.

> **Suggested answers**
> **Description 1:** sitting; body; side; turning; head; calm and relaxed; head scarf; Holland = picture 1
> **Description 2:** working; market; London, happy; poor; left; funny; moving quickly = picture 4

B Grammar action or state verbs

5 Go through the instructions and direct student to audio scripts **11B.1** and **11B.2** on >> **p.158**. Do a couple of examples as a class and point out that students underline the verb phrases, e.g. *are standing, doesn't seem*. Set a short time limit for students to find the verb phrases in the audio script. Put students in pairs to compare before checking answers as a class.

Direct students to the grammar box, the titles in the top row and the examples. Ask them to write the main verbs in the appropriate box. Monitor and help as necessary.

When students have finished, read the rule to the class. Check students understand by asking *What are the state verbs connected with? (Appearance, opinion, feelings.) Do these things generally change? (No.) Can you start and stop them? (No.) Can you start and stop actions like standing, looking, working and playing? (Yes.)*

> **verbs in the present continuous** (action verbs): stand look work think sit do turn enjoy play call
> **verbs in the present simple** (state verbs): be want hate have see seem remember

Teaching tip

Tell students to mime the action verbs then mime the state verbs. Ask which were harder to mime *(the state verbs)*. Point out that they can use this strategy to help decide if a verb describes an action or a state.

6 Do one or two examples as a class and put students in pairs to continue. Check answers. Say the state verbs and ask *What are these state verbs connected with? (Knowledge, feeling, senses.)*

> **action verbs:** walk listen write watch talk smile
> **state verbs:** know hear like understand

Extra help

Ask students to sit quietly and say what they can see and hear in the classroom. Then ask them to *look at* the clock, *look at* the board, *listen to* their watch and *listen to* the audio. Ask *Did you want or try to hear the traffic outside? (No.) Did you want or try to listen to your watch? (Yes.)* Students should see that *look at* and *listen to* require more conscious effort.

7 Go through the instructions and the example to check students understand the activity. Students do items 2–4 individually and compare in pairs. Nominate students to give answers. Make a note of any errors and give extra help at the end if necessary.

> 2 's smiling, likes   3 know, 's looking   4 seem, 're enjoying

8 Go through the example and point out that students must write the full verb phrase, e.g. *'s standing*. Students work individually to complete the text. Ask for volunteers to give answers.

> 2 's looking   3 isn't working   4 's smiling   5 is   6 seems
> 7 knows   8 like

9 Put students in pairs and explain that they should read each sentence in turn and look at the pictures and comment. Say the first sentence and ask students which picture it could be. Monitor and help as necessary. Check answers as a class and ask students which pieces of information helped them decide the picture. *(2 Mona Lisa.)*

C Pronunciation unstressed words

10 11B.3 Read the instructions and check students understand the activity. Direct students to the text in exercise 8 and read the instructions to the class. Ask *How can we tell if a word is stressed? (It sounds louder, clearer than the other words.)* Play the audio for students to listen. Play the audio a second time if necessary and elicit the answer

> The black words are stressed. The green words are 'grammar' words, e.g. prepositions, modals, articles, conjunctions, and some pronouns. These tend to be unstressed.

Extra help

Write *She's standing in front of you.* and *She's looking straight at you.* from the text in exercise 8 on the board. Read it aloud and ask *Why are some of the words underlined? (Because they are stressed.) Which words tend to be stressed? (The key words.)*

Do some intensive pronunciation work on stressed and unstressed sounds. Say the stressed words *standing, front, you, looking, straight, you* followed by the complete sentence. Then say the unstressed words *she's* /ʃɪz/, *in* /ɪn/, *of* /əv/, and /ən/, *she's* /ʃɪz/, *at* /at/, followed by the complete sentence. Ask students to say the sentence a few times and monitor and tap the rhythm to encourage students to produce the unstressed syllables.

11 Do the activity as a class first, tapping the table for rhythm. Put students into pairs to practise together. Monitor and praise effective use of sentence stress. When both students in each pair have read the text through a couple of times, ask for volunteers to read to the class. The class can clap the rhythm.

ABC Put it all together

12 Go through the instructions and the example as a class. Put students in pairs and remind them to use their dictionaries if necessary. When students have made their notes, ask them to underline key words.

13 Put students into groups. Remind them that they can hesitate and repeat words while they are speaking. Tell students to write their guesses on paper, and to say the picture at the end.

Student performance

Students should be able to give a short description.

Use this checklist for monitoring and feedback or to assess students' performance.

Content	Do students give sufficient information about the picture? exercise 4
Vocabulary	Do students use action and state verbs? exercise 5
Pronunciation	Do students try to place sentence stress correctly? exercise 11

I can **say how people appear.**

Students tick *on my own* if they can give a description using key words in their notes. They tick *with some help* if they need to read phrases from their notes two or three times.

Early finishers

Students change groups and repeat the activity. Listeners make a note of key words. Students compare notes and decide who used the most detail to describe their picture.

Additional material

www.oup.com/elt/result for extra practice material
www.oup.com/elt/teacher/result for extra teacher resources

How to say how people appear

A Listen for key words

1 Look at the paintings opposite. Which one do you like the most? Why? Tell a partner.

2 **11B.1▶** Listen and read **Portrait of a young woman** opposite. Which painting is the text about?

3 Which key words in the text helped you answer exercise 2? Underline them. Compare with a partner.

4 **11B.2▶** Listen to two more descriptions and note the key words. Match the descriptions with two of the other paintings.

B Grammar action or state verbs

5 Read audio scripts 11B.1 and 11B.2 on >> p.158. Underline all the verbs in the present continuous tense and circle all the verbs in the present simple tense. Write the verbs in the table.

verbs in the present continuous (action verbs)	verbs in the present simple (state verbs)
look	seem

Rule We do not normally use continuous tenses with state verbs.

Example   ~~She's hating her job.~~
~~I'm not knowing him.~~

6 Do you think the verbs below are action or state verbs? Decide with a partner.

know walk listen hear like write understand watch talk smile

7 In each pair of sentences, put one verb in the present simple and the other in the present continuous.

1 They're *speaking* a foreign language.
 I *don't understand* them. speak / not understand

2 She _____ at me. I think she _____ me.
 smile / like

3 Do you _____ that man? He _____ at you.
 know / look

4 They _____ unhappy. I don't think they _____ the party. seem / enjoy

8 Put the verbs in brackets in the present simple or continuous tense.

¹She *'s standing* (stand) in front of you and ²she_____ (look) straight at you. ³She_____ (not work) or doing anything else. ⁴She_____ (smile). Behind her you can see countryside with a river. ⁵She _____ (be) very calm and relaxed. ⁶It _____ (seem) like ⁷she _____ (know) your thoughts. ⁸I _____ (like) this picture.

9 Which painting is the text in exercise 8 about? Do you agree with it? Tell your partner.
More practice? **Grammar Bank** >> p.146.

C Pronunciation unstressed words

10 **11B.3▶** Listen to the text in exercise 8. Which words are stressed?
a the black words
b the green words

11 Practise reading the text in pairs. Does your partner stress the correct words?

ABC Put it all together

12 Work with a partner. Look at these four portraits. Choose one and write notes to describe it. Look at audio scripts 11B.1, 11B.2, and 11B.3 on >> p.158 for ideas.

Example   standing, wearing red, thinking, looking down, seems calm

13 Work in groups. Use your notes to describe one of the portraits. Remember – don't stress all the words. Guess which picture the other students in your group are describing.

I can say how people appear.

Tick ✓ the line.   with a lot of help   with some help   on my own   very easily

C Grammar past simple passive

6 Introduce students to the use of the passive. Go through the instructions and do the first item together as a class. Read the question and options a–c before giving students time to look at the text again and decide on an answer in pairs. Tell students the answer *(c)* and check they understand why *(Jo Allen was the make-up artist)*. Monitor and help as students match questions 2 and 3 to the answers. Go over the answers as a class.

> 2 b (the article isn't about photos or who took them)   3 a

7 Introduce students to the form of the passive. Write the sentence *Bardem's hair was shaved.* on the board and go through items 1–3 as a class.

> 1 The person who did the action isn't important, you don't know who did the action, you can put the topic in the subject position of the sentence.
> 2 *was* = singular noun in subject position, *were* = plural noun in subject position
> 3 past participle *(done)*

8 Write *subject + be + past participle* on the board and tell students to underline examples of the past passive in the text. Put students in pairs before asking for examples around the class. Monitor for accuracy when students give examples.

Extra help

Transformation drill. Say the following prompts about the make-up for students to change into passive sentences, e.g. *T She shaved his hair. SS His hair was shaved.*
She removed his eyebrows. She cut his eyebrows. She changed the shape of his nose. She added bags under his eyes. She painted spots on his skin.

9 Go through the instructions and the example to demonstrate the activity. Ask students to read items 2–6 and check any vocabulary. Put students in pairs to make the sentences. Ask for volunteers to say the sentences.

Extra plus

Ask for volunteers to say all the sentences so they are run together to form a continuous explanation.

10 Ask students if they have seen *The Lord of the Rings*. Elicit or give two or three facts about it and write them on the board, e.g. *it was very long, it was filmed in New Zealand*.

Ask students to read the text quickly to see if the information on the board is in the text.

Go through the instructions and the example as a class. Ask students why the passive tense is correct here *(because the text is about the film, not the writer)*. Monitor and help as students continue individually. Students check answers in pairs. Nominate different students to give the answers.

> 2 was made   3 were made   4 took   5 won   6 was filmed
> 7 visited

D Listen for detail in a conversation

In this section, students listen to a conversation for gist and specific information.

11 11D.1 Read the information and questions to the class. Ask students how they are going to listen, for the general idea or for detailed information *(for the general idea)*. Play the audio and ask for answers and a couple of examples of what Ben says and Kath does. Do not play the audio a second time or go into detail at this stage.

> 1 No. Ben says he wouldn't do it again.   2 Yes. Kath responds by asking questions for more information.

12 Go through the instructions and question 1 to check students understand the activity. Play the audio, pausing briefly for students to make notes. Ask students to compare their notes and play the audio a second time if necessary.

Remind students to write the answers in complete sentences. Monitor and check for accuracy. Direct them to audio script 11D.1 on **» p.158** or play the audio again to check their answers. Go over answers as a class and remind students that they can find a list of past participles on **» p.148**.

> 2 We were given a hostel to sleep in.
> 3 We were woken up at five every morning.
> 4 We were given an uncomfortable outfit to wear.
> 5 We were given an hour for lunch.
> 6 We were given sandwiches to eat.
> 7 We were told to talk to each other.

Extra plus

Students look again at exercise 11, question 2. In pairs, they list from memory anything about the conversation which suggested Kath showed she was interested in his story *(her intonation in responses and questions)*. Ask students to think about Kath's questions and write notes on the board. Play the audio again for students to listen and check. Direct students to audio script 11D.1 on **» p.158** to read again. In pairs, students practise having the conversation.

ABCD Put it all together

13 Go through the instructions and answer any questions. Give students time to think about an event, real or imaginary. Tell students to make notes and to use their dictionaries and the list of past participles on **» p.148** to help. Give students time to practise saying their stories.

14 Go through the instructions and read the example introduction. Put students in pairs to describe their experience to their partner. Tell the listeners to show their partner they are listening by saying 'ehm' at different points in the description. At the end, ask students to tell the class interesting facts about their partner's experiences.

Student performance

Students should be able to provide details of an event.

Use this checklist for monitoring and feedback or to assess students' performance.

Content	Do students give sufficient detail about the story? exercise 10
Accuracy	Do student mostly use *was* and *were* accurately? exercise 10 Do students mostly use the past participle after *was* and *were*? exercise 10

I can **say how something was done.**

Students tick *on my own* if they have told their story occasionally using their notes. They tick *with some help* if they have looked at their notes all the time.

Early finishers

Students retell their partner's story in small groups. Groups guess if the stories where real or imaginary.

Additional material

www.oup.com/elt/result for extra practice material
www.oup.com/elt/teacher/result for extra teacher resources

How to say how something was done

G past passive **v** the face

A **Vocabulary** the face

1 Make a list of words for parts of the face.
Example eye, ear …

2 Look at **The face** opposite. Match the words with the numbers in the pictures. Do you know who this is?
Example 1 = nose

B **Read and understand detail**

3 Read **The Power of Make-up** opposite. What do you find out about these people? Tell a partner.
Javier Bardem   Ramón Sampedro
Jo Allen   Alejandro Amenábar

4 Read the text again and answer the questions. Compare with a partner.
  1 How long did it take to do Bardem's make up?
  2 What changes were made to Bardem's …
     a hair?   c eyelashes?   e eyes?
     b eyebrows? d nose?   f skin?
  3 What time did Jo Allen finish doing his make-up?

5 Would you like to see this film? Why? / Why not?

C **Grammar** past simple passive

6 Read the sentences below from **The Power of Make-up**. Match questions 1–3 with answers a–c.
  1 'Bardem's hair was shaved.' Who shaved it?
  2 'Photos were taken at every stage.' Who did this?
  3 'The film was also given an Oscar for best make-up.' Who gave the Oscar?

  a Maybe a famous person. The article isn't about the Oscar ceremony.
  b We don't know. It isn't important.
  c Probably Jo Allen, but the article isn't about her, it's about the make-up.

7 Sentences 1–3 in exercise 6 are in the past simple passive. Answer the questions.
  1 In a passive sentence, you can say what happened *without* saying who did it. This is sometimes useful. Why? (Clue – look at answers a, b, and c in exercise 6.)
  2 When do you use *was* and when do you use *were*?
  3 Which verb form follows *was / were*?
     a infinitive (*to do*)
     b past simple (*did*)
     c past participle (*done*)

8 <u>Underline</u> examples of the past passive in **The Power of Make-up**.

9 Imagine you're a star. Say how you were treated on a recent trip.
  1 invite / New York   4 give / best room
     I was invited to New York. 5 serve / breakfast in bed
  2 meet / airport   6 show / on the evening
  3 take / five-star hotel   news

10 Read the text and <u>underline</u> the correct option.
The Lord of the Rings [1]write / <u>was written</u> by JR Tolkien. It [2]made / was made into three films by Peter Jackson. The three films [3]made / were made at the same time. The project [4]took / was taken eight years to complete, and it cost $270 million. The film [5]won / was won seventeen prizes. It [6]filmed / was filmed in New Zealand. The scenery was very beautiful and many people [7]visited / were visited New Zealand because of the film.

More practice? **Grammar Bank** >> p.146.

D **Listen for detail in a conversation**

11 **11D.1▶** Ben worked as an extra in the film *Emma*. He's telling his friend Kath about it. Answer the questions.
  1 Did Ben enjoy the work?
  2 Is Kath interested in his story?

12 Listen again. What are Ben's answers to these questions?
  1 Where did you go? *We were taken to a place in the middle of nowhere.*
  2 Were you given a place to sleep?
  3 What time were you woken up?
  4 What were you given to wear?
  5 How long were you given for lunch?
  6 Were you given anything to eat?
  7 What were you told to do?

ABCD **Put it all together**

13 Have you ever had any of these experiences? Choose one and make notes to answer these questions.
Where was it?   When was it?   What happened to you?
What was it like?   What were you told to do?
Were you given anything to eat?
  1 a stay in hospital
  2 your first day at school
  3 a school or business trip
  4 a part in a play
  5 *your ideas*

14 Tell your partner about your experience. Does your partner's experience sound good? Why? / Why not?
Example A few years ago I had a job as an extra in a film. We were told to arrive at 8.00 a.m. and …

I can say how something was done.

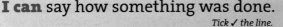

Tick ✓ the line.   with a lot of help   with some help   on my own   very easily

Pairwork

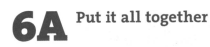

6A Put it all together

Caller cards

Choose any of these cards and 'phone' your partner.

> You phone Central College (726 8915). You want to speak to Ms Breen, Mrs Wilson, or Mr Nailer.

> You phone Central College (726 8915). You want to speak to Ms Green, Mrs Nilson, or Mr Mailer.

> You phone Kwikfix Garage (726 8515). You want to speak to Don or Tim.

> You phone Kwikfix Garage (726 8515). You want to speak to Dan or Tom.

Answerer cards

Choose any of these cards and answer the call from your partner.

> You are a secretary at Central College (726 8915). Here are some of the people in your department:
> **Ms Green** She's in class at the moment. Her class finishes at 17.15.
> **Mr Nailer** He's talking on the phone at the moment.
> **Mrs Wilson** She's free. You can put the caller through.

> You are a secretary at Central College (726 8915). Here are some of the people in your department:
> **Mr Mailer** He's on holiday at the moment. He's back on the 13th.
> **Ms Breen** She's talking on the phone at the moment.
> **Mrs Nilson** She's in class at the moment. Her class finishes at 9.50.

> You work at Kwikfix Garage (726 8515). You work with two other people:
> **Don** He's busy at the moment.
> **Tom** He's in the office. You can put the caller through.

> You work at Kwikfix Garage (726 8515). You work with two other people:
> **Tim** He's busy at the moment.
> **Dan** He's gone home. He starts work at 9.15 in the morning.

6B Put it all together
Different forms of transport

Choose two forms of transport. Make notes about the obligations connected with them. Use some of the ideas below.

> wear a helmet   wear a seat-belt   go through security
> wait for a long time   smoke   eat   drive   buy petrol
> get a licence   buy a ticket   book a seat   *your ideas*

> *Example*   Cycling   have to   wear helmet
>   don't have to   get licence
>   mustn't   ride on pavement

Use your notes to say which form of transport you prefer.

> *Example*   **A** I prefer driving to travelling by bus. You can
>   smoke if you want, and you don't have to
>   wait for a long time.
>   **B** Yes, but you have to buy petrol …

6C Put it all together
Student A Picture story

6D Exercise 12
Student A What were they doing?

Ask and answer questions about the pictures with your partner. Ask about Benny, Jerry, Gareth, and Ernest and Frances.

> *Example*   **A** What was Benny doing when the police
>   arrived?
>   **B** He was talking on the phone.

7B Exercise 12
Team A Jobs Quiz

What do you call...
- a doctor who does operations? (surgeon)
- the room where hospital patients sleep? (ward)
- a person who makes and mends shoes? (cobbler)
- a person who makes things with wood? (carpenter)
- a thing which you use to cut wood? (saw)
- a building where a farmer keeps animal food? (barn)

You can ask for clues:
- What's the first letter?
- And the second letter?
- How many letters are there in the word?
- Is the word similar in our language?
- Is the word _____ in our language?

7B Put it all together
Describing a job

Answer these questions about your job (or a job that you'd like to have).

1 What's your occupation?
2 Who do you work with or for?
3 What place or places do you spend time in at work?
4 What are the things that you use in your job?

Write definitions to explain your answers to the questions.

Example I'm a motorcycle courier. That's a person who delivers packages on a motorcycle. I work with ...

7C Exercise 11
Student A Office

8B Put it all together
Describing objects

8D Put it all together
Options

1 New computer ...  desktop? / laptop?	**2** Language lessons ... Latin? / Chinese?
3 Holiday ... hotel? / camping?	**4** New home ... house? / flat?
5 Journey ... train? / car?	**6** Birthday dinner ... restaurant? / home?
7 Music lessons ... piano? / guitar?	**8** New pet ... 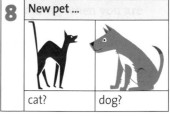cat? / dog?

7B defining relative clauses

Use defining relative clauses to say which person, thing, or place you are talking about.

for people	who / that	Fred's the man who cleans the school. A dentist is someone that takes care of people's teeth.
for things	which / that	A watch is a thing which shows the time. A dictionary is a book that tells you the meanings of words.
for places	where	This is the office where I work.

- When you use a relative pronoun (*who / which / that / where*) you don't need to use a subject or object pronoun (*he / they / it / her / them*, etc.).

>> Now go to **exercises 7.1 and 7.2** to practise.

7C *can / can't* (permission)

Use *can* to give permission (to say it's OK to do something).

Use *can't* (= *cannot*) to refuse permission (to say it *isn't* OK to do something).

+	–	?
I / You / We / They can borrow the bike.	I / You / We / They can't smoke here.	Can I / you / we / they go out?
He / She / It can use my mobile phone.	He / She / It can't park here.	Can he / she / it use your car?

Short answers	
Yes, I / you / we / they can.	No, I / you / we / they can't.
Yes, he / she / it can.	No, he / she / it can't.

- Use an infinitive without *to* after *can*.

>> Now go to **exercises 7.3 and 7.4** to practise.

7D *because, so*

Use *because* to explain why something happens.	I was late for work because I missed the bus.
Use *so* to explain what the result is.	I missed the bus so I was late for work.

>> Now go to **exercises 7.5** to practise.

prepositions of place: *in / on / at*

in	for an enclosed space (e.g. rooms, towns, continents)	My brother works in a big hotel. The children are in the playground.
	for private cars and taxis	He went to work in his car.
on	for surfaces (e.g. rivers, mountains) and lines (e.g. paths, coasts, roads)	We've got a villa on the Mediterranean coast. We had a lovely holiday on the River Thames.
	for public transport (e.g. planes, trains, buses, boats)	She got a job on a ship. I don't like travelling on buses.
at	for a particular point, or building	We met at the station. Wait at the reception desk.
	with *home* and *work*	They're at work. He's working at home.
	to say where people study	He's a pupil at Park School. My daughter is at university.

>> Now go to **exercise 7.6** to practise.

7.1 Match 1–8 with a–h.

1. ☑ *e* A chemist is a person
2. ☐ A canteen is a place
3. ☐ A mechanic is someone
4. ☐ A bus is a vehicle
5. ☐ A postman is someone
6. ☐ A camera phone is a phone
7. ☐ An airport is a place
8. ☐ A classroom is a place

a. that mends cars.
b. where planes arrive and leave.
c. which carries people around town.
d. that takes pictures.
e. ~~who sells medicines.~~
f. where you have lessons.
g. who brings letters to your house.
h. where you eat in a school.

7.2 Underline the correct word.
Example He's the man <u>that</u> / he mended our car.

1. This is the house where / which we had a party.
2. He's the man who / he teaches my children.
3. Our college has a machine that / who makes hot drinks.
4. A nurse is someone that / where works in a hospital.
5. What do you call a shop where / which you buy newspapers?
6. French is one of the subjects that / it we study at school.

7.3 Order the words to make sentences and questions.
Example photocopy can a make I ?
    Can I make a photocopy?

1. have a can today we lunch break long ?
2. can't you in office smoke the
3. jeans you at wear work can ?
4. the use can't you computer boss'
5. classroom in we eat our can't

7.4 Complete the library rules with *can / can't* and a verb from the box.

✓ read make do	✗ play eat bring ~~write~~

Example You _can't write_ in the library books.

1. You _____ photocopies on the library photocopier.
2. You _____ food in the library.
3. You _____ newspapers in the library.
4. You _____ computer games at the library.
5. You _____ your homework here.
6. You _____ animals into the library.

7.5 Complete the sentences using *because* or *so*.
Example I was ill _so_ I stayed at home.

1. Your boss was angry _____ you were late this morning.
2. The roads aren't very good, _____ Rajendra uses a bicycle to deliver the mail.
3. I joined a travel agency _____ I can get cheap holidays.
4. Sua doesn't sign her name, _____ she can't write.
5. It's the weekend, _____ we don't have to work today.
6. He's learning English _____ he wants to work in the USA.

7.6 Right or wrong? Tick (✓) or correct the sentences.
Example Don't run on the corridor.
    Don't run in the corridor.

1. I don't like travelling at busy trains.
2. My sister's studying Maths at university.
3. Their house is in the south coast.
4. Meet me in the coffee machine.
5. Holly and Anna work in an office.
6. They got on the taxi and sat down.

8A possessive pronouns

Use possessive pronouns to talk about possessions.

subject pronouns	possessive adjectives	possessive pronouns
I	my bag	Her bag is black, so she's borrowing mine.
you	your drink	That's not my drink, it's yours.
he	his umbrella	My umbrella is broken, so Jake lent me his.
she	her coat	I want a coat that's similar to hers.
we	our car	Mike and Stella's car is larger than ours.
they	their flat	Our flat is too small for a party, so we're using theirs.

>> Now go to **exercises 8.1** and **8.2** to practise.

8B present passive

Use the present passive when you don't know who does an action, or when the action is more important than the person who does it.

	subject	verb		object
active	I / We / You / They	see		me / him / her / it / you / us / them.
	He / She / It	sees		me / him / her / it / you / us / them.
passive	I	'm	seen	
	He / She / It	's	seen	
	We / You / They	're	seen	

- To form the present passive, use *am / is / are* + a past participle.

>> Now go to **exercises 8.3** to practise.

8C will (prediction)

Use *will / won't* to make predictions about the future.

+	–	?
I / You / He / She / It / We / They 'll win the race.		Will

short answers	
Yes, you / we / they will.	No, you / we / they won't.
Yes, he / she / it will.	No, he / she / it won't.

- Use an infinitive without *to* after *will* or *won't*.

>> Now go to **exercise 8.4** to practise.

8D first conditional

Use first conditionals to talk about possible future actions and their results.

If you give me your email address,	I'll write to you.
If he doesn't know how to use a computer,	he won't get a good job.
You'll save money	if you don't go out tonight.
The camera won't work	if you drop it in the water.

- Use *if* + present simple for a possible future action, and *will / won't* for its result.
- When a conditional sentence begins with an *if* clause, use a comma to separate the two clauses.

>> Now go to **exercises 8.5** and **8.6** to practise.

8.1 Replace the underlined words with a possessive pronoun.
Example Are these your books?   *Are these yours?*
1 This camera is good but their camera is better.
2 Are these History books your books?
3 Which computer is her computer, the desktop or the laptop?
4 He left his phone at home so I lent him my phone.
5 Our car is red, their car is blue.
6 This isn't Mike's coat, that's his coat on the chair.

8.2 Underline the correct words.
Example It isn't your bag, it's my / mine.
1 Their / Theirs house is bigger than our / ours.
2 Our / Ours children go to that school.
3 My / Mine pen doesn't work. Can I borrow your / yours?
4 Her / Hers computer is broken but his / her isn't.
5 Are they your / yours?
6 What's his / hers phone number?

8.3 Complete the sentences. Use the present passive of the verbs.
Example Coffee *is grown* in Africa and South America.   grow
1 The coffee beans _____ from the coffee plant.   take
2 The beans _____ to factories.   drive
3 They _____ to make coffee.   use
4 The coffee _____ into boxes.   put
5 The boxes _____ to other countries.   send
6 Cups of coffee _____ in shops and cafés.   sell
7 Coffee _____ all over the world.   drink

8.4 Make sentences and questions with *will / won't*.
Example they / pass / the / exam ?   *Will they pass the exam?*
1 everyone / have / a computer.
2 houses / be / more expensive.
3 there / be / more cars / on the roads?
4 there / not / be / diseases or hospitals.
5 we / not / have / TVs.
6 everything / be / very expensive?
7 we / have / school / on / the Internet.
8 he / go / to university?
9 I / not / get married.
10 more people / work / at home?

8.5 Match 1–7 with a–g to make first conditional sentences.
1 [e] I won't delete this file
2 ☐ This window will close
3 ☐ If you don't go to the interview,
4 ☐ We'll call a computer technician
5 ☐ If you download that song,
6 ☐ I'll send you a message
7 ☐ If you lend me your laptop,

a if you tell me your email address.
b you won't get the job.
c I'll listen to it.
d if we get a virus.
e ~~if you need it for work.~~
f I won't break it.
g if you click on that button.

8.6 Correct the sentences.
Example I'll call the police if someone will steal my money.
        I'll call the police if someone steals my money.
1 If you'll buy your ticket on the Internet, you'll save money.
2 He'll be sick if he ate all the biscuits.
3 If she not go to the meeting, her boss will be angry.
4 I have time, I'll phone you.
5 If we don't have any money, we won't to go out.
6 If their car has problems again, they are calling a mechanic.
7 He doesn't pass his exam if he doesn't study.
8 You'll be tired if you won't go to bed.

3C.3

1 What shall we watch?
2 Shall we watch the news?
3 How about playing a game?
4 Let's switch off the TV.
5 We could go out.

3C.4

A What shall we do?
B Shall we just stay at home and watch TV?
A OK. What's on?
B Let's see ... We could watch *Sports Week*.
A No, let's watch the *National Geographic* programme.
B OK. Good idea!

3D.1

actor star story crime
director thriller

character horror Harrison Ford
Laurel and Hardy

Harry Potter Star Wars

3E.1

Hi Zofia
I've got two tickets to see the *Phantom of the Opera* on Thursday evening. Would you like to come? It's at the *Palladium* at 7.00 . We could meet at 6.30 at *Esperanto's*. What do you think?
Marek

4

4A.1

The bed's too hard
The blanket's old
The pillow's small
The sheets are cold

The towel's wet
The floor is too
The taps don't work
There's no shampoo

The lamps don't work
The room's too hot
The ashtray's full
And the mini-bar's not

No glass, no soap
No toilet roll
And someone stole
The remote control!

4A.2

A Can I help you?
B Yes, I'd like a room please.
A Just for one night?
B Yes. How much is it?
A It's €80, breakfast included.
B OK.
A Could I see your passport, please?
B Yes, here you are.
A Thanks. Here's your key. It's room 224 on the second floor.
B Thanks. What time's breakfast, please?
A Breakfast's from 7.30 to 10 a.m.
B 7.30 to ten. Thanks.

4A.3

Can I have an alarm call at 7.30 a.m., please?

Could I have a cup of coffee, please?

The TV doesn't work. Could you

send someone to look at it, please?
Can you give me an outside line, please?

4B.1

M Oh no!
W What's happened? What have you done?
M I've burnt the toast!
W Yeah, I can smell it!

4B.2

M Oh no!
W What's happened? What have you done?
M I've burnt the toast!
W Yeah, I can smell it!

M Oh no! Look!
W What's happened? What have you done?
M I've broken my glasses.
W Oh no!

W Oh no!
M What's happened? Are you OK?
W The plates have fallen out of the cupboard.
M Ooops! What a mess!

W Ouch!
M What's happened?
W I've burnt my finger!
M Are you alright?
W Yeah, it's not too bad.

M Oh no!
W What's happened?
M I've dropped an egg on the floor!
W Has it broken?
M What do YOU think?!

M Yuck!
W What?
M I've put salt in my coffee!
W You idiot!
M It's disgusting!

M Oh no!
W What've you done?
M I've dropped my breakfast and it's gone all over the floor.
W Oh dear ...

M Oh no!
W What have you done now?
M I've dropped the sugar and it's gone all over the floor.
W Oh no, What a mess!

W Ouch!
M What's happened?
W I've cut my finger!
M Let's see ... oh, that looks bad ...

M Oh no, help!
W What's happened?
M The bottles have fallen on the floor!
W Ooops.

W What's that smell?
M Oops, um.. I've had a little accident.
W What?
M I've burnt a shirt ... .
W Oh you idiot!

W Oh no!
M What's happened?
W I've broken a cup!
M Are you all right?
W Yeah, but the cup isn't!

4B.3

I've cut my hand.
You've burnt the toast.
She's dropped an egg.
He's broken a glass.

4C.1

Home Alone
Lisa Hello?
Mum Hi Lisa, it's Mum here. Is everything OK? How's the house?
L It's fine.
M Have you fed Toby?
L Yes.
M   And have you taken him for a walk?
L Yes.
M Have you cleaned the bathroom?
L Yes.
M And have you watered the plants?
L Yes.
M And the cactus?
L Yes. I mean no! I haven't watered the cactus.
M Good girl. And have you kept the kitchen clean?
L Yes. I've washed up and put everything away, and I've cleaned the floor.
M What's that noise? You haven't invited all your friends for a party, I hope!
L No, don't worry. It's just a TV programme. Just a moment ... ssshhh! ... I've turned it off.
M Have you done the shopping?
L Yes.
M Have you turned on the heating?
L Yes. Anyway, Mum, how's the holiday?
M We've decided to come home early. We'll be there in ten minutes.
L What?!

4C.2

What have you **done** this **morn**ing?
What have you **done** to**day**?
Have you **cleaned** the **floors**?
Have you **cleaned** the **doors**?
What have you **done** to**day**?

I **haven't washed** the **sheets**
I **haven't made** the **bed**
I've **cleaned** the **floors**
I've **cleaned** the **doors**
But I **haven't bought** the **bread**

4C.3

I'm really tired 'cause um, I've got Mum and Dad coming to stay for the weekend. So you know, I'm trying to clean the house, and I've washed the sheets and made the bed for them and everything, and towels, I've washed all the towels and um, I've cleaned the bathroom. But there's still lots to do, I mean, I haven't started in the kitchen yet. It's really dirty and I haven't cleaned the cooker or the fridge and um, or the floors, and I haven't got time, you know, so ... . Yeah, and I'm really busy at work too.

4D.1

A OK Callum, so first I need to know how old you are. Are you under 18, between 18 and 22 or over 22?
B I'm 24.
A All right, so *over 22* then. OK, first question. Have you ever lived alone?
B No, I haven't.
A And have you ever lived in another town or country?
B No, I haven't.
A No, OK, and ... um ... have you ever paid for the shopping?
B Yes, uh huh.
A What about the electricity, gas or telephone bill?
B No, I haven't paid that.
A And rent. Have you ever paid rent?
B No.
A OK, and have you ever bought any of these things - a towel, knives, forks and spoons or a fridge?
B Well, I've bought a towel, but not the other things.
A A towel, OK. Have you ever had your own room?
B Yes.
A And your own house keys?
B Yeah, uh huh.
A And your own home?
B My own home? No, I haven't.
A Have you ever turned on the cooker?
B Yes, sure.
A And what about the heating and electricity?
B Yes, I've turned those on.
A Have you ever cooked a meal for yourself?
B Yes, I have.
A And for your family?
B Yes.
A And for guests?
B Um ... let's see ... No, I don't think so.
A Right. Have you ever put a battery in the TV remote control?
B Yes, sure.
A And have you ever put soap in the washing machine?
B Yeah, uh huh.
A And last question, have you ever put a shelf on the wall?
B Um ... no, I haven't done that, no.
A OK, thanks Callum.

4D.2

James Have you ever broken your arm?
Alice No, I haven't. Have you?
J Yes, once, my left arm.
A When was that?
J It was, er, in 2001.
A What happened?
J I fell downstairs.
A Ouch!

4E.1

Hi Phillipa
I've had a great time!
I've fed the cat.
I've left the keys with your neighbour.

Sorry, I dropped your box of eggs on the floor. I've cleaned the floor and bought some more eggs.
My towel was wet so I've left it in the washing machine.
Thanks for everything!
Ana

5

5A.1
Gavin Nice suit Jeff! Everybody's looking at it, have you noticed?
Jeff Well, that's because it's half price in the sales.
G No, but it's really nice. Very smart. And the jacket's a really good fit.
J Thanks. Don't you think the trousers are too short?
G They're quite short, yes, but long enough. And I love the colour. It really suits you.
J Thanks. What do you think of the shirt?
G Well, the colour's a bit bright, perhaps …
J Oh, I quite like it … Hey, quiet somebody's coming.
G You see! *She* looked at you.
J What, the woman in the red top? I thought she looked at *you*.
G Me? Oh no! *I* haven't got anything on!

5A.2
G It's **really nice.**
G It **really suits** you.
J They're **quite short** …
J The **colour's** a bit **bright**, perhaps …

5B.1
Sadie Hi Vic! Where are you?
Vic I'm in Bridge Street Market. I'm going for a coffee and cake in *Maxine's*. Do you want to come?
S Yeah, sure. I'll be there in fifteen minutes.
V OK. I'll see you there.
S What's the bill?
V Let's see, um … it's six pounds fifty.
S Oh no – I'm sorry, I haven't got enough. Could I borrow some from you and I'll go to the cash machine and pay you back.
V Oh, don't worry about it. I'll pay for it. You can pay next time!
S Well, OK then. Thanks.
S There's a sale at *Style Factory*. Let's go and see.
V Yeah, OK.
S Shall I carry one of your bags for you?
V Oh, yes please.
S Wow, that's heavy. What's in here?
V A set of plates. They were cheap in the market, so …
S Ha ha. And what's in the other?
V Cups.
V I like this scarf, but I haven't got enough money for it …

S Why? How much is it?
V £19.99. I've only got £15.
S I'll lend you five pounds. I've just got fifty from the cash machine.
V Will you? Oh great, thanks. I'll pay you back tomorrow.
S OK. Go and pay. I'll hold your bag for you.
V Thanks.
Woman That's £19.99, please. And there's a penny change. Shall I wrap it for you?
V No, thanks. I can just wear it.
M OK, then. Bye now.
V Bye.

5B.2
We'll **call** you **later.**
I **won't** forget.
Shall **I carry** it?

5B.3
We'll **call** you **later.**
I'll **hold** your **umbrella.**
I'll **lend** you my **jacket.**
I'll **pay** you **back.**
I **won't** forget.
You **won't** be **sorry.**
Shall **I carry** it?
Shall **I pay** for **you?**

5C.1
Dean's Jeans
Clean jeans, neat jeans
Sitting on your seat jeans
Dear jeans, cheap jeans
Wear them on the beach jeans
Wear them with a sweater
Great in any weather
Dirty jeans, clean jeans
The trousers of your dreams
Dean's Jeans!

5C.2
S Can I help you?
A Yes, I'm looking for a pair of jeans.
S Do you like these ones?
A Yes. How much are they?
S £54.99.
A Can I try a pair on?
S Yes, of course. What size are you?
A I'm not sure.
S OK, try this pair on. The changing room's over there.
S How are they?
A They're a bit small.
S OK, Try the next size. Here you are.
A Thanks
S What do you think?
A Yes, they're fine. I'll take them.
S How would you like to pay?
A I'll pay in cash.

5C.3
Do you like these ones?
Do you like this one?
How much are they?
How much is it?
Try this pair on.
Try this one on.
They're fine.
It's fine.
I'll take them.
I'll take it.

How are they?
How is it?
They're a bit small.
It's a bit small.
I'm looking for a pair of jeans.
I'm looking for a sweater.
Can I try a pair on?
Can I try one on?

5D.1
1 You mustn't cycle here.
2 You must walk on the path.
3 You mustn't enter in your swimming costume.
4 You must take off your cap or hood before you enter.

5D.2
Simon OK, now it's a good idea to put your membership card with your gym stuff. Don't forget it, 'cause you must show it at the door – I sometimes forget, and can't come in.
Judy What a pain!
S Yeah, I know. OK, so these are the machines.
J Wow! This place is big, isn't it?
S You must have a towel with you on the machines, to put over the seat.
J Right, OK.
S And you mustn't wear your street shoes in here.
J Oh, there's a pool.
S Yeah. Have you got your swimming stuff with you?
J Sorry?
S Your swimming costume and stuff. Have you got them with you?
J Oh, um … no. I'll bring them next time.
S Yeah – and remember, you must have a swimming cap to go in there.
J Swimming cap, OK. There are lots of rules. Are there any more?
S Um … let's see … Oh yeah, you mustn't eat when you're on the machines, but it's OK to drink water. And if you want to join the aerobics class, it's free. But remember, you must put your name on the list. it fills up very quickly.
J OK, is that all?
S I think so.
J Great. So we can smoke, then!
S Ha ha!

6

6A.1
Recep Hello, Central College?
Paola Yes, can I speak to Mr Hardy please?
R Yes, who's calling?
P Paola Nes.. . *(phone cuts off)*
Mechanic Hello, Kwikfix Motors.
P Kwikfix Motors? Oops, sorry, wrong number!
R Hello, Central College?
P Yes, can I speak to Mr Hardy, please?

R Did you say Mr Ardy?
P No, Mr *Hardy* – with an *H*.
R Ah, Mr Hardy, OK. Who's calling?
P Paola Nesta. I called a moment ago but I got cut off.
R Oh, yes. Just a moment … I'm sorry, he's busy at the moment. Would you like to leave a message?
P No, thanks. I'll call back later. Thanks.
R Hello, Central College?
A Yes, can I speak to Mr Hardy, please? This is Paola Nesta. I called earlier.
R Oh, yes. Hold the line, Ms Nesta. Don't hang up. I'll put you through

Mr Hardy Hello?
P Oh hi … Is that Mike Hardy? This is Paola Nesta speaking.
H Hi Paola! I can't speak now. Can I call you back later?
P Aaaaarrrgggghhhhhh!

6A.2
Can I speak to …
Sorry, wrong number!
I called a moment ago.
I got cut off.
I'll call back later.
Is that … ?
This is … speaking.
Who's calling?
Just a moment.
He's busy at the moment.
Would you like to leave a message?
Hold the line.
Don't hang up.
I'll put you through.

6A.3
Automated Message
Thank you for calling, hold the line
Please press one and we'll waste your time
Press two and we'll put you through
Don't hang up, you're in a queue
Hello, my name's Caroline
Please press three
And hold the line
Hold the line
If you want some music, just press four
Then press five and hear some more

Press six to speak to an operator
Sorry, she's busy, please call back later
Press seven for an answerphone
And leave a message after the tone
Press eight and wait and then press nine
If no one answers
Just hold the line
Just hold the line
If you're calling from abroad, press ten
Get cut off and dial again

Unit 6 Test Services

Date: _____

Grammar

1 **Past of irregular verbs** Write sentences using the past form of the verbs.

Example   I / have / breakfast at 7 o'clock
   I had breakfast at 7 o'clock.

1 Pat / buy / a new car last week

   _____

2 We / go / to the cinema last night

   _____

3 I / send / you an email yesterday

   _____

4 Jim / find / some money in the street

   _____

5 I / see / your cousin at the bank

   _____

   5

2 *have to*, *don't have to*, *mustn't* Complete the text with *have to*, *don't have to*, or *mustn't* and the verbs in (brackets).

Tips for driving in Britain

If you're going to drive a car in Britain, remember that you *have to have* (have) a driving licence and insurance. You also ¹_____ (wear) a seatbelt – it's the law!

In winter, it's a good idea to carry some warm clothes and a blanket in the car. You ²_____ (carry) spare petrol, but it's a good idea.

Don't forget that you ³_____ (drink) and drive in Britain – it's illegal. And you ⁴_____ (use) your mobile phone when you are driving. Finally, don't park your car in dark empty streets, because someone could break into it. You ⁵_____ (have) a car alarm, but it's a good idea.

   5

3 **Past continuous** Complete the sentences with the past continuous form of the verbs in (brackets).

Example   *Were you waiting* (you / wait) for the bus when you saw the accident?

1 I _____ (take) some money out of the cash machine when the man ran out of the bank.

2 We _____ (not live) in the house when someone broke in and stole the furniture.

3 _____ (it / rain) when you came home?

4 My friends _____ (have) dinner when I arrived at their house.

5 Jerry _____ (not work) at the post office when he wrote his novel.

   5

Vocabulary

4 **Telephone phrases** Choose the correct word to complete the telephone conversation.

> **A** Hello, can I *speak* to Mr Green, please?
> **B** Just a moment. I'll ¹_____ you through. Who's ²_____?
> **A** Jennifer Robinson.
> **B** ³_____ the line, please. ... I'm sorry. Mr Green is ⁴_____ at the moment. Would you like to ⁵_____ a message?
> **A** No thanks. I'll call back later.

Example   a call   b cut   c ~~speak~~

1 a hold   b put   c call
2 a calling   b telling   c called
3 a Through   b Put   c Hold
4 a speaking   b busy   c leaving
5 a cut   b tell   c leave

   5

5 **Bank and post office** Match words 1–6 with a–f.

1 ☐e You need this when you buy something on the Internet.
2 ☐ Someone who works in a bank or post office.
3 ☐ This is money in coins and notes, not cards.
4 ☐ You need to buy this when you send a letter.
5 ☐ This is usually at the bank. You can get cash there.
6 ☐ A passport and driving licence are examples of this.

a cash   c cash machine   e credit card
b cashier   d ID   f a stamp

   5

Pronunciation

6 **Stress in corrections** Think about the sound of these sentences. <u>Underline</u> the stressed word in the replies.

Example   **A** Did you say Thursday?
          B No, I said <u>Friday</u>.

1 **A** Did you say two thirty?
   B No, I said three thirty.

2 **A** Did you say Mrs Shaw?
   B No, I said Mr Shaw.

3 **A** Was that seven six five one?
   B No, seven six four one.

4 **A** Was that Mr Law?
   B No, Mr Tor – T-O-R.

5 **A** Did you say fifteen pounds?
   B No, fifty pounds.

   5

   GVP Total **30**

Reading and Writing An insurance claim

1 Read the text and complete the insurance claim form.

Part 4	*On this page, please describe what happened in more detail.*

I was riding my bike in the mountains in Snowdonia when the accident happened. I was on holiday with my girlfriend, but I was on my own at the time of the accident because my girlfriend wanted to go shopping. It was Wednesday 24th August, at about three o'clock in the afternoon. I had cycled about 60 km that day. The weather wasn't very good — it was raining and the road was wet.

I was going round a corner when a cow walked into the road. I turned and crashed into a tree. My bike was broken, but I was lucky. I was wearing a helmet and I wasn't hurt. Immediately after the accident, a car came and the driver stopped. We didn't call the police because we didn't have a mobile phone, but the driver took me to hospital. I had some tests at the hospital, but everything was OK.

Finally I called my girlfriend and she came to meet me. We returned to the hotel for five more days, but I couldn't go cycling. I would like to claim on my insurance to buy a new bike.

Signed	R J Hall

Insurance Claim Form

Name	Richard Hall	
Part 3 Accident Details		
A Context	**What were you doing?** *(please tick)* ☐ walking ☐ sitting in a car ☐ driving ☑ riding a bike	
	When did the accident happen? In the _____ in Snowdonia.	
	Where did the accident happen? At 3 o'clock on _____ 24th August.	
B Event	**What happened?** I was cycling and a cow walked into the road. I crashed into a _____.	
C Result	**Did you tell the police?** *(please tick)* ☐ yes ☐ no	
	Were you hurt? *(please tick)* ☐ yes ☐ no	
	Did you go to hospital? *(please tick)* ☐ yes ☐ no	

▢ 6

2 Read the text again. Choose the best answer a, b, or c.

Example Richard was on holiday in _____.
  a London ☐ b Scotland ☐ c Snowdonia ☑

1 He went cycling _____.
  a alone ☐ b with his girlfriend ☐ c with friends ☐
2 The accident happened in the _____.
  a morning ☐ b afternoon ☐ c evening ☐
3 Richard cycled _____ kilometres before the accident happened.
  a sixteen ☐ b sixty ☐ c eighty ☐
4 Richard was wearing a _____.
  a seatbelt ☐ b cycle helmet ☐ c sun hat ☐
5 Richard's _____ was broken.
  a arm ☐ b leg ☐ c bike ☐
6 Richard didn't have a _____.
  a car ☐ b mobile phone ☐ c helmet ☐
7 The driver took Richard _____.
  a home ☐ b to the hotel ☐ c to hospital ☐
8 Richard wants to claim for _____.
  a a new bike ☐ b the cost of the holiday ☐
  c the hospital tests ☐

▢ 8

3 Read Sam's claim form. Tick ✓ True, False, or Doesn't say.

Insurance Claim Form

Name	Sam Jones	
Part 3 Accident Details		
A Context	**What were you doing?** *(please tick)* ☑ walking ☐ sitting in a car ☐ driving ☐ riding a bike	
	When did the accident happen? in the city centre, opposite the post office	
	Where did the accident happen? on Saturday evening at about 8 o'clock	
B Event	**What happened?** I was crossing the road and a car didn't stop at the traffic lights. I was knocked down.	
C Result	**Did you tell the police?** *(please tick)* ☑ yes ☐ no	
	Were you hurt? *(please tick)* ☑ yes ☐ no	
	Did you go to hospital? *(please tick)* ☑ yes ☐ no	

Example Sam was driving when the accident happened.
  True ☐ False ☑ Doesn't say ☐

1 The accident happened in a small village.
  True ☐ False ☐ Doesn't say ☐
2 The accident happened in the evening.
  True ☐ False ☐ Doesn't say ☐
3 A young man was driving the car.
  True ☐ False ☐ Doesn't say ☐
4 The accident happened at the traffic lights.
  True ☐ False ☐ Doesn't say ☐
5 Sam wasn't hurt.
  True ☐ False ☐ Doesn't say ☐
6 Sam broke his leg.
  True ☐ False ☐ Doesn't say ☐

▢ 6

4 Imagine you completed the claim form in exercise 3. Describe what happened in more detail. Write 50–60 words.

▢ 10

Reading and Writing Total		30

Unit 7 Test Work

Date: _____

Grammar

1 **Defining relative clauses** Complete the sentences and questions with *who*, *which*, or *where*.

Example What do you call a person _who_ works in a library?

1 A bookshop is a place _____ you buy books.
2 Are these the computers _____ students can use?
3 Was Velázquez the artist _____ painted 'Las Meninas'?
4 A photocopier is a machine _____ copies text or pictures.
5 Prague is the city _____ Chris met his wife.

[5]

2 ***can/can't* (permission)** Make affirmative and negative sentences and questions with *can*.

Example I go out in the lunch hour? [?]
Can I go out in the lunch hour?

1 You smoke here. [-]
_____

2 Where I put my bag? [?]
_____

3 We wear jeans to work? [?]
_____

4 The rule is you arrive late. [-]
_____

5 You wear anything you want. [+]
_____

[5]

3 ***because, so*** Rewrite the sentences with *so* or *because*.

Example They came on the bus. Their car has broken down.
They came on the bus because their car has broken down.

1 I haven't got the key. I can't open the door.
_____

2 Ana was wearing a suit. She had a job interview.
_____

3 I've lost my phone. I can't call you.
_____

4 Justin is ill. He can't come to work today.
_____

5 I'm happy. I passed the test.
_____

[5]

Vocabulary

4 **Job conditions** Choose the correct word to complete the job advert.

Example a ~~staff~~   b interview   c salary

1 a nights   b flexible   c staff
2 a well   b attractive   c company
3 a salary   b money   c expenses
4 a team   b experience   c uniform
5 a experience b interest   c interview

> ### WANTED
> # Regional sales *staff*
> **We offer:**
> • 1 _____ hours
> • a 2 _____ car
> • an attractive 3 _____
> **Applicants must have 2 years'**
> 4 _____ in sales.
> Call 01435 877988 for an 5 _____.

[5]

5 **Jobs and workplaces** <u>Underline</u> the correct word.

Example When I was a *secretary*/*mechanic*/*dentist* I worked in an office in London.

1 Picasso was a famous artist. His *laboratory*/*studio*/*cockpit* was in Paris.
2 Linda's sister is a *mechanic*/*nurse*/*cashier*. She works at the bank on the High Street.
3 My friend's a scientist. This is the *garage*/*laboratory*/*surgery* where she works.
4 Did you work at the General Hospital when you were a *pilot*/*mechanic*/*nurse*?
5 Carmen is a *receptionist*/*secretary*/*cashier* at the Grand Hotel in London.

[5]

Pronunciation

6 **Short and long *o*** Think about the sound of the letter *o* in these words. Write the words under the correct sound.

boss closes don't not office ~~smoking~~

long /ɒ/	short /əʊ/
smoking	

[5]

GVP Total	30

7

Reading and Writing A job description

1 Read the job adverts. Tick ✓ True, False, or Doesn't say.

1

> We are looking for experienced English teachers for a residential summer school in July and August only.
> - Minimum 3 years' experience.
> - Candidates must be energetic and friendly, and work well in a team.
> - Competitive salary.
>
> Email david @LanguageSchool.com for more details and an application form.

2

> **WANTED**
> # Magicians
> for children's parties and special events.
> Must be experienced and have own equipment and car.
> Attractive pay and travel expenses.
> Call Ellen on 01987 458976 for an interview (you will also need to demonstrate your magic skills).

3

> **IT TECHNICIANS REQUIRED**
> to take care of our clients' computers in offices through the region.
> Car provided, and you must have a valid driving licence.
> **Working hours: 9.00–5.00, Monday– Friday, plus one Saturday per month.**
> Please email your CV (no attachments) to FionaWells@Tech-care.co.uk

Example   For job 1, you don't need experience.
   True ☐   False ✓   Doesn't say ☐

1 The contract for the teaching job is 12 months.
   True ☐   False ☐   Doesn't say ☐
2 You earn £1,000 for the teaching job.
   True ☐   False ☐   Doesn't say ☐
3 The magicians must be able to drive.
   True ☐   False ☐   Doesn't say ☐
4 The magicians don't have to go for an interview.
   True ☐   False ☐   Doesn't say ☐
5 For the third job, you have to look smart.
   True ☐   False ☐   Doesn't say ☐
6 You get a company car with the IT technician job.
   True ☐   False ☐   Doesn't say ☐

☐ 6

2 Read Jane's description of her job. Then complete the table with three more good points and three bad points.

I'm a postwoman on the Isle of Mull in Scotland. The best thing about my job is that it's very sociable because I know lots of
05 people on the island, and I can talk to them every day! Also, I get very long holidays so I can go away with my children when they are on school holidays. The working hours
10 are also good for me. My daughter is only five, so I can meet her when she finishes school at half past three. Another good thing is that I don't have to worry about what to wear for work, because I've got a uniform. It's a dark blue coat and jumper, with trousers
15 in winter and shorts in summer. I like working as the postwoman on Mull because I've lived here all my life.

The worst thing about my job is that I have to get up very early because I start at five o'clock. But I'm not really a 'late-night' person so I don't mind. Also, my husband works
20 in the evenings so I don't see him very much during the week, but we spend more time together at the weekends. One other bad point is that I have to work outside in all weathers so I sometimes get very wet. But on the whole, I really enjoy my job. There are more good things than bad
25 things about it!

good points	bad points
very sociable	4
1	5
2	6
3	

☐ 6

3 What do the highlighted words in the text refer to?
Example   it (line 3) *my job*

1 them (line 6) _____
2 they (line 8) _____
3 her (line 11) _____
4 It (line 14) _____
5 here (line 16) _____
6 him (line 20) _____
7 we (line 21) _____
8 it (line 25) _____

☐ 8

4 Imagine you have one of these jobs. Write a description, including the good and bad points. Use the text in exercise 2 to help you. Write 50–60 words.

teacher   graphic designer   fitness instructor
actor   nurse   taxi driver

☐ 10

Reading and Writing Total   ☐ 30

Unit 8 Test Gadgets and technology

Date: _____

Grammar

1 Possessive pronouns Replace the **bold** words with a possessive pronoun.

Example They're Ann's glasses, and I think that bag is **her bag,** too. *hers*

1 I've lost my phone. Can I use **your phone**? _____
2 If you haven't got a camera, you can borrow **our camera.** _____
3 Robert's got your number, but have you got **his number**? _____
4 Our house is nice but I prefer **their house**! _____
5 Can I use your Internet access? **My Internet access** isn't working. _____

▢ **5**

2 Present passive Rewrite the text in the passive.

- They cut the plastic into circles.
- They record the songs onto the CD.
- They print the information on the disc.
- They put each disc in a plastic box.
- They send the CDs to the shops.
- They sell millions of CDs around the world.

Example The plastic *is cut* into circles.

1 The songs _____ onto the CD.
2 The information _____ on the disc.
3 Each disc _____ in a plastic box.
4 The CDs _____ to the shops.
5 Millions of CDs _____ around the world.

▢ **5**

3 1st conditional Complete the sentences with the correct form of the verbs in (brackets).

Example If you *open* the attachment, you'll get a virus. (open)

1 If you give me your email address, I _____ you the document. (send)
2 The computer will download the new programme if you _____ on this button. (click)
3 She _____ if you send her junk mail. (not reply)
4 _____ Sally with the broadband connection if she has a problem? (you / help)
5 If they _____ the computers today, we'll work at home tomorrow. (not repair)

▢ **5**

Vocabulary

4 Material and shape Match the descriptions 1–6 with the objects a–f.

1 ▢ c It's made of cloth, and it's long and thin.
2 ▢ It's usually round or square, and it's made of glass.
3 ▢ It's long and thin. It's made of wood, and sometimes it's got an eraser at the end.
4 ▢ It's long and thin, and it's usually made of plastic.
5 ▢ It's flat and round. It's made of plastic.
6 ▢ It's made of metal. It's round and it's got a handle.

a a pan
b a pencil
c ~~a tie~~
d a CD
e a mirror
f a toothbrush

▢ **5**

5 Email Choose the correct word or phrase to complete the email.

✉ ▢
Hi Adam,
Be careful if you _receive_ an email from someone called Hugo. It says 'It's your lucky day!' in the ¹_____ at the top, and it's got an ²_____. Don't open it – it's a ³_____! Just highlight it, ⁴_____ on the button and ⁵_____ it. It's junk mail – it isn't from me!
Your friend,
Hugo

Example a delete   b ~~receive~~   c send

1 a icon   b subject   c button
2 a attachment b icon   c email
3 a button   b message   c virus
4 a click   b delete   c send
5 a receive   b delete   c send

▢ **5**

Pronunciation

6 Pronoun + 'll Think about the sound of these words. Match the words with the correct pronunciation.

1 ▢ c we'll   4 ▢ they'll   a /juːl/   d /aɪl/
2 ▢ you'll   5 ▢ it'll   b /ʃiːl/   e /ðeɪl/
3 ▢ I'll   6 ▢ she'll   c /wiːl/   f /ɪtl/

▢ **5**

GVP Total ▢ **30**

Reading and Writing A message of apology

1 Read the text and match the highlighted words with the correct definition.

> **Laptop 'thief' apologizes and returns missing computer**
>
> A businesswoman who accidentally took a laptop containing an important unfinished novel has apologized and finally returned the computer.
> Thirty-year-old manager Helen Goode put her own laptop on the luggage rack above her seat on the 15.30 train from London to Edinburgh. In the seat next to hers was the well-known author Mrs Tara Penn. Her laptop was also on the luggage rack. When Ms Goode left the train at Leeds, she took the wrong laptop. Mrs Penn realized the mistake immediately. She shouted after the woman, but it was too late. Ms Goode didn't hear and the train left the station.
> Mrs Penn contacted the train manager and he called the police, who soon identified Ms Goode from her seat reservation. However, when they tried to contact her, she didn't reply. After two weeks they sent a letter saying they would prosecute her if she didn't return the laptop.
> Unfortunately Ms Goode was on holiday in the Caribbean for a fortnight, so she didn't open the laptop or realize it wasn't hers. When she returned, she received the letter and immediately contacted the police. She apologized to Mrs Penn and returned the computer. Mrs Penn is delighted that she can now complete her novel.

1 laptop ☐   a period of two weeks
2 unfinished ☐   b portable computer
3 luggage ☐   c incomplete
4 prosecute ☐   d bags and suitcases
5 fortnight ☐   e very happy
6 delighted ☐   f make a legal case against someone

 6

2 Read the text again and answer the questions.

1 Why was the laptop important?
_____

2 Where were the two laptops on the train?
_____

3 What did Mrs Penn do when she realized the mistake?
_____

4 How did the police identify Ms Goode?
_____

5 Why didn't Ms Goode reply when the police tried to contact her?
_____

6 What did the police do after two weeks?
_____

7 What happened to the computer when Ms Goode returned?
_____

8 Why was Mrs Penn delighted?
_____

☐ **8**

3 Read the emails and tick ✓ True, False, or Doesn't say.

> ✉   ☐
>
> Hello Lisa,
> I'm really sorry – I think I deleted your message by mistake. I thought it was junk mail because it had an attachment and there wasn't a subject. I'm afraid it was too late when I realized, and so I've lost the file you sent me. Could you resend your original email? I'm really sorry about this.
> All the best,
> Gary

> ✉   ☐
>
> Hi Gary,
> No problem! Here's the original message again, and the attachment. It's just a document with this month's sales figures. If you look below, you'll see that I've sent you all the annual figures, too.
> Have fun!
> Lisa

Example   Gary deleted Lisa's email by mistake.
          True ✓ False ☐ Doesn't say ☐

1 Lisa's original email contained a lot of attachments.
   True ☐   False ☐   Doesn't say ☐
2 Lisa sent her first email yesterday afternoon.
   True ☐   False ☐   Doesn't say ☐
3 Gary asked Lisa to send her message again.
   True ☐   False ☐   Doesn't say ☐
4 Lisa was angry because Gary deleted the message.
   True ☐   False ☐   Doesn't say ☐
5 The sales figures were for the month of June.
   True ☐   False ☐   Doesn't say ☐
6 Lisa sent Gary more information about the sales figures.
   True ☐   False ☐   Doesn't say ☐

 6

4 Choose <u>one</u> of the situations and write a message of apology. Use the emails in exercise 3 to help you. Write 50–60 words.

a you forgot your sister's birthday
b you spilt coffee on your friend's computer keyboard
c you borrowed your cousin's digital camera and it broke while you were using it

☐ **10**

☐ Reading and Writing Total ☐ **30**

Unit 10 Test Journeys

Date: _____

Grammar

1 Present perfect with *yet*, *just*, and *already* Write the words in (brackets) in the correct place in each sentence.

Example   Have you visited Oxford? (yet)
Have you visited Oxford yet? _____

1 We've been to Cambridge and York. (already)
_____

2 I've finished my English exams! (just)
_____

3 Have you had the results? (yet)
_____

4 I've registered for the next English course. (already)
_____

5 We've finished our first week of classes. (just)
_____

☐ **5**

2 Present perfect with *for* and *since* Complete the conversation with *for* or *since*.

A How long have you lived in London?
B Oh, I've been here *for* about five years.
A Really? I've only been here ¹_____ last year.
B But have you studied English ²_____ a long time?
A Yes – ³_____ I was five years old!
B I've only studied English ⁴_____ I left school. That's when I decided to come and live here.
A And how long have you been at this school?
B ⁵_____ one year now. I have lessons twice a week after work.

☐ **5**

3 *used to* Replace the **bold** words with phrases with *used to*.

Example   It **was** very expensive to travel by plane.
used to be _____

1 People **went** through security more quickly.
_____

2 They **used** pesetas in Spain. _____
3 We **got** our euros at the bank. _____
4 My uncle **visited** Mallorca every summer. _____
5 They **brought** me a present every year. _____

☐ **5**

Vocabulary

4 Prepositions of direction Complete the directions with these words.

cross   follow   ~~leave~~   past   reach   takes   until

You *leave* the station, walk ¹_____ the pub, and ²_____ the main road at the traffic lights. You can then see the river. ³_____ the river for a short distance ⁴_____ you ⁵_____ the university. The walk ⁶_____ about twenty minutes.

☐ **6**

5 Air travel Complete the text with these words.

~~arrived~~   boarded   checked   landed   took   went

My journey home

I *arrived* at the airport in Paris and ¹_____ in my bags, then I went through passport control and had a look round the shops. When I ²_____ to the departure gate, I got a big surprise. Rob, my ex-boyfriend, was sitting there! We ³_____ the plane together, and his seat was next to mine! Anyway, the plane ⁴_____ off, and we chatted for the whole journey. An hour later, we ⁵_____ at Heathrow, and when we went out into the arrivals hall, someone was waiting for Rob. It was my best friend Judith!

☐ **5**

Pronunciation

6 *yet* /j/ or *jet* /dʒ/ Think about the sound of these words. Write the words in the correct column.

~~yet~~   yours   ~~jet~~   journey   yes   just

/dʒ/	/j/
jet	yet

☐ **4**

☐ GVP Total   **30**

Reading and Writing
A letter to a holiday friend

1 Read the holiday route and match paragraphs 1–6 with headings a–f.

ACTIVE IN THE ANDES

Take a journey of adventure and activity through Peru.

Includes: – Trip to Machu Picchu   15 days / 14 nights
– Lake Titicaca and Cuzco   £1,699
– Canoeing in the rainforest   Maximum group size: 12

1 _____ Your tour guide will meet you after your flight from London, and accompany you to your hotel. You'll have time to explore Lima, which used to be Latin America's principal city.

2 _____ Next we'll fly from Lima to Juliaca, up in the Andes. There we'll meet our driver, who will take us by minibus to Puno, next to Lake Titicaca, at an altitude of 3,800 metres.

3 _____ When you've had time to acclimatize, we'll continue in the minibus to the La Raya pass (4,330m). On the way, we'll see lots of local wildlife including llama and alpaca. We'll arrive in Cuzco in the evening, where we'll check into a hotel for two nights.

4 _____ Next we'll do a short walk to get ready for the Inca Trail to the high village of Chinchero. We'll ascend about 900m in four hours, seeing fascinating bird life on the way, including parrots and hummingbirds. We'll stay in a traditional village house.

5 _____ We then meet the rest of our team (four porters and two chefs) before beginning our three-day walk. You'll stay in comfortable tents along the way, and enjoy excellent local cuisine. Reaching Machu Picchu is a fabulous experience.

6 _____ For a fascinating finish to the holiday, we'll fly to Puerto Maldonado and into the rainforest. There we'll meet our local wildlife guide. You'll stay in an eco-lodge surrounded by animals like otters and monkeys, and explore the local area on foot and by canoe.

a Prepare for the Inca Trail   d Drive to Lake Titicaca
b Fly to Lima   e To Machu Picchu
c Amazon adventure   f Journey to Cuzco

□ 6

2 Read the holiday route again and complete the summary.

1 Transport: plane, minibus, on foot, _____
2 Accommodation: hotel, village house, _____, eco-lodge
3 Villages, towns and cities: Lima, Juliaca, _____, Cuzco, Chinchero, Puerto Maldonado
4 The team: guide, driver, _____, chefs, wildlife guide
5 Wildlife (birds): _____, hummingbirds
6 Wildlife (animals): llama, alpaca, otters, _____

□ 6

3 Read the letter and tick ✓ True, False, or Doesn't say.

Dear Jake,

Remember me? We met at Machu Picchu when you asked me to take your photo. Well, I've just printed my photos, and I'm sending these ones of you as promised. I'm also sending some pictures from the trek as I guess you followed the same route. Hopefully they'll bring back happy memories! Sorry it's taken me so long to get in touch. I've been really busy since I got back. I've just moved house!

After Machu Picchu, I flew to Puerto Maldonado and stayed in the rainforest for a few days. We saw some amazing wildlife and took a canoe trip down the river! I've been back in London for a month now and I really miss travelling. It's rained every day here and I've had a bad cold.

How about you? Did you get back to Lima OK? And what about the rest of your journey? Did you go to Patagonia in the end?

Next time you're in London for work, give me a ring. It would be great to see you again.

All the best,

Katie

Example   Katie went on holiday to Peru.
      True ☑   False □   Doesn't say □

1 Katie knew Jake before she went on holiday.
   True □   False □   Doesn't say □
2 Katie lives with some friends.
   True □   False □   Doesn't say □
3 Katie went to Puerto Maldonado by minibus.
   True □   False □   Doesn't say □
4 She stayed in the rainforest after Machu Picchu.
   True □   False □   Doesn't say □
5 The weather hasn't been good in London since Katie returned.
   True □   False □   Doesn't say □
6 Jake was planning to cycle to Patagonia.
   True □   False □   Doesn't say □
7 Katie would like to see Jake again.
   True □   False □   Doesn't say □
8 Jake sometimes visits London for work.
   True □   False □   Doesn't say □

□ 8

4 Imagine you've been on this holiday. Write a letter to a friend you met on the trip. Use the text in exercise 3 to help you. Write 50–60 words.

Walk to Santiago!
Looking for others to join me on the Camino de Santiago, June–July. Must be fit and sociable! Spanish language would be an advantage.
Call Chris on 020 456987

□ 10

Reading and Writing Total   30

Unit 11 Test Body and mind

Date: _____

Grammar

1 Action or state verbs Underline the correct verb forms in the text.

This is my favourite painting. It's full of strange people. Some of them *are eating* / *eat* fruit, and some ¹ *are smiling* / *smile*. In fact, most of them ² *are seeming* / *seem* to be happy. There are also fish and birds. One of them ³ *is giving* / *gives* a man a red berry. I ⁴ *am liking* / *like* this picture, but I ⁵ *don't understand* / *am not understanding* it!

5

2 Verb + infinitive (with *to*) Rewrite the sentences using the verbs in (brackets).

Example Jack said he would help me. (promise)
Jack *promised to help* me.

1 Ellen isn't 18 but she said she was. (pretend)
Ellen _____ 18.
2 Sam said he would look for a job. (agree)
Sam _____ for a job.
3 Sarah didn't buy the medicine. (forget)
Sarah _____ the medicine.
4 I'm going to study law at university. (plan)
I'm _____ law at university.
5 My brother wouldn't lend me the money. (refuse)
My brother _____ me the money.

5

3 Past simple passive Complete the text with the correct form of the verbs in (brackets).

'Pride and Prejudice' *was written* by Jane Austen between 1796 and 1797. The film ¹_____ (make) in 2006. The young English actress, Keira Knightley, ²_____ (choose) to play Elizabeth. Some scenes ³_____ (film) at Chatsworth House in Derbyshire in England. The costumes ⁴_____ (make) by an expert, which were beautiful. Unfortunately, 'Pride and Prejudice' ⁵_____ (give) an Oscar.

5

Vocabulary

4 Symptoms of illness Complete the conversation with these words. There are two words you don't need to use.

aching better feel headache matter sick sore ~~well~~

A I don't feel very _well_ .
B What's the ¹_____?
A I've got a ²_____, a ³_____ throat, and I'm ⁴_____ all over.
B Maybe you should go to the doctor's.
A Yes, you're right. I hope I ⁵_____ better tomorrow – it's my birthday!

5

5 The face Write the words for the parts of the face.

1 *n o s e*
2 _ _ _ _
3 _ _ _ _ _ _ _ _ _
4 _ _ _ _ _
5 _ _ _ _
6 _ _ _ _ _ _ _ _

5

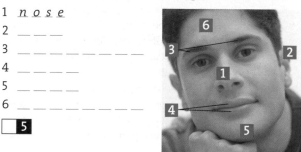

Pronunciation

6 Stress in two-syllable verbs and nouns Think about the sound of these words. Underline the stressed syllable.

Example lifestyle

1 become
2 promise
3 reason
4 exam
5 prefer

5

GVP Total **30**

11

Reading and Writing A complaint

1 Read the instructions and answer the questions.

SLIM©
A natural method that might help people to lose weight
SCIENTIFICALLY TESTED!
90 tablets – No prescription required
USE SLIM FOR FAST EFFECTIVE WEIGHT LOSS

HOW TO USE SLIM©:
– Take three tablets three times a day before meals with a glass
of water
– You should also take regular exercise while using *Slim*

* **You must not use *Slim* if you are under 18 years of age**
Always ask your doctor for advice about dieting, or if you suffer
particular health problems.

Never exceed the stated dose.
KEEP OUT OF REACH OF CHILDREN

Expiry date June 2014

Example   Who is this product for?
people who want to lose weight

1 How many tablets are there in the box?

2 How often should you take the tablets?

3 When should you take the tablets?

4 To lose weight, what should people do as well as
taking these tablets?

5 Who mustn't use these tablets?

6 When should you talk to your doctor?

☐ **6**

2 Read the letter of complaint and complete the notes.

---

34 Green Road, Manchester, M23 7GH

23rd July

Dear Sir / Madam,

I am writing to you because I wish to make a complaint about
your product 'Slim' which I have used recently. Last year I
gained a lot of weight and I didn't feel happy about it. I was
recommended your product 'Slim' by my local chemist.

In April I bought three boxes of Slim at £24.99 per box, and I
have taken them now for three months. However, I have not
lost any weight at all. In fact, I have gained five kilos during this
time. Clearly, this product does not do what was promised on
the box.

I would like to request a refund of the £74.97 I have spent on
your product without getting any results.

I hope to hear from you soon.

Yours faithfully, Clarissa Biggs

Name: Clarissa Biggs
1 Date of complaint: _____
2 Product: _____
3 Product price: _____ per box
4 Date product bought: _____
5 Product used for: _____ months
6 Action requested: Customer asks for _____.

☐ **6**

3 Read the letter again. Choose the best answer, a, b, or c.
Example   Clarissa lives in _____.
a London. ☐ b Manchester ☑ c Birmingham ☐

1 Clarissa is writing to _____ Slim.
a recommend ☐ b order ☐ c complain about ☐
2 She gained weight _____.
a five years ago ☐ b last year ☐ c last month ☐
3 Clarissa's _____ recommended the product to her.
a doctor ☐ b friend ☐ c chemist ☐
4 Clarissa bought _____ of Slim.
a three boxes ☐ b six boxes ☐ c three bottles ☐
5 While she was taking Slim, Clarissa _____.
a didn't gain any weight ☐ b lost five kilos ☐
c gained five kilos ☐
6 Clarissa spent _____ on this product.
a £24.99 ☐ b £74.97 ☐ c all her money ☐
7 She is _____ with the results of the product.
a delighted ☐ b disappointed ☐ c impressed ☐
8 Clarissa wants _____.
a a refund ☐ b more tablets ☐
c more instructions ☐

☐ **8**

4 Imagine you have been in one of these situations.
Write a letter of complaint. Use the letter in exercise 2
to help you. Write 50–60 words.
a you have taken some medicine which hasn't
worked
b you had a terrible meal at a restaurant, and
became ill afterwards
c the doctor at your health centre wasn't very helpful

☐ **10**

| Reading and Writing Total | **30** |

Unit 12 Test Getting together

Date: _____

Grammar

1 Gerund or infinitive Complete the text with the correct form of the verbs in (brackets).

A few weeks ago I was having dinner with some friends and they said they'd like *to go* (go) to the Wickerman Festival in Scotland. So we decided ¹_____ (get) some tickets and take a couple of days off work. I don't mind ²_____ ' (drive) so we went up in my car. We planned ³_____ (stay) in a tent, but it rained all the time. Everyone enjoyed ⁴_____ (go) to the festival, but we want ⁵_____ (book) a hotel next time!

 5

2 Indefinite pronouns / adverbs Choose the correct word to complete the sentences.

Example Myfriends often get bored in the summer because there's _____ to do.
a nothing ☑ b nowhere ☐ c nobody ☐

1 Last summer we went to a festival _____ in the south of Spain.
a nowhere ☐ b somewhere ☐ c someone ☐

2 _____ was wearing traditional costumes at the festival.
a Everyone ☐ b Somebody ☐ c Everything ☐

3 The town was really busy and there was _____ to stay the night.
a no one ☐ b somewhere ☐ c nowhere ☐

4 We decided to find _____ to eat and then stay up all night.
a anything ☐ b something ☐ c everyone ☐

5 It was a good idea because _____ went to bed that night!
a nowhere ☐ b anyone ☐ c no one ☐

☐ **5**

3 2nd conditional Underline the correct form of the verbs.

Example IfI were rich, I *buy / bought / 'd buy* a fast car.

1 If we *lived / would live / live* in an ideal world, no one would be hungry.

2 Poor countries *get / would get / got* richer if we helped them more.

3 If I *have / had / would have* a car, I'd go out more.

4 If there was a cinema in my town, I *watched / watch / 'd watch* more films.

5 My mum would travel if she *had / has / 'd have* more time.

☐ **5**

Vocabulary

4 Polite requests Match 1–6 with a–f to make polite requests.

1 ☐c☐ Would you like to
2 ☐ Would you mind
3 ☐ Do you mind if
4 ☐ Could you
5 ☐ Would you like
6 ☐ Could you tell me

a I bring some friends?
b how to get to the festival?
c ~~come through now?~~
d helping me with the food?
e help the children with their costumes?
f to come to the carnival with me on Saturday?

☐ **5**

5 Festivals and celebrations Complete the text with these words.

competition costumes dancing party ~~procession~~ tropical

Every year the world's biggest carnival *procession* takes place in Rio de Janeiro, Brazil. There's plenty of music and ¹_____, with some people wearing traditional ²_____ and others wearing very little! Every year there's a ³_____ to find the best samba band.

As Brazil is a ⁴_____ country with fantastic beaches, a lot of celebrations take place there. On New Year's Eve, two million people gather on Copacabana beach. There are always fantastic fireworks and everybody enjoys the ⁵_____!

 5

Pronunciation

6 Stress in words ending -ion Think about the sound of these words. Underline the stressed syllable.

1 procession   4 tradition
2 pronunciation   5 congratulations
3 information   6 competition

☐ **5**

GVP Total	30

12

Reading and Writing An email conversation

1 Read the email conversation. Match the subject lines a–f with emails 1–6.

a   Dates etc.
b   Coming to London!
c   See you soon!
d   Fantastic! Want to stay?
e   Ideas for the weekend
f   Peanut butter?!

---

1 _____

Hi Katie,
Guess what – I'm coming to London in September for work. Are you going to be there? I'm not sure exactly when I'm coming yet, but I'll let you know as soon as possible. I'll have to work Monday – Friday but then I'll be free at the weekend. Hope we can meet up!
Best wishes, Jake
ps Patagonia was amazing – can't wait to tell you all about it!

---

2 _____

Hi Jake,
That's great news! I'd love to meet up. Do you want to stay at my place? Just let me know when you have the dates. I'd love to show you round and take you to all my favourite places. It'll be great to see you again!
All the best, Katie
ps glad you got to Patagonia in the end!

---

3 _____

Katie,
Thanks for inviting me to stay, but my company has already booked a hotel and I can stay there at the weekend too. But I'd love to meet up! I've got the exact dates now – I arrive 15ᵗʰ September and leave on the 21ˢᵗ. Are you free the weekend of 20ᵗʰ / 21ˢᵗ? Can't wait to visit all your favourite places! J

---

4 _____

How about meeting for dinner on the Friday evening? What time do you finish work? If you come round to my place, I'll show you all the photos from Peru. On Saturday we could go up to Camden and have a look round the markets, etc. Then on Sunday we could take a picnic to the Heath if the weather's OK – but you never know here! Bring an umbrella just in case! K

---

5 _____

That sounds great. I'll call you when I arrive.
See you soon, J
ps Would you like me to bring you anything from the States?

---

6 _____

Hi Jake,
How about bringing me some authentic peanut butter?! It's just not the same here – that's the only thing I miss from the States! Can't wait to see you.
Katie x

    ☐ **6**

2 Read the email conversation again. Answer the questions.

1   Why is Jake going to London?
_____

2   When does Jake arrive in London?
_____

3   When does Katie want to meet?
_____

4   Why does Katie want Jake to go to her house?
_____

5   Where is Jake at the moment?
_____

6   What would Katie like Jake to bring with him?
_____

    ☐ **6**

3 Underline the best *informal* expressions in the email.

Come to a party?

¹ *Dear Katie /* <u>*Hi Katie!*</u>

² *How are you? / How do you do?* There's a party on Friday 19th September at ³ *a friend's /an acquaintance's* house. ⁴ *I'd like to invite you / Do you want* to come with me? I hope you can make it – I ⁵ *can't wait to see you / look forward to seeing you* again. It's been a long time!

⁶ *Can you let me know / Would you mind letting me know* if you can come?

⁷ *Yours sincerely / Best wishes,* Alison

ps ⁸ *Do you want to stay at my place / Would you like to sleep at my house* after the party? It isn't far from here.

pps ⁹ *Would you mind bringing a bottle of wine? / Bring a bottle!*

    ☐ **8**

4 Write two more short emails to complete the conversation in exercise 1. Write 50–60 words. Include this information: exact arrangements for meeting; confirm plans for the weekend; up-to-date weather.

    ☐ **10**

 Reading and Writing Total ☐ **30**

Tests key

Unit 1

Grammar
1 1 s' 2 s 3 's 4 's 5 s'

2 1 finishes 2 watch 3 goes 4 has
   5 teaches

3 1 did 2 are 3 does 4 were 5 do

Vocabulary
4 1 grandmother   4 husband
   2 uncle   5 sister
   3 daughter

5 1 Where 2 how 3 When 4 Which
   5 What

Pronunciation
6 1 2 2 1 3 3 4 1 5 2

Reading and Writing
1 1 a 2 b 3 c 4 a 5 b 6 c

2 1 False 2 True 3 Doesn't say 4 False
   5 False 6 True

3 1 German
   2 Mondays
   3 7.00 to 8.30
   4 Ute
   5 (to be able to) speak to husband's
     family
   6 Deutsch Direkt
   7 study notes after class
   8 read German books

4 Students' own answers.

Marking guidelines		marks
Task	Have students included appropriate information? Have students explained why and how they are studying the language?	4
Grammar	Have students used the present simple and present continuous appropriately?	4
Vocabulary	Have students used a variety of words for ways of studying?	2

Unit 2

Grammar
1 1 We had a lovely big room.
   2 We visited some pretty white villages.
   3 We went to an interesting old castle.
   4 There were some beautiful long
     beaches.
   5 We bought some fine Spanish wine.

2 1 b 2 c 3 a 4 b 5 c

3 1 gave 2 bought 3 went 4 took
   5 saw

Vocabulary
4 1 hot 2 sunny 3 snowy 4 cold
   5 cloudy

5 2 mug 3 plate 4 postcard 5 cap
   6 rug

Pronunciation
6 1 1 2 1 3 3 4 2 5 2

Reading and Writing
1 1 Christ Church College
   2 take a boat trip
   3 43 metres
   4 Blenheim Palace
   5 the number 20
   6 half an hour
   7 £4.20
   8 about 3,000 years old
   9 near (the village of) Uffington
   10 about an hour

2 1 a 2 b 3 c 4 a 5 b 6 b
   Students can write the letter a, b, or
   c, or the word. They should not lose
   marks if they just write the letter or
   the word.

3 1 Doesn't say 2 True 3 False
   4 Doesn't say

4 Students' own answers.

Marking guidelines		marks
Task	Have students included the information a reader expects?	4
Grammar	Have students used adjectives in the correct position? Have students used comparative and superlative adjectives correctly?	4
Vocabulary	Have students used a variety of words for tourist attractions? Have students used a variety of fact and opinion adjectives?	2

Unit 3

Grammar
1 1 would like to 2 don't like 3 like
   4 would like to 5 wouldn't like to

2 1 c 2 a 3 c 4 a 5 b

3 1 is going to watch
   2 aren't going to win
   3 am going to cry
   4 isn't going to rain
   5 are going to play

Vocabulary
4 2 c 3 f 4 a 5 d 6 b

5 1 stay 2 let's 3 go 4 could 5 about

Pronunciation
6 1 roller skating 2 weather 3 camera
   4 surf 5 rock

Reading and Writing
1 1 cinema 2 Saturday 3 8.30
   4 Showroom Cinema 5 snowboarding
   6 Sunday 7 2.00 8 Sheffield Ski Centre
   Students can write one-word answers or
   fuller answers. They can write the times
   as figures or in full, e.g. half past eight,
   two o'clock.

2 1 True 2 False 3 Doesn't say 4 False
   5 True 6 False

3 1 you like to come 2 do you think
   3 If you're free 4 send me an email
   5 at 3 o'clock tomorrow 6 could meet

4 Students' own answers.

Marking guidelines		marks
Task	Have students included the information a reader expects? Have students used informal language consistently?	4
Grammar	Have students used the present simple and present continuous accurately? Have students used capital letters correctly?	4
Vocabulary	Have students used phrases for suggestions accurately?	2

Unit 4

Grammar

1 1 a 2 b 3 c 4 b 5 a

2 1 Have you ever lived in England?
2 Have you ever broken your leg?
3 Have you ever done an extreme sport?
4 Have you ever had an accident?
5 Have you ever taken shampoo from a hotel?

3 1 Could you send 4 Can I have
2 Can I use 5 Could you call
3 Could you change

Vocabulary

4 2 plate 3 cup 4 glass 5 knife
6 fork

5 1 burnt 2 cut 3 broken 4 put
5 fallen

Pronunciation

6 1 shampoo 2 pillow 3 towel 4 taps
5 sheets

Reading and Writing

1 B Places around town D Our holiday
C Moving around E About us

2 1 Doesn't say 2 No 3 Yes 4 Yes
5 Doesn't say 6 Yes 7 Doesn't say
8 Yes 9 No 10 Doesn't say

3 1 c 2 b 3 b 4 a 5 b 6 c

4 Students' own answers.

Marking guidelines		marks
Task	Have students covered all the points?
Have students used appropriate greeting and closing phrases?	4
Grammar	Have students used the present perfect appropriately?	4
Vocabulary	Have students spelt the words for things around the house correctly?	2

Unit 5

Grammar

1 1 too 2 really 3 enough 4 very
5 quite

2 1 a 2 b 3 a 4 a 5 c

3 1 must 2 mustn't 3 must 4 must
5 mustn't

Vocabulary

4 1 carry 2 borrow 3 wrap 4 lend
5 hold

5 1 (Size) 40. 2 Yes. Can I try it on?
3 It's nice. I'll take it. 4 How much is it?
5 I'll pay in cash.

Pronunciation

6 1 /e/ 2 /iː/ 3 /eɪ/ 4 /eə/ 5 /ɪə/

Reading and Writing

1 1 more unusual shops 2 clothes shop
3 Jenner's 4 kilts 5 Dundàs Street
6 shortbread biscuits
7 around the castle 8 THISTLE STREET
Students can write short answers or longer answers for these questions.

2 1 False 2 True 3 Doesn't say 4 True
5 Doesn't say 6 True

3 b 3 c 6 d 1 e 7 f 4 g 5

4 Students' own answers.

Marking guidelines		marks
Task	Does the information match the headings?
Would the reader be able to understand the tips?	4
Grammar	Have students used the present simple correctly?	4
Vocabulary	Have students spelt the words for things to take correctly?	2

Unit 6

Grammar

1 1 Pat bought a new car last week.
2 We went to the cinema last night.
3 I sent you an email yesterday.
4 Jim found some money in the street.
5 I saw your cousin at the bank.
Students should spell the irregular past verb correctly in each sentence, but do not deduct marks for spelling errors in the rest of the sentence, as the focus is on the past of irregular verbs.

2 1 have to wear 2 don't have to carry
3 mustn't drink 4 mustn't use
5 don't have to have

3 1 was taking 4 were having
2 weren't living 5 wasn't working
3 Was it raining

Vocabulary

4 1 b 2 a 3 c 4 b 5 c
5 2 b 3 a 4 f 5 c 6 d

Pronunciation

6 1 three 2 Mr 3 four 4 Tor 5 fifty

Reading and Writing

1 2 mountains 3 Wednesday 4 tree
5 no 6 no 7 yes

2 1 a 2 b 3 b 4 b 5 c 6 b 7 c 8 a

3 1 False 2 True 3 Doesn't say
4 True 5 False 6 Doesn't say

4 Students' own answers.

Marking guidelines		marks
Task	Have students included sufficient detail?
Have students organized their ideas logically?	4
Grammar	Have students used the past simple and past continuous appropriately?	4
Vocabulary	Have students spelt irregular past tenses correctly?	2

Tests key

Unit 7

Grammar
1 1 where 2 which 3 who
  4 which 5 where

2 1 You can't smoke here.
  2 Where can I put my bag?
  3 Can we wear jeans to work?
  4 The rule is you can't arrive late.
  5 You can wear anything you want.

3 1 I haven't got the key so I can't open the door.
  2 Ana was wearing a suit because she had a job interview.
  3 I've lost my phone so I can't call you.
  4 Justin is ill so he can't come to work today.
  5 I'm happy because I passed the test.

Vocabulary
4 1 b 2 c 3 a 4 b 5 c

5 1 studio 2 cashier 3 laboratory
  4 nurse 5 receptionist

Pronunciation
6 **long** /ɒ/: closes, don't
  short /əʊ/: boss, not, office

Reading and Writing
1 1 False 2 Doesn't say 3 True 4 False
  5 Doesn't say 6 True

2 **good points**
  1 long holidays (or go away with children)
  2 working hours (or meet daughter after school)
  3 (have) uniform (or no worries about clothes)
  bad points
  4 get up early (or start at 5 o'clock)
  5 don't see husband much during week
  6 work outside in bad weather (or get wet)

  Students' answers can be in note form, expressing the above ideas. Do not penalize for inaccurate grammar.

3 1 the people I know on the island
  2 my children 3 my daughter
  4 the uniform 5 Mull 6 my husband
  7 my husband and I 8 my job

4 Students' own answers.

Marking guidelines		marks
Task	Have students joined sentences with *because* or *so*? Have students written about both good and bad points?	4
Grammar	Have students *used have to, don't have to, must* and *mustn't* appropriately?	4
Vocabulary	Have students used a variety of words related to jobs?	2

Unit 8

Grammar
1 1 yours 2 ours 3 his 4 theirs
  5 Mine

2 1 are recorded 2 is printed 3 is put
  4 are sent 5 are sold

3 1 'll send 2 click 3 won't reply
  4 Will you help 5 don't repair
  Do not deduct marks if students use full forms instead of contractions.

Vocabulary
4 2 e 3 b 4 f 5 d 6 a

5 1 b 2 a 3 c 4 a 5 b

Pronunciation
6 2 a 3 d 4 e 5 f 6 b

Reading and Writing
1 1 b 2 c 3 d 4 f 5 a 6 e

2 1 because it contained an important unfinished novel
  2 in the luggage rack
  3 she shouted after the woman
  4 from her seat reservation
  5 she was on holiday
  6 sent Ms Goode a letter
  7 Ms Goode returned it to Mrs Penn
  8 because she could complete her novel

3 1 False   4 False
  2 Doesn't say   5 Doesn't say
  3 True   6 True

4 Students' own answers.

Marking guidelines		marks
Task	Have students included the information a reader expects? Have students organized the information logically?	4
Grammar	Do students use pronouns appropriately? Do students use past tenses appropriately?	4
Vocabulary	Do students have enough vocabulary to express their ideas?	2

Unit 9

Grammar
1 1 C 2 U 3 C 4 U 5 C

2 1 a little 2 many 3 None 4 a few
  5 much

3 1 mustn't 2 should 3 must
  4 shouldn't 5 mustn't

Vocabulary
4 1 d 2 e 3 c 4 a 5 f

5 1 do 2 do 3 make 4 Have 5 do

Pronunciation
6 1 a boiled_egg with sliced bread
  2 an_orange for me, please
  3 some_ice cream with your fruit?
  4 some scrambled_egg, please
  5 a sliced_apple for dessert?

Reading and Writing
1 1 chocolates (or flowers)
  2 when the meal is pizza or burgers
  3 smoke or use a mobile phone
  4 pass food to someone else
  5 'Itadakimasu'/I will receive
  6 because it's very impolite

2 1 Irish stew
  2 potatoes
  3 colcannon (or mashed potatoes with butter and cabbage)
  4 barm brack (or sweet bread with spices and dried fruit)
  5 Guinness
  6 King Sitric's Restaurant

3 1 b 2 c 3 c 4 a 5 b 6 b 7 a 8 b

4 Students' own answers.

Marking guidelines		marks
Task	Have students given sufficient information? Have students linked sentences with *and, also,* or *as well*?	4
Grammar	Have students used countable and uncountable nouns correctly? Have students used adjectives in the correct position?	4
Vocabulary	Have students used a variety of food words? Have students used verbs with nouns correctly?	2

Unit 10

Grammar

1 1 We've already been to Cambridge and York.
2 I've just finished my English exams!
3 Have you had the results yet?
4 I've already registered for the next English course.
5 We've just finished our first week of classes.
If students get *yet, just* and *already* in the correct place in the sentence, award the full mark.

2 1 since 2 for 3 since 4 since 5 For

3 1 used to go   4 used to visit
2 used to use   5 used to bring
3 used to get

Vocabulary

4 1 past 2 cross 3 Follow 4 until
5 reach 6 takes

5 1 checked 2 went 3 boarded 4 took
5 landed

Pronunciation

6 /dʒ/ journey, just
/j/ yes, yours

Reading and Writing

1 1 b 2 d 3 f 4 a 5 e 6 c
Students can write the letter a–f, or the words. They should not lose marks if they just write the letter or the words.

2 1 by canoe 2 tents 3 Puno
4 porters 5 parrots 6 monkeys

3 1 False 2 Doesn't say 3 False 4 True
5 True 6 Doesn't say 7 True 8 True

4 Students' own answers.

Marking guidelines		marks
Task	Have students used informal language consistently? Have students included all the information?	4
Grammar	Have students used the present perfect appropriately? Have students used prepositions of direction accurately?	4
Vocabulary	Have students spelt irregular past tenses correctly? Have students used a variety of travel-related words?	2

Unit 11

Grammar

1 1 are smiling 2 seem 3 is giving
4 like 5 don't understand

2 1 pretended to be 4 planning to study
2 agreed to look 5 refused to lend
3 forgot to buy

3 1 was made   4 were made
2 was chosen   5 wasn't given
3 were filmed

Vocabulary

4 1 matter 2 headache 3 sore
4 aching 5 feel

5 2 ear 3 eyebrows 4 lips 5 chin
6 forehead

Pronunciation

6 1 be<u>come</u> 2 <u>pro</u>mise 3 <u>reason</u>
4 ex<u>am</u> 5 <u>prefer</u>

Reading and Writing

1 1 90
2 three times a day
3 before meals
4 take regular exercise
5 people under 18
6 if you want advice about dieting or if you suffer particular health problems

2 1 23rd July   4 April
2 Slim   5 three
3 £24.99   6 refund (of £74.97 or money back)

3 1 c 2 b 3 c 4 a 5 c 6 b 7 b 8 a

4 Students' own answers.

Marking guidelines		marks
Task	Have students described the situation in sufficient detail? Have students described the events in chronological order?	4
Grammar	Have students used a variety of past tenses? Do students use action and state verbs accurately?	4
Vocabulary	Have students got enough vocabulary to express their ideas?	2

Unit 12

Grammar

1 1 to get 2 driving 3 to stay 4 going
5 to book

2 1 b 2 a 3 c 4 b 5 c

3 1 lived 2 would get 3 had
4 'd watch 5 had

Vocabulary

4 2 d 3 a 4 e 5 f 6 b

5 1 dancing 2 costumes 3 competition
4 tropical 5 party

Pronunciation

6 2 pronun<u>cia</u>tion   5 congratu<u>la</u>tions
3 infor<u>ma</u>tion   6 compe<u>ti</u>tion
4 tra<u>di</u>tion

Reading and Writing

1 1 b 2 d 3 a 4 e 5 c 6 f

2 1 for work
2 15th September
3 Friday evening
4 She wants to show him her photos from Peru.
5 in the States
6 (authentic) peanut butter

3 2 How are you?
3 a friend's
4 Do you want
5 can't wait to see you
6 Can you let me know
7 Best wishes
8 Do you want to stay at my place
9 Bring a bottle!

4 Students' own answers.

Marking guidelines		marks
Task	Have students used informal language consistently? Have students included the information a reader expects?	4
Grammar	Have students used gerunds and infinitives accurately? Have students used future forms appropriately?	4
Vocabulary	Have students used going out phrases accurately?	2

OXFORD
UNIVERSITY PRESS

Great Clarendon Street, Oxford OX2 6DP

Oxford University Press is a department of the University of Oxford. It furthers the University's objective of excellence in research, scholarship, and education by publishing worldwide in

Oxford New York

Auckland Cape Town Dar es Salaam
Hong Kong Karachi Kuala Lumpur Madrid
Melbourne Mexico-City Nairobi New Delhi
Shanghai Taipei Toronto

With offices in

Argentina Austria Brazil Chile Czech Republic
France Greece Guatemala Hungary Italy Japan
Poland Portugal Singapore South Korea
Switzerland Thailand Turkey Ukraine Vietnam

OXFORD and OXFORD ENGLISH are registered trade marks of Oxford University Press in the UK and in certain other countries

© Oxford University Press 2008

The moral rights of the author have been asserted

Database right Oxford University Press (maker)

First published 2008

2012 2011 2010 2009 2008
10 9 8 7 6 5 4 3 2 1

Photocopying

The Publisher grants permission for the photocopying of those pages marked 'photocopiable' according to the following conditions. Individual purchasers may make copies for their own use or for use by classes that they teach. School purchasers may make copies for use by staff and students, but this permission does not extend to additional schools or branches

Under no circumstances may any part of this book be photocopied for resale

Any websites referred to in this publication are in the public domain and their addresses are provided by Oxford University Press for information only. Oxford University Press disclaims any responsibility for the content

ISBN-13: 978 0 19 430483 2

Printed in Europe

ACKNOWLEDGEMENTS

Illustrations by: Joanna Kerr p294

Photographs by: Hemera Technologies Inc. p298(plate); OUP pp292(gym/Photodisc), 292(corridor/Photodisc), 293(Spanish flag/EyeWire), 295(Radcliffe camera/Photodisc), 296(couple/Gareth Boden), 296(cup and spoon/Ingram), 298(glass/Photodisc), 298(knife/Stockbyte), 298(fork/Stockbyte), 300(shopping/image100), 302(girl in car/Brand X Pictures), 304(office/Gareth Boden), 305(young woman/Photodisc), 306(girl in shop/Digital Vision), 308(desert/Corbis/Digital Stock), 309(tulips/Photodisc), 309(rice/Photodisc), 310(friends/Phil James), 310(airplane/Photodisc), 312(photo frame/Stockbyte), 312(young man/Photodisc), 314(fireworks/Photodisc).

Illustrations by: David Atkinson p25; Cyrille Berger p18; Annie Boberg p48; Stuart Briers p110; Gary Bullock 126

(holiday picture), 132; Bob Dewar pp40, 127(Lisa's house); Mark Duffin pp15, 53, 60(bank & post office a/w), 75, 78 (making pencils & objects), 85, 90, 129 (objects); Scott Garrett pp19, 29, 61; John Goodwin p56; Simon Gurr p62; Andy Hammond pp43, 59, 79; Peter Harper p102; Terry Kennett p36; Joanna Kerr pp13, 55, 129(computer, holiday, journey etc); Ken Laidlaw p10; Gavin Reece pp46, 47, 100, 126(film studio), 127(the kitchen), 128(what were they doing?), 133(film studio & kitchen), 134(what were they doing?); Mark Ruffle pp91, 107; Terry Wong pp128 (robber), 129(office), 134(handbag thief & office).

Commissioned photography by: Gareth Boden pp38(picture 'B'), 50(Buying Jeans), 70, 106, 120; Mark Mason pp 8, 10

Thanks to the following for providing locations: Six TV, Oxford; Roberto Gerrards, Hertford.

The publishers would like to thank the following for permission to reproduce photographs: Alamy Images pp6(Ericsson/vario images GmbH & Co.KG), 6(McDonalds/Ferruccio), 6(airplane/EuroStyle Graphics), 6(Ford car/picturesbyrob), 6(Schweppes advert/John Ferro Sims), 6(Porsche/vario images GmbH & Co.KG), 6(Dior shoes/PCL), 6(Suzuki GSX750R/Motoring Picture Library), 6(Fifth Avenue/Frances Roberts), 6(Michelin logo/artpartner-images.com), 6(Chanel/Andrew Holt), 6(Honda logo/Gari Wyn Williams), 6(Yamaha/Peter Coombs), 6(Ferrari/Mick Broughton), 12(watch/Synthetic Alan King), 12(Allianz Arena/imagebroker),12(Cannon Hill Park/Images of Birmingham), 12(match/Rob Walls), 12(Maple leaf/imagebroker), 20(Hyde Park/The Photolibrary Wales), 20(winter/Robert Harding Picture Library), 20(girls/Pegaz), 20(Tower Bridge/SCPhotos), 20(Siberia/Images&Stories), 22(Cairo/Authors Image), 22(Oriental knifes/FAN Travelstock), 22(souvenirs/Jon Arnold Images Ltd), 22(beerjugs/David Crossland), 22(Soviet advertising posters/Iain Masterton), 22(souvenir cups/Jack Sullivan), 22(Egyptian souvenirs/Westend 61), 22(Panama t-shirts/M. Timothy O'Keefe), 22(fans/Robert Fried), 22(baseball caps/Lightworks Media), 22(postcards/Jeronimo Alba), 22(keyrings/Stuart Crump), 22(cairo/Authors Image), 26(sky diving/StockShot), 30('Psycho'/Pictorial Press Ltd), 40(spoon/Maximilian Weinzierl), 40(sink/Patrick Eden), 40(gas burners/Mark Sykes), 40(cooker/Sam Morgan Moore), 40(radiator/Leslie Garland Picture Library), 40(tap/Stephen Cobb), 52(keep off sign/Nick David), 52(Prohibited sign/Kim Karpeles), 52(admission sign/Paul Carstairs), 52(sailing club sign/alam), 52(St Elli shopping centre/Walespix), 52(youth/Janine Wiedel Photolibrary), 58(traffic lights/vario images GmbH & Co.KG), 58(road sign/Chris Howarth), 58(motorway/Tony Charnock), 58(L Plate/Dominic Burke), 58(dispatch rider/Ianni Dimitrov), 58(zebra crossing/Paul Mayall), 58(man on phone in car/Fredrik Skold), 58(accident/Aspix), 58(petrol station/Rob Walls), 68(staffroom/Janine Wiedel Photolibrary), 76(wireless symbol/Ewan Stevenson), 76(Singapore/Eye Ubiquitous), 76(frustration/David J. Green), 76(drying mobile/Scott Hortop), 76(mobile/Andrew Curran), 80(schoolchildren/Sally and Richard Greenhill), 86(fried egg/Jochen Tack), 86(chicken/Michael Soo), 86(scrambled eggs/foodfolio), 86(egg/The Anthony Blake Photo Library), 86(bread/D. Hurst), 88(street vendor/David Leadbitter), 90(food pyramid/D. Hurst), 92(knife/Roger Eritja), 92(India/Eye Ubiquitous), 92(breaking bread/ArtMediaPix), 96(England/David Gregs), 96(Cornwall/Celia Mannings), 96(public house/Graham Oliver), 98(airport/joeysworld.com), 98(check in sign/graficart.net), 98(airport signs/Peter Horree), 98(duty free/Helios), 98(Airport gate sign/David R. Frazier Photolibrary. Inc), 98(toilet sign/Wilmar Photography), 98(Boeing 747/Gary Crabbe), 98(airport sign/John Rensten), 98(customs/geogphotos), 98(exit sign/Oote Boe Photography), 102(dragon on silk/Panorama Media (Beijing) Ltd), 102(silk seller/Tamir Niv), 102(Samarkand/Tibor Bognar), 108(Girl with a Pearl Earring c1665/6 oil on canvas/Visual Arts Library London), 108(Portrait of Lisa del Giocondo (Mona Lisa) 1503–1506 by Leonardo da Vinci/Dennis Hallinan), 108(The Shrimp Girl c1745/Visual Arts Library London), 112(Mar Adentro 2004 film poster/Photos 12), 112(Jennifer Lopez/Photos 12), 113(Emma 1996/Pictorial Press Ltd), 116(clampers/Ruby), 116(street canvasser/Gary Roebuck), 116(police chase/Harry Sheridan), 118(snow festival/Pacific Press Service), 118(Moss Man Tribe/Doug Steley), 118(rainbow/Keren Su/China Span), 118(Berber men/Anders Ryman), 118(carnival, Brazil/Sue Cunningham Photographic), 118(Holi Festival/Keren Su/China Span), 118(camel wrestling/Jeremy Nicholl), (Elephant football/Robert Harding Picture Library Ltd); Anthony Blake Photo Library pp40(pint glass/ATW Photography), 86(jacket potato/Norman Hollands), 86(mashed potato/Scott Morrison), 86(grated cheese/Tim Hill), 86(frozen peas/Robert Lawson), 86(grilled sardines/Martin Brigdale); Axiom Photographic Agency p94 (pumpkin seller/Sue Carpenter); Bridgeman Art Library Ltd pp60(Drug Store, 1927 (oil on canvas), Hopper, Edward (1882–1967)/Museum of Fine Arts, Boston, Massachusetts, USA, Bequest of John T. Spaulding), 108(A Bar at the Folies-Bergere, 1881–82 (oil on canvas), Manet, Edouard (1832–83)/©Samuel Courtauld Trust, Courtauld Institute of Art Gallery); Corbis pp6 (Maria Sharapova/Michael Cole), 6(Bjork/Alessandra Benedetti), 12 (woman with dog/Tony West), 17(Eiffel Tower/William Manning), 17(London Eye/Skyscan), 20(ice formation/Remi Benali), 24(volcano & rapids/Hubert Stadler), 26(ice climber/Beat Glanzmann), 26(diver/Stuart Westmoreland), 26(snowboarder/Mike Chew), 26(waterskier/Rick Doyle), 30(iceberg/Paul Souders), 42(teens with pizza/C. Devan/zefa), 42(mother & son/Freitag/zefa), 52(rollerblader/Benelux/zefa), 67(man serving/Patrik Giardino), 67(tennis player/Joe McBride), 68(cleaner/Shannon Fagan), 96(Cornwall/Jason Hawkes), 98(baggage/Patrik Giardino), 102(desert/Keren Su), 118(Tomatina/

Reuters); DK Images p46(swimming shorts/Dorling Kindersley); Getty Images pp(woman on mobile/Miguel Salmeron/Photographer's Choice), 6(Gabriel Garcia Marquez/Piero Pomponi), 14(female runner/Dirk Anschutz/ Stone), 14(smiling girl/Photographer's Choice RR), 19(woman in glasses/David Young-Wolff/Photographer's Choice), 28(Waikiki beach/Marc Schechter/Stone), 28(Men surfing at Waikiki Club/Frank Scherschel/Time Life Pictures), 38 (broken egg/Harry Sheridan/Photonica), 38(man in kitchen/Joos Mind/Taxi), 38(woman clearing up/David C. Ellis/Stone+), 38(broken glasses/Dag Sundberg/The Image Bank), 38(spilt cereal/Philip J. Brittan/Photonica), 38(housework/Donna Day/Stone), 38(spilt flour/Olaf Tiedje/Photonica), 38 (woman in kitchen/Trujillo-Paumier/Stone+), 38(man with cleaning products/Didier Robcis/Stone), 46(pants/Jacobs Stock Photography/Photographer's Choice), 46(tights/Olle Lindstedt/Nordic Photos), 54(Chinese New Year/Sylvain Grandadam/Stone), 68(office/Gregory Kramer/The Image Bank), 68(canteen/Yellow Dog Productions/The Image Bank), 68(science class/Sean Justice/ Photonica), 68(computer class/Andy Sacks/Photographer's Choice), 84(man with laptop/bilderlounge), 88(woman cooking/Tai Power Seeff/The Image Bank), 88(tent/Melissa McManus/Stone), 88 (potatoes/Petri Artturi Asikainen/Gorilla Creative Images), 88(camping/Andrew Shennan/Taxi), 88(barbecue/Riser), 88(street vendor/Rich LaSalle/Photographer's Choice), 88(preparing vegetables/Riser), 88(tea ceremony/Bruno Morandi/Reportage), 88(Ndebele woman/Martin Harvey/Gallo Images), 88(mangoes/Livia Corona/Stone), 88(kebab/Bill Arce/StockFood Creative), 89(salad/David Loftus/StockFood Creative), 89(egg salad/Chris Alack/StockFood Creative), 89(pasta/Spencer Jones/StockFood Creative), 92(eating/Todd Warnock/Stone), 98(newspaper/amana images/Photonica), 102(Jiayuguan Fortress/Keren Su/The Image Bank), 102(Xi'an, China/Greg Elms/Lonely Planet Images), 102(Pamir Mountains/David Sanger/The Image Bank), 109(Detail from St. Augustine in his Study/Sandro Botticelli/The Bridgeman Art Library), 109(Portrait of Paul Scarron (1610–60) (oil on canvas)/French School/The Bridgeman Art Library), 109(Young Man with a Hat, 1888 (oil on canvas)/Vincent van Gogh/The Bridgeman Art Library), 112(The Sea Inside 2004 film poster/Stephen Shugerrman), 116(policeman/Peter Dazeley/Photographer's Choice), 116(computer demonstration/Erik Dreyer/Stone), 116 (prison/Benelux Press/Taxi), 116(waiting room/Silvia Otte/Photonica), 116(army/Robert Daly/Stone), 116(mature man/altrendo images), 118(cheese rolling/Peter Macdiarmid), 122(Les Saintes, Guadaloupe(oil on canvas), Claude Salez/The Bridgeman Art Library), 122(Cleopatra (69–30 BC) on the Terraces of Philae, 1896 (oil on canvas), Frederick Arthur Bridgman/The Bridgeman Art Library), 122(Be Free Three (oil & acrylic on canvas), Kaaria Mucherera/The Bridgeman Art Library), 122(Shakira/Krafft Angerer/AFP), 122(Brad Pitt/Piyal Hosain/Fotos International), 122(First Carpet-Cat-Patch, 1992/The Bridgeman Art Library), 130(family/Britt Erlanson/Stone), 133(family/Britt Erlanson/Stone); KEO Films p20 (Dr Nick Middleton with an Afar cowboy en route to Dallol/KEO Films/Andrew Palmer); Kobal Collection pp32(Laurel & Hardy/Hal Roach/MGM), 32(Dracula 1931/Universal), 32(Gone with the Wind/Selznick/MGM), 32(Julius Caesar 1953/MGM), 32(Psycho 1960/DANJAQ/EON/UA), 32(Dr No/DANJAQ/EON/UA), 32(Blade Runner/Ladd Company/Warner Bros), 32(Titanic 1997/Twentieth Century Fox/Paramount), 33(Laurel & Hardy/Hal Roach/MGM); OUP pp30(tv/Chris King), 68(school/Photodisc), 78(wood/Photodisc), 78(metal/Photodisc), 78(material/Photodisc), 78(colour hoops/Corel), 78(glass/Photodisc), 78(box/Ingram), 78(clock/Stockbyte), 122(young woman/Photodisc); PunchStock pp12(trying on shoes/Corbis), 12(coins/Brand X Pictures), 14(woman/Stockbyte), 14(woman/Valueline), 22(smiling man/Photodisc), 22(bags/Brand X Pictures), 26(rollerblading/Digital Vision), 30(illustration/Digital Vision), 36(hotel receptionist/BananaStock), 36(hotel room/BananaStock), 38(rinsing finger/Image Source), 38(cut finger/Image Source), 43(young man/Digital Vision), 46(socks/Photodisc), 46(top/Photodisc), 48(shopping/Corbis), 52(youth/Brand X Pictures), 54(Chinese boy/IZA Stock), 56(mannequins/Digital Vision), 58(car/Creatas), 58(changing tyre/Stockbyte), 68(teacher/Stockbyte), 68(classroom/Stockbyte), 68(class/Digital Vision), 74(home office/BananaStock), 76(spilt coffee/Digital Vision), 78(ruler/Corbis), 92(salami/Westend61), 98 (currency exchange/Creatas), 98(departure board/Brand X Pictures), 98(on time/ Brand X Pictures), 98(welcome home/Creatas), 102(Mogao Caves/Digital Archive Japan), 104(man/imageshop), 104(man on dock/imageshop), 109(Portrait of Giuliano dé Medici/Valueline), 115Federico II of Montefeltro/Photodisc), 116(carrying parcels/Photodisc), 116(autograph signing/image100); Rex Features pp6(JK Rowling/Maggie Hardie), 6(Jackie Chan/Maria Laura Antonelli), 6(Wolfgang Peterson/Sipa Press), 30(Anaconda/Columbia/Everett), 50 (Rebel Without a Cause filmstill/SNAP), 52(youth/Brand X Pictures); Science Photo Library p96(Cornwall/M-Sat Ltd); Surfpix p28 (Rabbit Kekai surfing/Jim Russi).

The Publishers and Authors would particularly like to thank the following readers and teachers for their help with the initial research and piloting: Maggie Baigent, Jo Cooke, Ana Deptula, Jon Fitch, Anne Fowles, Rachel Godfrey, Amanda Jeffries, Colin Lockhart, Fiona McLelland, Marisa Perazzo, Graham Rumbelow, Enda Scott, Joanna Sosnowska, Meriel Steele, Carol Tabor, Michael Terry.

Recordings directed by: Leon Chambers
Words and music in songs by: Mark Hancock
Musical arrangements by: Phil Chambon
Vocals in songs by: Jo Servi and Jude Sim